D1282721

Tell Me
Good Things

Tell Me Good Things

On Love, Death, and Marriage

JAMES RUNCIE

BLOOMSBURY PUBLISHING

NEW YORK · LONDON · OXFORD · NEW DELHI · SYDNEY

BLOOMSBURY PUBLISHING
Bloomsbury Publishing Inc.
1385 Broadway, New York, NY 10018, USA

BLOOMSBURY, BLOOMSBURY PUBLISHING, and the Diana logo
are trademarks of Bloomsbury Publishing Plc

First published in 2022 in Great Britain
First published in the United States 2023

ISBN: HB: 978-1-63973-152-7; eBook: 978-1-63973-197-8

Library of Congress Cataloging-in-Publication Data is available.

2 4 6 8 10 9 7 5 3 1

Typeset by Newgen KnowledgeWorks Pvt. Ltd., Chennai, India
Printed and bound in the U.S.A.

To find out more about our authors and books visit
www.bloomsbury.com and sign up for our newsletters.

Bloomsbury books may be purchased for business or promotional use. For information
on bulk purchases please contact Macmillan Corporate and Premium Sales Department at
specialmarkets@macmillan.com.

For Rosie and Charlotte

Everyone in the world has to face the loss of someone they love. There are countless tributes, biographies and laments written by the recently bereaved. In the best of them, the writing reaches out beyond therapy and recollection to share what Dr Johnson called 'moral instruction in the art of bearing calamities'. They help those facing a similar devastation.

My wife, Marilyn Imrie, died of motor neurone disease at five o'clock in the morning on 21 August 2020. She was a drama director, a singer and an artist: mother to two girls, wife, sister, aunt and grandmother. She was seventy-two years old.

We had thirty-five years together. This is our story, and this book is a love letter to her. But, as well as an account of trauma, it's the memoir of a woman who was an effervescent force for good in the world, a person who thought the best of people, embraced adventure and delighted in greeting her friends: 'Hello, Gorgeousness! Tell me good things!'

This is not only my way of reclaiming her from the last months of a terminal illness but an attempt to provide my own version of Johnson's 'moral instruction' and to offer both the consolation of sorrow and the possibility of hope in the face of despair.

So here you have it. Bereavement: a comedy.

The End

In November 2014, we were staying at Gladstone's Library in Flintshire, some eight miles west of Chester. I had given a talk the previous evening, and Marilyn and I had booked in for a few days to read, think and write in Britain's finest residential library, founded by the Victorian scholar, polymath and prime minister, William Ewart Gladstone. The plan was for a restorative retreat but, on our first morning, Marilyn woke up with a sharp pain down her left arm.

I was making tea. I came back to the bed and touched her wrist, very gently, to ask where it hurt, and she called out in anguish. She gave such a sharp cry that I couldn't quite believe the sound was coming from her. What was this severe and frightening discomfort that had come on overnight?

Marilyn wondered if it was the result of a recent flu jab, even though she had never had such a reaction before. The pain went up to her shoulder and down her left leg. She didn't feel at all well.

We had booked in for the week but decided, during breakfast, that staying on was going to be no good. It would be better to get back home to Edinburgh. Marilyn saw a doctor as soon as we returned and, although the soreness eased, she was thrown by the peculiarity of the inflammation and the inexplicable speed of its arrival.

Over the next few years there were what doctors explained away as 'the aches and pains of ageing': tiredness, moments of numbness, a weakening in the wrists and arms. Marilyn found it hard to twist the tops off jam jars, and we developed a routine where she stopped bothering and handed them straight to me. She complained that the saucepans had become unwieldy, and I was told off for buying a griddle because it was too heavy. 'How do you expect me to lift that?' she asked.

Soon, there were other health issues: oedema in the right ankle, a watery eye, and a pain in her upper leg which reminded us of the joke I had made at my sister's wedding: 'Our mother has just had a hip replacement operation. We did wonder whether it might have been simpler to keep the hip and replace the rest of her.'

These were still days in which illness came and went and we always got better; when we could laugh as if nothing could ever go wrong, or, if it did, we would find a solution and get on with our lives. Marilyn continued to work as she had always done, producing and directing *Rumpole* and *The Ferryhill Philosophers* for Radio 4, the voice-overs for an animation series, a stage musical about Dusty Springfield, and an adaptation of Alice Munro's *The View from Castle Rock* at the Edinburgh Book Festival. We worked on three of my plays together, two about Dr Johnson and one about an imaginary meeting in Paris between Fred Astaire, Audrey Hepburn and Jean-Paul Sartre. We described it as the world's first and probably last musical about existentialism: *Tap Dancing with Jean-Paul Sartre*.

Marilyn had always had amazing energy but started to tire. 'It's not surprising,' I said, 'you never stop.' The children asked if she had thought about taking it more easily, but no one dared suggest the word 'retirement' and in 2017 we celebrated her seventieth birthday in Venice. We bought a house, right by the sea, in the fishing village of St Monans in the East Neuk of Fife, not far from where Marilyn was born. Our daughter, Charlotte, was working as a journalist and writer of non-fiction, and she had just given birth to a baby girl. My stepdaughter Rosie worked in the theatre as a dramaturg. At the time, we did not realise that things could not possibly be this good. We were too busy.

Then came the fall. A slip on a wet stone during the interval of a concert in August 2019. ('My foot just gave way.') Then another on her birthday in November. ('I must have tripped on the leg of a sofa.') Then she fell in the garden but didn't tell me about it until there was another in the living room as she turned away from the window. The doctors asked if she had been drinking. She laughed and looked at me. 'No,' I explained. 'I'm the one who drinks. Marilyn hardly touches the stuff.'

They told us it was probably sciatica. She had physiotherapy but her legs and hips did not seem able to respond as they should have done.

A few weeks later, teaching a course in radio drama at LAMDA, she found that she could not get her mouth to say the word 'vintage'. Alarmingly, she complained that there was something wrong with the accelerator on the car. 'It won't go down.' She lost more strength in her legs. Every time there was a new symptom, she went to the GP. He referred her to what he called a 'one-stop shop', which turned out to be a polyclinic for geriatric patients. They thought she was just getting old. There were no further appointments available for three months.

At Christmas, Marilyn could not lift the turkey in and out of the oven and asked Rosie to accompany her to the shops because she didn't want to go out alone. She was frightened of another fall.

She felt tired and heavy and took more and more painkillers. She never told us how many she was taking. They were hidden by her side of the bed, in the bathroom, in her handbag and in make-up pouches. We were aware something was wrong, but no one knew what, and we started to worry about the big things: a brain tumour, MS, and something called myasthenia gravis, except her watery eye did not seem to be consistent with the disease.

Eventually, we saw the doctor at the one-stop shop. He tested Marilyn's reflexes and asked about her voice and her swallow. At the time, she did not have any problems eating or chewing and he was puzzled by a variety of symptoms that 'didn't add up'.

I could see that the weakness in her voice terrified her. Marilyn was a singer. I had always thought she had the most beautiful voice in the world. Now, it was quiet and hesitant, and I could tell that she was frightened.

'Don't worry,' the doctor told us. 'It's not going to get any worse.'

But it did. The gap between appointments narrowed so that in January and early February we were going for tests twice a week. They said there was a neurologist we should see: a Dr D. But he wasn't available. There was a long waiting list. It was going to be five more months.

Separately, and without telling each other, we looked up the symptoms on the internet. We tried to find out if we could see Dr D privately but, even then, it was going to be a ten-week wait. It seemed that he was just about the only neurologist in Scotland but that couldn't be right. I spoke to my friend Ali, a private doctor in London, who told me to come down south as soon as we could. We needed clarity. She would get a diagnosis immediately. 'Just throw money at it, James. What matters more than this?'

But Marilyn was tired and in pain and could not face the journey. Surely, we could get all this done in Scotland?

We went to the one-stop clinic again. They had lost the last blood test, so Marilyn was asked to give blood by a nurse who told her, 'I hate doing this and I'm not very good at it.' Blood poured everywhere. Marilyn tried to be patient but muttered to me afterwards, 'For God's sake.'

We googled myasthenia gravis and brain tumours and avoided talking about the one illness that we feared the most. Her voice faltered, some food became difficult to chew (although Marilyn disguised this because she didn't want to alarm us, even though we all knew). She asked Charlotte to cut up her green beans for her at one Sunday lunch because she said she couldn't face big mouthfuls.

The doctor asked about her swallow once more, and we pushed for more tests, and he mentioned Dr D again and said that there were more things to investigate because none of this made sense, until he finally ended a sentence with the words that no one had ever dared to say out loud. His voice was gentle and even, but to me it sounded as if he spoke entirely in capital letters. MOTOR NEURONE DISEASE.

I know now, because doctors have told me, that these are the three words they most dread having to say to a patient. They only do so when they have ruled out absolutely everything else. It is the 'last man standing' in a diagnosis, the one disease that you really, *really* don't want to get. MND is the degeneration and death of the specialised nerve cells in the brain and spinal cord (motor neurones) which transmit the electrical signals to muscles for the generation of movement. It is a form of slow and inexorable paralysis. There is no treatment for it; only the delaying tactic of the drug Riluzole, which does not work on everyone. And even then, it only prolongs life by, on average, three months.

Apart from that, there is absolutely nothing to be done. The paralysis takes hold until you are no longer able to speak, move, eat, drink, or, eventually, breathe. With incapacity comes humiliation. MND is not so much insidious as relentless. It is ravenous and without pity. Thickening saliva makes the patient prone to choking. Incapacity causes painful constipation. You never know quite what is going to happen next but there will always be something awful. You can't 'fight' it or 'battle' it. You can't be 'determined to beat this', or any of the other clichés that people say in the wake of a cancer diagnosis. MND is fatal in every single case. And it is not even rare. In the United Kingdom, 1 in 50,000 people get it every year. The individual lifetime risk is 1 in 300 and, according to a recent study, this is increasing. No one seems to know why, despite the millions of pounds and dollars spent on research.

The doctor tried to reassure us that he didn't think it *was* necessarily MND because Marilyn still had her swallow, and so we tried hoping that it was myasthenia gravis or even a brain tumour. 'Imagine hoping for a brain tumour,' she said. We were told that the nearest-best diagnostic tool for motor neurone disease was an electromagnetic test of her nerve responses (an EMT) and there was a three-month wait for that too.

Marilyn now had immense difficulty walking, couldn't drive and was scared of stairs. She was fearful of falling, even when she was walking across a clear carpeted floor. She needed to be sure that she always had something to hold on to. We discussed it and we did not discuss it. Everyone was too terrified to express their true feelings. Did looking up motor neurone disease on the internet make it more likely that she had it?

I tried to find out about the fabled neurologist Dr D who was so busy that there appeared to be no real difference between his private or his NHS waiting list. I discovered his personal email and wrote to him in desperation, but this had no effect. We would have to wait. It would be 'foolish', he said, to rush into this.

Foolish.

Marilyn was getting worse by the day, and it seemed we could not see any specialist in Scotland or get a diagnosis at all. It had been three months since she first 'presented', and six months since the first fall. Now there was the possibility of a pandemic, although no one talked about that much either. It was only in Italy and China. It wasn't going to affect people in Britain too much, was it?

Ali phoned to check how things were going. 'For God's sake,' she said. 'Come down to London while you still can. I can find you a neurologist in twenty-four hours.'

And so, at the end of February 2020, as the signs first appeared in GPs' surgeries and hospitals warning of the imminent Coronavirus, we boarded the train to London and found ourselves in Queen Square talking to a charming doctor – Nick – who ran through all the reflex testing that we had come to know by heart, before sending us next door to the London Hospital of Neurology for an

EMT. It was administered by a kind Estonian doctor, who apologised. 'This can be quite painful.'

We saw Ali who looked guarded and shocked and loving and resigned all at the same time. She said we had to stay on in London until they had the results. 'There's no point returning to Scotland if you're going to have to come back down again in a week. Just wait.'

We made another appointment with Dr Nick and he was charming but sheepish and told us that he wanted a second opinion. There was a very good man, another Nik but without the 'c'. He could see us the next day. When I googled his name, I saw that his main field of expertise was MND. Ali phoned to say that she was 'so sorry'. She had already been told, of course, but even then, I couldn't quite believe this was happening. I heard the sadness in her voice.

Perhaps if I refused to accept it then it would disappear?

So, when we went to see Dr Nik without the 'c', we were given to understand that this was a formality, as if we already knew but it hadn't quite been spelt out. He looked at the EMT result, did the briefest of reflex tests ('Do you have to?' Marilyn asked) and then confirmed the diagnosis without, it seemed, quite mentioning the disease.

'How did I get it?' said Marilyn, as if there was something, anything, she could have done to avoid it: more exercise, more vitamin D, not being born in Scotland – a country where, along with multiple sclerosis, MND seems to be more prevalent (one report suggests that its incidence is 67 per cent higher in Scotland than in other Northern European countries).

'We don't know,' Dr Nik replied. 'But I can tell you that the people in Edinburgh are very good. You will be well looked after.'

'If we ever meet them,' I said.

'Oh, you'll see them now,' he assured us. 'I'll write to them. In fact, I'd like to dictate the letter in front of you so that you know what I am saying and can correct any errors. We'll get it off today. Is that all right?'

Was that all right? We didn't have much of a choice.

And so, we watched and listened as he spoke into his Dictaphone. Neither of us could quite believe that this was happening, that we were in this room, and there was nothing we could do. Our luck, our good fortune, our happiness, whatever you liked to call it, had run out at last and forever. There was no future to look forward to any more: only the fled past and a frightening present.

This is what Dr Nik dictated:

'Marilyn is a 72-year-old lady with no significant medical past. For the last six months she has fallen a number of times and has noticed that her hands are significantly weaker. Marilyn works as a director of audio and theatre and she is unable to maintain her voice as normal. She is unable to sing.'

Marilyn looked at me. I held her hand. She held mine. Was this the end of us? We returned to the doctor and his dictation.

'On examination she clearly found it difficult to get up from her chair. Whistling was more challenging. The tongue appeared to be normal.

'There is a suggestion of weakness of head flexion $(4+/5)$.'

[What did this mean?]

'In the upper limb there was wasting and weakness, distally more so on the left (FDI $4-/5$).'

[What was FDI? Later I looked it up. First dorsal interosseous.]

'Bedside testing of power in the lower limb was unremarkable.'

['It would have been remarkable if I'd been doing it,' I said, trying to be funny, because it was so awful.]

'I reviewed the investigations including EMG. Unfortunately, the history and examination are consistent with MND. We spoke at length about the diagnosis. It is a highly variable disorder which makes predicting prognosis futile ...'

Futile.

We listened as he concluded, shook our hands, put on his bicycle clips and wished us well. He couldn't have been any nicer. It's just that the words were all wrong.

We took the train home and Marilyn said, 'It's strange. I will never see London again.'

We texted the girls, Marilyn's sister, my sister. I had given up alcohol, but I had two beers. It was late at night. Rosie met us at the station with a kind and cheerful guard from LNER who had a station wheelchair and a taxi waiting.

We went home and drank tea. Ali phoned again. She told us that the Covid situation was going to get a lot worse. We should see our closest friends as soon as we could.

The next morning, Marilyn dictated an email:

I wanted to let you know that yesterday, after a barrage of tests and scans, they have diagnosed that I have motor neurone disease. At the moment I feel fit and well though I tire quite easily and I sound and walk like Margaret Rutherford on a bad day. Rest assured that I am still very much on email, though talking on the phone is tricky; and I am still working away on various projects.

As you can imagine, we are still in the early stages of processing this news, and I am spending all my time with

James, Rosie, Charlotte, Sean and Bea. You can still email me, or even better James, but please understand if we don't reply speedily.

With much love
Marilyn

We realised that we would now have to embark on a crash course in the disease; rather like doing a university degree you had never intended to sign up for, or being involved in a play in a language you couldn't speak that should never have been staged in the first place.

There was one question we still had to ask Ali.

'How long have we got?'

'It's impossible to say. Every case is different; but you can look up the average.'

Motor neurone disease is called 'the thousand-day disease', because that's the average life expectancy after diagnosis. However, this diagnosis seemed to have taken ages, and what were we going to count as the first symptoms? The pain at Gladstone's Library? The first fall at the concert?

'Two years?' I asked.

'If you're lucky,' said Ali.

'That seems a long time, given how she is now.'

'I know.'

'It says six months to two years. Could it be as short as six months?'

'If you're lucky,' Ali said again, meaning that brevity would at least cut short the distress. 'It's horrible. I am so sorry.'

In the end, it was five months and twenty-two days.

Before …

How We Met

In 1983, I was working as a producer in the BBC Radio Drama Script Unit in London on a non-renewable fixed-term contract. I was twenty-four years old. If I wanted to stay in the Corporation when it came to an end, I would have to find another job within it. There were three possibilities: one in Belfast, one in Birmingham and then a one-year 'attachment' (the irony is not lost on me now) in Edinburgh. One of the three radio drama producers there, a woman called Marilyn Imrie, was going to work as a script editor in television for a year and they needed someone to replace her. Because my grandfather was Scottish, and because I loved the festival and the city, I thought that the only non-permanent job, in Edinburgh, was the best option and, if it didn't work out, I would just come back to London.

I had never met Marilyn properly before, but we had sat next to each other on a sofa in a BBC script meeting. I had been struck by how extraordinarily pale she was. She had the gentlest and warmest of voices and she smelled of hyacinth, jasmine and coriander, the perfume I later came to know as Mystère de Rochas. She had just produced David Rudkin's *Ashes* and Jessie Kesson's *The White Bird*

Passes and won an award for Trisha Fine's play *Can You Hear Me?* She had come down to London from Edinburgh to secure commissions for plays by Bernard MacLaverty and Liz Lochhead and discuss her plans for an adaptation of Robert Louis Stevenson's *Kidnapped*. Because the room was full and crowded, we never actually spoke to one another.

'Who was that pale woman?' I asked my boss afterwards.

'Why? Are you interested?'

'No, it's just that … her skin is like milk.'

'She's been through a lot. Perhaps it's what makes her a good director.'

'Do you need to be unhappy to direct?' I wondered.

I was talking to Ronald Mason, a generous hard-drinking chain-smoker from Belfast who had been Head of Programming in Northern Ireland at the start of the Troubles. He had incredibly elegant fingers and he wore a crisp, perfectly ironed white shirt with a lemon-yellow tie and gold cufflinks. He looked like a benevolent gangster who spent his free time reading Yeats.

'You need to understand desperation,' he said, as if this was the most obvious thing in the world.

(When Marilyn and I married, he gave us a black marble rolling pin with the injunction: 'Not to be used in disputes.')

A year later, after I had got the job and arrived in Edinburgh, my new boss thought it would be a good idea if we all met together to have a bit of a lunch and, this being the 1980s, 'a bit of a lunch' meant a nice restaurant, gin and tonics, a lot of wine and not much work afterwards, especially for men who didn't have to worry too much about childcare.

It was just before Easter. Marilyn was very late, she always was in those days, and arrived at Black's Restaurant in Jeffrey Street, in a red summer coat over a black-and-white gingham dress, with a chunky fake pearl necklace and matching earrings. I stood up as she arrived (I had been well brought up) and she came over, smiled, and kissed me hello.

'You sat next to me on that grey sofa. I remember. Shall we sit next to each other now? I can let you in on all the things they won't have dared to tell you.'

Who is this extraordinary woman? I thought, astonished by the velocity of her character and the enveloping warmth of her presence. And then, almost immediately: I wonder if she has a boyfriend?

She was eleven years older than me, divorced, and living as a single mother with Rosie, her five-year-old daughter from a subsequent relationship. She told me that she had 'completely given up on men', but I could phone her for a chat about work any time and we could, perhaps, go to a film sometime, although it was hard for her to get a babysitter when she was already commuting to Glasgow every day.

'I'll babysit,' I said.

'You don't mean that.'

'I do. I hardly know anyone here. How else am I going to fill my time?'

'I'll have to get to know you a bit better first.'

'Well, let's go to a film, then.'

Marilyn chose *Rumble Fish*, Francis Ford Coppola's now cult American Noir film about boy gangs in Tulsa, Oklahoma, starring Matt Dillon, Mickey Rourke, Dennis Hopper, Nicolas Cage and Diane Lane. For anyone at all interested in pursuing a career in film or television this was essential viewing. Shot principally in black and white, it combines French New Wave freshness with German expressionist lighting techniques and *Koyaanisqatsi*-style time-lapse. It also features a soundtrack by Stewart Copeland from the Police. This was just the kind of thing any would-be cineaste should be watching, and I had form on this, having been chucked by my girlfriend Mary in the middle of Tarkovsky's *Mirror* in the Hampstead Everyman.

Now, however, sitting next to this lovely woman and watching what seemed to me to be a piece of self-indulgent nonsense, even by Francis Ford Coppola's standards, I wanted to walk out. This was going to be ninety-four minutes in the cinema when I could have been talking to Marilyn. She didn't have the endless free time of youth. She needed to pack in a film that she could talk about at work and get back to the midweek babysitter for ten o'clock.

'Are you enjoying this?' I whispered, as a black-and-white Mickey Rourke was mesmerised by a full-colour Siamese fighting fish in an Oklahoma pet shop.

'I think it's really interesting. Are you not?'

'I'd rather be with you.'

'I never walk out of films,' she replied, but noticing my restlessness after all the pets in the pet shop had been set free and I had let out an audible 'Oh, for God's sake', Marilyn agreed to leave. We went into Dario's Pizza in the Lothian Road for a Four Seasons and a bottle of Valpolicella. I explained why I had hated the film and she told me how I had missed the point. In the rom-com of our lives, I suppose this would count as the first argument.

I was grumpy, I told her, not just about the film and the limited time we had together, but also because there was so little to do at work. There was no radio drama to be made until I had commissioned a few writers, and no one seemed to be in any particular hurry to get on with anything. I was encouraged to 'use the time to think creatively' and so I told Marilyn that I was toying with the idea of directing some Chekhov in the theatre.

'*The Cherry Orchard* is my favourite play.'

'I want to do *Three Sisters*.'

'Why?'

She leant forward, curious about the possibility, clearly interested in the opportunity to discuss how such a production might proceed. It was a look of hers that I later came to love and adore, the look of expectation, intrigue, the beginning of something new. Filled with the confidence of youth, I set out my plans for the show, oblivious to the irony of my mansplaining feminine frustration and marital disappointment to the experienced woman opposite.

I told her that I thought the play was about ignorance and limitations of privilege, how all of the characters apart from the maid and the army doctor assume that the action is about them. They think they have been marked out for something special, and it takes them the course of the play to realise that they have not. They are as susceptible to the quiet desperation of everyday lives as anyone else. I wanted to think of ways in which self-centred individuals, concentrating too much on their own ambition, were brought to a place where a beautiful melancholy could be the beginning of hope. Marilyn smiled and said, 'Go on.'

I did, for far too long, and then she told me how important she thought it was to make the world off-stage as convincing as what happens on it: the fire in the town, the soldiers marching, the duel between Tuzenbach and Soliony. We have to want to go to Moscow as badly as the Three Sisters; just as we hear the music across the lake at the beginning of *The Seagull*. We imagine the beauty of *The Cherry Orchard* even if we cannot see it, we can't bear for it to be chopped down, and we have to understand how hard it is for the family to return to their old home and how desperate is their melancholy when they leave it for the last time: 'Goodbye old house, goodbye old life!'

Marilyn said that when she had been very sad, the previous year, and 'couldn't stay cheerful any longer', her daughter Rosie wanted to make her feel better. 'What's your favourite play?' she asked, and then performed her own version of what she thought *The Cherry Orchard* might be like with her dolls, her toys and her puppets.

And so there we were, eating pizza and using Chekhov to talk about the comedy and pathos of everyday life, the desire of the characters to be more than they were, the disappointments of those who felt that life had passed them by, and how to make the future a realistic possibility rather than a dream.

A week later Marilyn phoned up and asked, 'Did you mean what you said about babysitting? I'm really stuck.'

'I'll do it,' I said and came to a spacious ground-floor flat in Craigmillar Park where I was introduced to Rosie, her equally pale and even more suspicious daughter. I think we read stories and watched some television and Rosie showed me a wooden chair that had been bound with red-and-white ribbons, odd bits of material, rope and string.

How I came to be tied to this chair, I cannot fully remember, apart from Rosie saying, 'You're my prisoner,' but by the time Marilyn came home I was still stuck, even though I could easily get out, because I didn't want to let Rosie down and because I thought it would amuse Marilyn.

'Well, that's one way of getting a man to stay,' she said when she returned, 'but I'm still sworn off them.'

Over the next few weeks, we saw each other several times. I made what I thought was my famous minestrone soup, as if no one had ever made such a thing before, and brought it round to her house where we talked even more about my profit-share production of *Three Sisters*. It was going to be staged at the Netherbow in the Royal Mile.

Although I had been to drama school and was youthfully confident about my directing, this had all been in England with actors who were used to doing a lot of talking about Peter Brook and Stanislavski, arc and action, method and motivation. Scottish actors were more instinctive and impatient. They weren't so interested in poetic understanding or the writer's intention. Their preparation was more visceral. Perhaps there was more of the tradition of variety and the music hall in their DNA.

I was reminded of a teacher at drama school who kept repeating the phrase: 'It's SHOW-business, not TELL-business, darling.' These Scottish actors wanted to act with their bodies as well as their heads. They preferred to stand up and get on with it rather than sit around discussing the difference between intention and action.

Whenever I tried to 'do a bit of directing' or give a note, I was met with the response: 'I thought I was doing that.'

One of them told me about the actor John Stahl, who, after listening to twenty minutes of notes from an English director on how he should deliver a line, replied, 'I'll do it with a look.'

After one of the (male) actors said to me, 'I don't do vulnerability,' I phoned Marilyn to ask for tips. She told me about the need to be clear and patient and let the actors find their way. 'Don't think you have to give them all the answers.'

'But I feel like I'm failing them.'

'It's a process. You've got three weeks. You have to let things bed down.'

'The only thing I want to bed down—'

'Yes, yes, that's quite enough of that.'

In the end I learned so much from the actors, not just about the play and the art of performance but what it might mean to live in Scotland and how it was a different country inside Mrs Thatcher's Britain. They said what they thought, were warm and challenging, and I came to understand what some people in Glasgow call their 'aggressive friendliness'. They didn't like bullshit, they couldn't stand pretension, they wanted to be loved (don't we all?) and they wanted a laugh and a drink and to be paid on time.

And then I realised that this was not just another production. It was a crash-course degree in how to behave in Scotland, a lesson in how generous and creative people in a different country think, and it was the best accidental preparation I could have had for loving Marilyn.

I continued to talk to her, and she said that the designer and I could come round to her flat after the technical rehearsal and turn our anxieties into excitement over a bottle of red wine. Kevin and I went over to Craigmillar Park and told her all our hilarious and extraordinary anecdotes about the amazing time we were having. Marilyn listened to us *two boys* as if she had never heard such stories in her life, even though she had been married to a theatre director for five years and seemed to know every performer in Scotland.

On the day of the first night, she sent me a telegram to wish me good luck: YOU SAY IRENA AND I SAY IRENA. DON'T CALL THE WHOLE THING OFF!

That evening she sat next to the theatre critic of the *Scotsman*. 'Don't worry,' she said to me, 'I'll see her right.'

The next day I received a card promising that she had loved the production. It was a pen-and-ink cartoon 'Biff Kard', satirising the *Guardian*-reader set, entitled 'How to Behave at a Preview', with a louche John Grierson film director lookalike holding a dry martini and saying, 'This is my masterpiece – hand and glass locked in a tension of opposites,' and his glamorous date replying, 'Don't be a wally, Nigel. People will hear you.'

Marilyn had added extra speech bubbles. The one at the top read: 'It certainly has all the hallmarks of genuine Runcie ... but is it Chekhov?'

And at the bottom: 'It certainly has all the hallmarks of Chekhov ... but is it authentic Runcie?'

She signed the card: 'With love as always'.

Always. I had only known her a few months. I started a notebook and began to write down all my thoughts about her, little memories, hopes and anxieties, and copied out Masha's confession in *Three Sisters*: 'I'm in love – all right, so that's my fate. So that's my lot in life. Somehow, we shall live our lives, whatever happens to us. You read some novel and you think, that's all so trite and obvious. But as soon as you fall in love yourself, you realise that no one knows anything, and that we each have to decide these things for ourselves.'

All my friends had assumed that, if I was ever going to marry, it would either be to some posh English girl (I had recently been to a Wodehousian wedding where I had sat between two women called Arabella Harcourt-Seeley and Jamanda Haddock) or to some scarily neurotic actress with a vodka problem. My most recent relationship had ended with an upturned bowl of spaghetti in my lap and a postcard with a razor blade sellotaped to it explaining what I should do to my penis. I should probably add that at this time my father was also the Archbishop of Canterbury and the idea of my marrying a woman who was eleven years older than me, a divorced single parent with a five-year-old daughter, would have sent my parents into a bit of a spin.

Marilyn took me in her yellow Citroën 2CV down to Skippers Bistro in Leith and we sat at a shared table so we couldn't speak as privately as I wanted to, and she showed me how to eat lobster properly. She had learned how to do so in France, and I wondered what on earth I could do to get this woman, who was dressed in what appeared to be a grey silk flying suit, to spend more time with me.

I told her that my favourite writer was Henry James and she replied, saying that she preferred Robert Louis Stevenson. Henry James 'always chewed more than he bit off'.

When I said that I was going to do a Scottish production of Strindberg's *Miss Julie* for Radio 3, she sent me a hand-drawn cartoon of a watching budgerigar saying: 'Jings! Whit's Jock daein' wi' thon chopper?'

Then I received a postcard from her, a painting by Phryne Frappa of a woman unveiling in front of three eager old men, with the words: 'Three elderly producers inspecting my credentials before joining Radio Drama – don't you love it?'

She left a box of rose-hip tea in my doorway.

Dearest James
This box of tea

Is spent with special love
From me.

She said she didn't want to ruin me (although I was perfectly prepared to be ruined if it meant being with her). It wasn't fair on either of us. She insisted over the next ten days that there was *absolutely no chance of a relationship.* We were friends. She encouraged me to 'find a proper girlfriend' and she would vet her for bonkersness, and I did manage, quite soon, too soon probably, to spend some time with a petite and extraordinarily attractive chain-smoking ballerina. We sat in gloomy pubs, even at the height of summer, with very little to say to each other and stayed in weekend getaway hotels with yellow nylon sheets and drank in pointless golf and tartan-styled lounge bars in St Andrews with me thinking, alternately, 'Shit, it's still only eight o'clock' and 'I wish I was with Marilyn.' I realise this does not put me in a particularly good light, but then I think the ballerina was only dating me to get her old boyfriend back which, in the end, she succeeded in doing.

Before returning for a production that I had to do in London, I dropped round a little toy that I had bought in Jenners department store for Rosie's sixth birthday. I arrived, not thinking, in the middle of her birthday party and left straight away. Marilyn sent me a note on red paper waiting for my return:

Welcome home James!
(a red-letter day!)
Hope studios, travels and sojourns were all smooth and pleasant. Craigmillar Park enterprises await your return for your participation in jolly summer jaunts – ring for details!

Please forgive my erratic and (I'm sure) seemingly thoughtless behaviour at times over the last few weeks. Life's a bit too bumpy for comfort – but I hope you and I are going to be friends. I look forward to it.

With love, Marilyn

PS. The lion continues to be much loved. It was so kind of you …

At the Edinburgh Festival that year she had so many people staying that it was almost impossible to see her, but she phoned me up and said she had an afternoon free and was desperate to escape. Would I like to go with her to the *Creation* exhibition at the Gallery of Modern Art?

This was, perhaps, one of the first shows to concentrate on environmental perception. It was about the human position in space, time and landscape, with areas devoted to The Beginning, The Heavens, The Earth, The Seas, The Planets, The Creatures and The Human Image: seven sections for the seven days of Creation.

Marilyn was tired and told me that all she wanted was quiet and beauty and space and company. It was a hot afternoon but the galleries were not crowded, and we walked between paintings before sitting down on a low bench in front of Emil Nolde's *Large Poppies (red, red, red)* from 1942, one of the few pictures he was able to paint in the Nazi period: a big, blowsy image of deep crimson, scarlet and mauve poppies at the height of summer in what looked to be a strong wind.

I had bought the catalogue and read from Nolde's autobiography: 'The blossoming colours of the flowers and the purity of those colours – I love them. I loved the flowers and their fate: shooting up, blooming, radiating, glowing, gladdening, bending, wilting, thrown away and dying.'

'Gladdening,' said Marilyn thoughtfully. 'They cheer my heart.'

She talked about wild poppies growing in the hedgerows of Fife, of her childhood and the country lanes and the sea at St Andrews. Then she stopped talking and we just sat there. I think something extraordinary then happened that we acknowledged but couldn't quite explain. It was a resting place, a coming-in to land, a feeling of security and companionship. This was where we were. We could stop here for a while without saying anything. It was a feeling of having come home. I knew then, more than ever, that this was all I needed, to be with this person at this time. Love need not be desperate or hasty, it could just be warm, tacit, accepting; the feeling I would later recognise when love was described as 'being with someone you can do nothing with'.

I do not know how long we sat there, but I think it was longer than I had ever sat in front of any other painting. I knew that neither of us wanted to leave, that love was a form of rescue and we had somehow saved each other from all our present anxieties if only for a short while in that time and space; and that, whenever we were nervous or anxious about each other in the future, we could come back to this moment when we were alone and together. Then, God willing, there would be other such moments, perhaps, over the future years, where we would know each other without speaking, and understand that no one and nothing else mattered.

But Marilyn was worried by what we had started and how everything was going to turn out. She wasn't sure if it was fair on me. Surely, I was too young? Perhaps she should let me go like the Marschallin does with her young lover in Strauss's *Rosenkavalier*. Did I know it? (No, of course I didn't.)

I refused to listen and said that I was only interested in her and she said, 'What about the ballerina?' and I said, 'You know that's hopeless. Even she thinks it's hopeless. We're both on the rebound.'

Then Marilyn and I went away from the bench in front of a painting of poppies in full flower and buffeted by the wind, back to our normal everyday jobs as if we too were characters from *Three Sisters* forced to come to terms with the fact that we had boring mundane everyday lives just like everybody else.

Except that we refused to accept this. I sent jaunty messages to Marilyn, basically saying HELLO! I AM HERE.

She came into the Radio Drama office over the weekend and wrote a little note on the back of a postcard of a Hugh Cameron painting called *A Lonely Life* and added: '*Sans toi, chéri, certainement!* The sun is pouring into my/your/our office this morning and I feel the need of your company.' Beneath, she added a riddle:

My first is in Jam but not in honey
My second is in rain but not in sunny
My third is in mine but not in yours
My fourth is in below and in above
My last is in kisses
It's you that I love.

And then, upside down at the bottom, just in case I hadn't understood, she wrote: 'Is James the answer?'

If we didn't see each other, we sent one another cards and letters and internal BBC memos with 'Private' scrawled across the back of the envelopes. I found out that her middle name was Elsie and that two of her female friends called her 'Marilyn Elsie Fatbottom'.

Then I received another riddle:

My first is in beetle
But never in ant
My second's in flower
But not in plant
My third is in tipple
But not in drink
My fourth is in tap
But not in the sink
My fifth is in orange but not in plum
My sixth is in mine
In short it's my …?
And this object, which is animal, vegetable and mineral, longs
   to be close to yours
Ever your own daft Elsie
Kisses on the bottom xxx

I told her I couldn't wait for us to be together, and she promised me: 'Everything will change soon. I have so many fears, insecurities and anxieties, but none of them are about you and me. I believe that we were meant to find each other.'

She went on yet another course, away at BBC Elstree, and I gave her a bottle of Mystère de Rochas and phoned to say that I would miss her and longed for her return. All I wanted was to see her again.

So, I had to wait for her and realised that love was as much about patience as anything else. At the same time I knew, instinctively and absolutely, that I had no choice because this was the woman I loved and wanted to be with at whatever cost. It wasn't a *coup de foudre*. It was worth everything. Marilyn was going to define my life.

However, I still had to earn her trust. I had to show that I cared passionately and, at the same time, demonstrate that I was ready to wait. I had to prove my love to a woman who said she no longer had faith in men, love or marriage; and yet, simultaneously, we had to make sure that we didn't analyse everything too much or go over things in a way that would destroy the unpredictability, the informality and the excitement of all that was possible. We had to learn all the lessons that the Three Sisters hadn't.

There was so much to say and yet it was also simple. We loved each other, whatever the difficulties that might lie ahead. We had to believe and trust that this was true. Christians talk about a leap of faith. We had to hold hands and jump without looking down, but both of us couldn't help but peek through the hands over our eyes and think: Oh God, what an abyss.

We spoke on the phone when she was on her course in London and acknowledged both that it was almost impossible and that we missed each other madly. I told her that I couldn't imagine a life without her, such a thing was inconceivable now, but perhaps we didn't have to do *everything* straight away. Maybe we could just make a start?

Marilyn told me that she had met up with her friend Liz, who had told her not to get in a state. 'Why are you making such a fuss? Just have a wee affair. You don't have to marry him.'

Then I got this message: *I think you are a wonderful and extraordinary man – the warmest I have ever known. I want you to believe how happy you make me – it's like being given a present of something you thought you'd lost. Also, the thing is, I fancy you rotten. Can anything be done about this?*

She told me that she was getting the sleeper back from London. She knew that she would be exhausted and

32

would need a rest as she never slept well on the train, but I could come round on Saturday afternoon. Rosie was staying with her grandparents in Fife. Could I just pop round and see her?

I brought her jonquils and honey and she opened the door and was so sleepy that, for a moment, I thought she had forgotten that I was coming, but then she smiled and made Earl Grey tea in her black velvet dressing gown with nothing underneath and said, 'Oh for goodness' sake, come to bed.'

And that was how it began.

Death as Theatre

Anyone who made the marriage vow 'in sickness and in health', however sincerely meant, would never have been able to envisage that a disease such as MND would transform their world.

Kevin Talbot and Rachael Marsden, *Motor Neuron Disease: The Facts*

Terminal illness is a full-time job. Given our background, the only way the family knew how to approach it was as some kind of weird and unexpected new production.

In the theatre, everything moves with gathering intensity towards the first night. Get that right, and you can refine and adapt and change as the run goes on. But we were working towards a last night, at an unspecified date, for one performance only.

Marilyn had taught us that the qualities necessary for any production were preparation, adaptability and holding your nerve. She was the calmest and most serene of directors, believing that anxiety was contagious. Her approach was to create a generous and inclusive atmosphere in which everyone could be at their best.

But what was this impromptu, unscheduled and unscripted production going to be like when she was not in charge and was undoubtedly going to be at her worst?

Soon, she would be unable to issue instructions or explain what she wanted, because her speech was disappearing almost as fast as her energy, hope and enthusiasm.

Her shows often began with the excitement of combining an idea and an author. She spent hours making sure that the building blocks of a production were right. Each scene had to progress the action and every character had to have a purpose, an arc and a direction. There had to be light and shade between main plot, character plot and all the little subplots. There needed to be opportunities for surprise and reversals (where, just as you think everything is going swimmingly, there is a dramatic shift for the worse). And then you had to knit it all together and make sure that no one in the audience could see the joins. Her job as a director was to provide a safe and creative framework in which everyone could feel secure without being constricted. She chose her music early, wanting to find the rhythm of the drama, believing that although some productions contained terrific moments, they couldn't always sustain their momentum.

'Lots of people can direct scenes, but they can't direct plays, James. It's not just about the good bits. It's about the piece as a whole. Everything has to be earned and paid off. Then you add the grace notes.'

Some plays might come with an existing character: *The Stanley Baxter Playhouse* for Radio 4, or John Mortimer's *Rumpole* with Benedict Cumberbatch and then Julian Rhind-Tutt. Or, it might start with an actor and an idea. The last production we did together was the aforementioned *Tap Dancing with Jean-Paul Sartre*. It started because our friend, the actor Ashley Smith, looks a little like Audrey Hepburn, and we wanted to find a vehicle for her. Marilyn had the idea that we could create something around the making of the film *Funny Face* with Fred Astaire. When we spoke about it together, I thought it would be fun to introduce Jean-Paul Sartre, on the principle that they could teach him about tap dancing and he could reveal the meaning of life at the same time. So, we started with the actor, the idea and the music ('It don't mean a thing if it ain't got that swing') and tried to be as playful as we could. It was entertainment, showbiz, joy and ridiculousness.

But this last production that we were forced into planning in real life without preparation or warning had none of these things. There was no script and we had no ideas about the casting. The first person we needed was a neurologist but, as previously discussed, Scotland's star neurologist had a waiting list of three months and so, as in the theatre, he 'wasn't available'. The company that had recently won an award for 'Scotland's Best Care Provider' was fully booked and wasn't taking on new patients. The Covid crisis meant that MND Scotland could not give us any physiotherapy or massage.

This was not a good start. But we were familiar with this kind of casting dilemma. You start by asking for Meryl Streep and work down.

So, we did finally manage to find a determined and helpful care company to provide two hours a day (leaving Rosie and me with the other twenty-two) while Charlotte was looking after her two-year-old daughter. She had no childcare and Covid had closed all the nurseries.

The carers that came were intrigued by our theatrical lifestyle.

'Have you worked with any famous actors?' one of them asked, and Marilyn nodded. 'Just a few.'

'Anyone I might have heard of?'

This is always a difficult question, because younger people want you to say Emma Watson and older people expect Laurence Olivier. None of them have actually 'heard' of the people you have actually worked with. Fame is not as extensive as we like to think. (I was reminded of David Sedaris's fine observation that people may be celebrities in this world, but what about the rest of the universe? All that vast space where no one knows them at all.)

During this production we had to work fast because it had started without us quite realising it had done so, as if we were filling in a slot that had become unexpectedly available. There was the feeling of accelerating panic that always accompanies an unprepared, underfunded and under-resourced production. There was no budget and no schedule, only a gradually accumulating cast of characters that came to resemble an eighteenth-century playbill.

The Reluctant Patient
A Tragic Farce in One Act

Dramatis Personae
Miss Marilyn Imrie, the Reluctant Patient
Mr James Runcie, her husband
Miss Rosie Kellagher, her eldest daughter
Miss Charlotte Runcie, her youngest daughter

Dr Ali Joy, friend of the above
Dr A-L, a Palliative Care Doctor
Dr R, a General Practitioner
Dr J, a Hospice Doctor
Miss A, an MND Nurse
Miss B, a Specialist in Ventilation
Miss L, a Speech Therapist
Miss S, a Social Carer
Miss K, a Physiotherapist

The Reverend Neil Gardner, a Minister

A Chorus of Carers: Anna, Fiona, Christie, Carol
Six District Nurses

Theatricals on the telephone (billed in alphabetical order
to avoid dispute):
Miss Hetty Baynes
Miss Deborah Findlay
Mr Bill Paterson
Miss Siobhán Redmond
Miss Gerda Stevenson
Mr Pip Torrens

Characters at the corner shop, the dry-cleaner's and the pharmacy
Local friends and townsfolk

The action takes place in the City of Edinburgh and in the village of St Monans.
In the midst of a plague.
The Year of Our Lord 2020.

Each of the medical characters had their own specialist skills. The trick was going to be to get them all to work together in a unified and coordinated production. Unfortunately, they didn't appear to know how to do this and, in a time of Covid, they were unable to see Marilyn in person.

This was not so much a play but a series of variety acts. We were also in the wrong venue. Our Edinburgh home had a bathroom and toilet that could not accommodate a wheelchair, the entrance to the bedroom was too narrow and there were awkwardly deep steps up to the front door. The possibility of adapting our flat to enable the best care was compromised by a Covid lockdown that prevented builders, carpenters and electricians coming into our home at all. At the same time, the acceleration of MND made the production 'schedule' tighter and tighter.

There was no designer, no stage manager, no prop master. New equipment was delivered to the door and we had no idea how to install or use it (and some of it didn't work). Rosie and I manipulated bath boards, bath chairs and walking frames; steps, ramps, rests, cushions and pillows; specialist cutlery, drinking cups and food blenders. Ventilators and nebulisers arrived and, although an utterly magnificent woman called Angela showed us how to use them, we had to keep checking the instruction manual and going online to find a way of nursing by YouTube.

Everything came to us at speed. There was hardly time to learn how each piece of kit worked before the pace of the illness made most of the props redundant within two weeks of their arrival.

In the early days, it seemed that we were involved in the bleakest of bedroom farces. Some of the actors weren't up to the job. Out of the first group of carers, lovely though they were, one didn't know how to support Marilyn as she still tried, vainly, to walk; another hadn't changed bedlinen before; a third did not know how to tie shoelaces. When a fourth told us that she couldn't take out Marilyn's earrings, because she had 'a thing' about 'anything that's been in the body', I phoned the organisation to tell them that this wasn't good enough. As a result, I was put through to the woman who ran it.

'Ah yes,' she explained, 'Jane's got a fetish about piercing.'

'You mean a phobia?'

'No, I mean a fetish.'

'I don't think you do.'

'We all have them, Mr Runcie. I've got one about belly buttons. In my early days, when I was caring myself, if I had to wash a patient, I could never catch a sight of their belly button. One glance and I was off. Thought I was going to be sick. Some people are funny like that, aren't they?'

I wanted to give her a badge, as I secretly planned to hand out to so many people over the coming months, saying: *This is not about you.*

That would have been mean. But I didn't know what I was doing any more. Illness makes you mad. It takes you into the opposite of a 'brave new world'. It is a stage on which you hoped you might never have to play a part and in which there is a savage, unreal humour. Our friend Anna told me that, after chemotherapy and the loss of her hair, she went to her local fishmonger who looked at her shaved head and said, 'Hello, Anna, haven't seen you for a bit. Fashion or cancer?'

Our production started running out of control from the very first week of 'rehearsals'. We changed our care provider and chucked more people and more money at the problem in an attempt to 'save the show' but this particular production was unsalvageable. As our GP, Dr R, told us: 'You just have to keep going but, in the end, there is nothing you can do. You have to give in. It just overwhelms you.'

Rosie moved the set around (the main sitting room) and tried to make backstage (the bedroom) as comfortable as possible. There was new furniture (an electric rise-and-recline mobility chair) and different lighting (candles). The initial design had developed into a site-specific show with no audience: or rather, an audience of one or two people at a time.

On Midsummer's Day we decided to visit St Monans. By this stage, travelling anywhere involved packing as if we were going on a family holiday. The car was filled with hospital equipment, walking aids, a ramp and a wheelchair. Getting in and out of it without a fall or some other accident was terrifying. Every movement required extreme concentration.

As we finally set off, the whole business of leaving the house having taken far longer than any of us had anticipated, each of us was thinking, Why are we doing this? Is it really worth the effort? After ten minutes on the road, Rosie insisted that we turn back. We had forgotten Marilyn's neck support and she could not manage the trip without it.

For God's sake, I thought as the journey elongated and felt even more futile.

But we arrived to a clear blue sky, no wind, calm seas and a light that felt as if it would never dim. There were so few people about we seemed to have the entire village to ourselves. It was a still point in a turning world, a time of calm and beauty in which, just for a moment, we could forget that Marilyn was ill. She asked to go to the far end of the harbour where we stopped to look back at the picture-postcard beauty of the houses on the shore. It was the perfect stage set.

Marilyn smiled. She was happy. Joy was still possible. Pleasure was still possible. We were at home on a flawless Scottish evening and none of us had any desire to be anywhere else. We did not want the day to end, determined to wring out every drop of bliss.

It was her last delight.

The following morning was dull and grey. It was spitting with rain. As Rosie helped her out of her chair, Marilyn froze, unable to walk, stand or support herself. Overnight, the illness had moved on to its next relentless stage. If the previous day had been like a dream dress rehearsal, now we could feel the curtain coming down. No more midsummer light, no more beauty, no more smiles, no more laughter, no more loveliness. *Finita la commedia.*

Even then, Marilyn tried to cheer us up, because that was who she was, always seeking out the positive, adding the grace notes, squeezing out the last pips of joy, knowing that life can be ridiculous even when it is at its most tragic. That evening, we watched television and the news reported that, because of the pandemic, the Paralympics were going to be postponed.

'Good,' she said loudly. 'Another year to prepare.'

She always had a fantastic sense of the larky and the ludicrous. When we were then introduced to the concept of a hoist to lift her from place to place and the carers told her that it was going to be quite difficult, Marilyn replied, 'Don't worry. I used to be a glider pilot.'

This was something I didn't know. She had done this in her early twenties. She closed her eyes as she was lifted into the air as if she was in an immersive production of *Peter*

Pan, and I wondered if she was remembering gliding over the fields and farms of Fife, being in another place, a more exciting world, a theatrical or filmic dream: anywhere that was not stuck within the inexorable mundanity of a terminal illness.

Our friend Siobhán told me that the last act in a play is always the least rehearsed and here we were, encountering a surreal version of the same thing, the actor's nightmare of going onstage without knowing the lines, or being unable to remember the play they were actually *in*.

Just as with a first night in the theatre, there were the cards and the flowers and the messages of goodwill. After the show there would be all the questions about 'how it went'. And then, after the one and only night of this particular and exclusive one-woman show, there would be 'the get-out' and the removal of all the props and furniture.

Marilyn and I spoke about her ideas for the funeral and the memorial service and all the actors and musicians she would like to take part and I realised that it was this that was going to be her final production. It was something she could script and plan and control and it would be *her* production at last, not something that had been foisted on her like *The MND Show*.

She wrote to me:

Darling

These are just some thoughts/suggestions for a possible future funeral/memorial service … of course none of this may be at all possible in the current situation … but you and the girls will decide and know best in the circumstances prevailing. I love you and totally trust that I will be delighted by whatever you arrange. You and the girls will know best.

I will be there in spirit
I promise faithfully.
MX

I couldn't really take this in, but this was her first draft of a service. It is, allegedly, one of the 'advantages' of a terminal illness. You have time to prepare.

My father did it when he had prostate cancer, writing his own memorial service and putting the script into a brown envelope called 'The Event'. He took great care over it and gave the script to me a few months before he died, saying, 'I'm rather looking forward to this.'

It's what we are all supposed to do in order to come to terms with our own mortality. We should, like stoics or medieval monks, imagine our own funeral, including the people we want to take part: the minister, the music, the friends and the readings. But very few of us do so, because we don't want to think about the end at all. It seems mawkish, sentimental, even self-indulgent, especially if you are not actually *dying* at the time. But now I think it's a good idea. And this was what was happening to us, all in a rush: this extra, unexpected, production. We could not shirk it. And we wanted it to be right.

When we talked about the idea of a ceremony, a funeral, a memorial or a show together, while Marilyn could still speak (we knew that it wouldn't be long before she could not talk at all) and with all the plans in front of us, she asked, rather tentatively, for something I had forgotten: the traditional, theatrical, 'final round' of applause.

'I will make sure that happens,' I said. 'People will do it anyway. Bill will start it off—' and, at that moment, I could not bear to imagine it.

It was going to be some show: the show of her life.

Venice

Marilyn had never been to Venice and so we decided to spend our honeymoon there. I knew the city well, having at one point wanted to become an art historian. When I was eighteen, I won an essay competition by writing about a Bellini altarpiece. The prize was a week's stay in the city, and I had already been back several times, drawn to its doomed magnificence, its floods and reflections, its mists and revelations. Here was a city that was like an ever-evolving stage set containing history, violence, romance, intrigue and despair. It made death and decay beautiful.

It was late November 1985. We stayed at the Hotel Luna Baglioni, just off St Mark's Square. On the first morning, we walked into the flooded Piazza San Marco, had a coffee at Caffè Florian and turned on to the seafront, passing the Doge's Palace and the Bridge of Sighs, until we reached the public gardens. When we looked back to the island of San Giorgio Maggiore and the Church of the Salute, it was midday. All the church bells started to ring. Marilyn said, 'I've never been so happy.'

We loved the theatricality of Venice. We spent a whole morning looking at a single room of Carpaccio paintings in San Giorgio degli Schiavoni. Marilyn drew her favourite details in her watercolour sketchbooks: a parrot nibbling at a lily, a fine greyhound, a patient little dog and an abandoned turban. We tried to imagine the music the trumpeters and drummers would be playing as St George brought back his slaughtered dragon for the approval of his patron. It was all colour, noise and sumptuous display. Later that day, the Venetians walking the streets for their evening *passeggiata* appeared to be the natural descendants of the characters in the paintings. We laughed to imagine what it might be like if people did this in Glasgow, as if they were performing their own local version of the walkdown in a Scottish pantomime, and Marilyn told me of a disastrous production of *Goodnight Vienna* in Paisley which had gone down 'about as well as a production of *Goodnight Paisley* would have gone down in Vienna'.

Four years later, when she was in labour for the birth of Charlotte, we remembered that morning walk out loud, imagining our steps to take the concentration away from the pain, and we knew then that we would always have this memory to return to; like the slip on two uneven flagstones that Proust makes at the end of *À la recherche du temps perdu* which brings all his memories flooding back, fills him with felicity and makes death indifferent to him.

Marilyn kept a notebook of everything we saw on our honeymoon. She had it specially bound and gilded by an Edinburgh bookbinder and gave it to me that Christmas:

Monday 25 November
We arrived in Venice in darkness, and a dark mist. Leaving the Hotel Luna, we walked to St Mark's Square and the moon shone down full and clear on to the Doge's Palace, the Campanile, the water and us. Some boys played football. The square and the sky were navy blue.

Wednesday 27 November
Today to the church of San Zaccaria – the saint who fathered
John the Baptist. His remains rest here, and a perfect Bellini
altarpiece of the Madonna with Saints (St Jerome in vivid
red). As is common here, you insert 200 lira for light on your
picture – after a short time you are plunged into darkness
again: life!!

The Frari
Thursday afternoon
The Assumption of the Virgin *by Titian. Set above the*
high altar is a piece of wonderful sumptuous craft. The vibrant
orange clothed figure in the foreground, the Virgin's pink robe
swirling around her, the blue of the sky below the gold of the
heavens. Tonight, James gave me a silver butterfly brooch –
farfallo. Delicate and perfect, like the time.

Our favourite place was the Ca' Rezzonico, and Marilyn
writes of it as 'the most beautiful chilled marble, an icy
palace of dead Poesy. Browning died here, and there is a
play to be written about it, a film to be made, pictures to
be painted!'

At the top of the building there are a series of pale
and playful eighteenth-century frescoes by Giandomenico
Tiepolo that tell the story of scenes from the life of
Pulcinella, celebrating the joys of love, courtship and
commedia dell'arte. Masked figures in white are walking on
their hands, attempting a tightrope crossing or drinking
and laughing after a game of badminton. It's a place of
light, summer and celebration.

One scene, *The New World*, puts the viewer at the back
of a crowd of people watching a puppetry act that we
can't see.

'I love this,' Marilyn said. 'It's like waiting for the lights to go down in the theatre, the anticipation that you're going to be in for an adventure, a show in which anything might happen. Just like us.'

I realised that I was now looking at the world through her eyes as well as my own and that I wanted to develop and expand her thoughts in order to continue our conversation. This was the beginning of my wanting to become a writer. In fact, looking back now, I realise that I only became a novelist because of Marilyn. All my books have been dedicated to her. This is not just an act of thankfulness. It is an acknowledgement that she was the first person who made it possible for me to think imaginatively about what it might be like to be someone entirely different.

When we returned home from Venice, I tried to write a novel about the Ca' Rezzonico but I could never quite get it right. Instead, I wrote *The Colour of Heaven*, which begins with the discovery of an abandoned baby in a little side canal in the midst of the Ascension Day festivities. The boy is short-sighted, as I am, and he grows up to go on a journey along the Silk Route, in the spirit of Marco Polo, to search for the perfect ultramarine blue. He finds it in the lapis lazuli caves of Afghanistan, where he meets and falls in love with Aisha, a woman in her thirties who already has a child. So, in fact, it was all about Marilyn.

Venice became our romantic, imaginary home. It was the place where we knew that if we were ever lost or doubted each other we could go back and fall in love all over again. We planned to return every year until we were too old or incapacitated to do so. We even told the children that, when the time came, we wanted to have our ashes scattered over the lagoon.

Fifteen years into our marriage, and celebrating our anniversary, we arrived at Gatwick Airport and I asked Marilyn if she had remembered her passport. Exasperated, she told me that of course she had, here it was, and she opened it to see Charlotte's face staring back at her. 'Oh, my God, I've packed the wrong one.'

This could have cued up all manner of accusation but there was an evening flight from Luton with one space left on it, and we decided that I would travel ahead with the luggage, Marilyn would go home and pick up the correct passport and then come on later. I said I would meet her, just around midnight, at the Piazzale Roma, and we did just that, without any argument, and got the slow vaporetto with no one else on it down the Grand Canal, listening to the slap of the water, the grinding of the gears, and a lone gondolier singing the last of his songs under a full winter moon:

'o sole mio sta nfronte a te!
'o sole, 'o sole mio
sta nfronte a te, sta nfronte a te!

His voice echoed against the old, indomitable stone. We listened as the boat moved through light and shadow. It was as if we were suspended in history. Marilyn cuddled into me and said, 'This is more romantic, isn't it? You see how it's all turned out for the best? Thank you for not being cross. Thank you for loving me.'

For her seventieth birthday, we took six friends and wandered through the rooms of the Ca' Rezzonico once more, sharing our secret favourite place. The next day, we went to the Locanda Cipriani on Torcello with Joanna and Richard, Jo and Stuart, Hildegard and Bill. We drank a crisp Verduzzo Amabile and ate fried courgette flowers and herb-scented grilled fish and talked of love and marriage and how much our friendship meant to each other. Marilyn laughed and laughed and encouraged Bill to tell one of his favourite anecdotes to get the party going. It was about Ken Dodd.

Following a gig in north-east Scotland, his friend Phil Cunningham, the great accordion-playing raconteur, was asked back to the manse by the local minister for a welcome gathering of the local great and the good. As he waited for his first drink of the evening, Phil couldn't help noticing a picture of Ken Dodd on the mantelpiece. He told the minister that he wouldn't normally have had him down as a fan of the buck-toothed Liverpudlian comic with the sticky-out hair. The host handed him his drink. When it was time for a refill, Phil tried again, talking of his love for Ken Dodd and his Diddymen. How tickled he was to have seen him in action. Surely the minister must have done so himself? Yet again, his host was reluctant to come clean. Still, Phil was determined to get the truth out. How did this man come to know Ken Dodd? It was only after his third enquiry, pointing to the picture on the mantelpiece yet again, that the minister grasped Phil's accordion-playing arm and said quietly but exceedingly firmly: 'That's my fucking wife.'

Marilyn had heard the story before but pretended not to have remembered it properly simply so that she could hear it again. She loved shared laughter and encouraging people to be their best selves. She knew the liberating freedom of true companionship where the cares of the world can disappear, if only for a while.

Afterwards we visited the Basilica of Santa Maria Assunta. The flooring was studded with stone and glass, designed in a swirl of cubes, semicircles and triangles that work as grounding to the most beautiful thirteenth-century Byzantine mosaics. We saw the Virgin Mary cradling the Christ Child. The gold background glimmered in the fading autumn light, as if lit by unseen candles, a shimmering glimpse of eternity.

We fell silent. Marilyn took my hand and we looked at an image of the Virgin in Glory filled with wisdom and grace. It had a knowledge of inevitability, but also a strange and lasting permanence. It was sure that it would always be there, long after we had all departed and died, waiting for the next visitors to be consoled by its serenity. We could have stayed there forever.

What Not to Say

Shortly after the diagnosis, a friend *who is a psychiatrist* told us that we should make sure we 'make the most of the precious time there is left'.

I told him that Marilyn and I didn't actually *need* a terminal illness to enjoy each other's company. *All* our time was precious. In another telephone call, he said that I could phone him 'whenever you like' but that 'Saturday afternoons are best for me'.

It's difficult to know what to say in these situations but I thought psychiatrists were supposed to be good at this sort of thing.

A friend in America emailed to say how shocked she was. She had a friend with MND in Bristol. Did I know him? Maybe she thought the diagnosis gave us access to its every victim.

Nurses with experiences of MND warned us that the disease was 'like a roller coaster' but, as the illness progressed, I thought, No, it's not. It's nothing like a roller coaster. Stop saying that. But all the professionals kept coming out with the same phrase, as if it were a mantra or a prayer or a way of filling the silence with a fact. 'Like a roller coaster'. Sometimes they added the word 'journey' for extra effect.

'The journey's like a roller coaster.'

'NO IT ISN'T,' I kept wanting to say. 'We're not going on a journey at all. We're stuck in this flat in Edinburgh in the middle of a lockdown. It is NOT A JOURNEY. And, more importantly, IT IS NOT A BLOODY ROLLER COASTER EITHER. With a roller coaster you have ups as well as downs. The ride is thrilling. With this disease there ARE NO UPS. It is down all the way and it is NEVER thrilling. Try to find some other metaphor. And, while you're at it, you might as well learn from us not to come out with such crap to your future patients.'

But I didn't ever say this. I just replied, 'Yes, I suppose it is.'

I sat on a sofa with the girls and said, 'If anyone tells us that we're going to come out of this stronger, I'm going to kill them.'

'MND,' said Rosie. 'The disease that brings families closer together.'

Dr R said, 'I'm sorry. You wouldn't wish this on your worst enemy.'

'Well, I don't know,' said Charlotte. 'I wouldn't rule it out. Maybe one day I'll meet someone really awful.'

If it was 'like' anything, it was similar to the myth of Sisyphus. No matter how far we pushed the stone up the hill it was always going to roll back down again.

Another friend, who is a therapist, sent me a text. *How are you?*

Three words that take under three seconds to write, requiring an answer that takes far longer. I have come to despise this phrase. There is an immediate answer. *Fine. Coping.* And there is a more hostile response too: *How the fuck do you think I am?*

What those caring for the sick need *least of all* is more work; more explanation, more *things to do*. To answer a friend's 'How are you?' takes time if you want to do it properly.

Almost as bad is 'I wish there was something I could do.'

Well unless you are prepared to help with the shopping, the feeding, the washing, there isn't anything really. I translated the phrase 'I wish there was something I could do' into 'There's nothing I can do' or even 'There's nothing I am prepared to do.'

All these remarks put the onus on the recipient.

Tip: 'Thinking of you' is better. As is 'Do not reply. Just to say that I know it must be impossible. I am sending all my love.'

Or this: 'James. Call any time if you want to, but not if you can't. Any time. Day or night. I mean it.'

Instead of Márquez's *Love in the Time of Cholera* we were faced with *Terminal Illness in the Time of Covid 19*. All our friends wanted to come and pay a visit but the one and only advantage of a pandemic was that we could legitimately say: 'No visitors.' Marilyn did not want to see anyone. She couldn't bear the idea of people witnessing her decline. She was determined to be remembered at her best. Furthermore, she didn't want to upset people. At the beginning of her illness, she could still send little texts and emails but speaking on the phone was hopeless. It exhausted her and she ran out of breath and sometimes she just couldn't face being brave and cheerful any more.

'This is your opportunity,' another carer said to me, 'to prove how much you love your wife.'

Bloody hell, I thought. Soon someone will be telling me that this has all been 'a blessing in disguise'.

'Yes it is,' I wanted to say, 'but I'm not sure I'd describe it as an "opportunity".'

But I said 'thank you' in any case because she was right. It *was* a way of showing, and yes, *proving*, how much we loved her. This love was not about bold romantic declaration or saying the right thing at the right time, or about carefully chosen presents. Those days had gone, even though I did not acknowledge that yet. Now it was about the small things: the slow, patient and deliberate acts of care which we could not mess up because if we did then the consequences would be accident, pain and a quicker decline.

Danger, as the signs say at electricity substations. *Risk of Sudden Death*.

So, what *do* you say when a friend is terminally ill? One of the main things I have learned is that love is nothing if it is not practical. We are not judged by our intentions but our actions. *By your deeds thus shall ye know them.*

This was what Rosie and I were doing. We did not talk about how we were feeling or what it all meant because we were too busy problem-solving. At the same time, we tried to anticipate each stage of the illness, never quite knowing when the next descent was going to come, how steep the fall or how long it might last. Each time we got used to one stage we were on to the next. We were all instinct, all action. Everything was caught up in the moment of caring.

Our friends Florence and Richard came with beautifully constructed soups every other day: curried lentil, spicy tomato, Stilton and broccoli. Alex and Ruth brought sourdough and risotto, Jock and Charlotte arrived with Parmesan and bolognese and our neighbour Jane blended up a different energy juice or smoothie every day for five months. These were simple, everyday acts of kindness from 'the supporting cast' that we will never forget. Rosie and

I then had to add 'Tupperware wrangling' to our stage management of the daily theatre of illness. The front hall became our very own prop store, stacked up with piles of labelled tubs belonging to different people.

The actors kicked in with personalised audiobooks that were sent as attachments directly to Marilyn's phone. Pip Torrens recorded every single one of P. G. Wodehouse's tales of Jeeves and Bertie Wooster. Siobhán Redmond and Deborah Findlay read their favourite stories, Hetty Baynes took on Daphne du Maurier's *Rebecca*. Richard Williams found extracts from actors' diaries and told a wealth of anecdotes. His wife Joanna MacGregor played Chopin mazurkas. Gerda Stevenson sang a song and wrote Marilyn a poem. They were all doing what they were best at.

We received so many flowers that I had to ask people to stop. Our home was looking like a crematorium.

'I haven't died yet,' Marilyn said as I wheeled her back to the bedroom. 'Just in case you were wondering.'

My sister, Rebecca, made it as simple as possible. 'I'm going to send you flowers every Wednesday, the same size for the same vase. You just take the old ones out and put the new ones in. You must have *some* flowers.'

The friends who were not actors (or florists) posted scented candles and soaps and body milks and exotic shower gels. They were thoughtful gestures that helped us to make the most of being at home and made the rooms feel fresh and clean and light and aired. Philip Howard arrived at the same time as the district nurses and handed over a bottle of Givenchy's Dahlia Divin which certainly made a change from the morphine.

It was dangerous and upsetting and sentimental to send memories of holidays and happier times, but this, too, proved strangely comforting. Each week, Bill and Hildegard posted packages containing seven envelopes, a postcard memory or moment of beauty for each day: Matisse's *Two Models Resting*, Elfie Semotan's photograph of a man with a pigeon on his head in Venice, Vallotton's portrait of his wife ('It reminds us of you: Grace and Beauty') and Brancusi's *The Kiss*: 'It says Marilyn and James.'

Comedy was helpful. This wasn't the time for Chekhov, since we were in the middle of a Russian play of our own, but we watched black-and-white classics: all the Fred and Ginger movies, *Some Like It Hot*, *Bringing Up Baby*, *All About Eve*. Siobhán sent DVDs of films we didn't know so well starring Barbara Stanwyck and Rosalind Russell. In the afternoons Rosie nursed and tended Marilyn and they managed to get through the whole series of *Mad Men*, rationing themselves to two episodes at a time. And just as every day of 'lockdown with a terminal illness' was like a Sunday, in the evenings it was time for a period drama. We watched all the Jane Austen, Charles Dickens, George Eliot and Anthony Trollope adaptations we could find, playing our favourite game:

'When did they make this? Who's that actor again? Have you worked with him? Isn't he the one that was in, oh you know, that thing with— oh God, was it Penelope Wilton? Bill was in it too, wasn't he, or was that something else? Look, it's Pip when he had hair! There's Deborah – she should be in it more. God, the music's terrible. It's so badly lit! Derek Jacobi's wig is ridiculous. Wasn't Siobhán in this?'

Sometimes our emotions were hijacked by a plot twist or the death of a character that we hadn't been expecting. On other occasions we decided to confront the eye of the storm by watching the National Theatre relay of *A Monster Calls* in which a young boy has to learn how to come to terms with his mother's death from cancer. Then there was the Royal Ballet's production of *The Cellist*, about the life and death of Jacqueline du Pré. Watching this latter production, in which the magnificent dancer Lauren Cuthbertson moved from graceful ebullience to faltering and falling as multiple sclerosis took hold, was an act of hallucinatory madness. We could not believe that we were following all this; that we had *consciously* chosen to watch a ballet about a woman brought low, literally, by a muscle-wasting disease. I offered to turn it off but Marilyn said, 'No, let's keep going,' as if we were witnessing an illness become an art form. It was, perhaps, a way of framing what was going on, of converting it into theatre. This was another performance that we were going through, or a dream or a parallel life. God knows what it was. When it finished, we sat in silence, acknowledging that the dance had a strange redemptive grace. We had seen the imagined, idealised, balletic version of what life might be like for us in the next few weeks and months. Perhaps this could even be a way of thinking that it was beautiful?

When we ran out of things to say or it all got too much, we listened to music and watched concerts. I read a selection of new novels, some of which I had to put aside as they had too much suffering in them (Maggie O'Farrell's *Hamnet* was abandoned very early on even though we could tell it was a fine piece of writing because it was too good at describing illness). I then read my own just completed novel about Bach, out loud, which, like all my work, is about love and death and Marilyn.

When I approached the last chapter of the book, however, I couldn't continue. I found myself crying, unable to speak at all, and I remembered Dr R's words: *You have to survive it as best you can but in the end you just have to throw up your hands.*

Had we reached that stage? Marilyn smiled, and cried too, and I knew that reading the novel about Bach wasn't the most helpful thing to have done but we both wanted to do it if only because the publication was something to look forward to. It was something to share, another last production.

Charlotte read the whole of *The Hobbit*, *Three Men in a Boat* and *Mallory Towers*, one chapter at a time, and then *The Wind in the Willows*. After that she went on to the collected Wordsworth and any other poem Marilyn requested. She even read Christina Rossetti's poem by a daughter to her mother because, she said, it was loving and essential and had to be done.

To this day I just don't know how she managed to get through reading it out loud at all:

Sonnets are full of love, and this my tome
Has many sonnets: so here now shall be
One sonnet more, a love sonnet, from me
To her whose heart is my heart's quiet home,
To my first Love, my Mother, on whose knee
I learnt love-lore that is not troublesome;
Whose service is my special dignity,
And she my loadstar while I go and come.
And so because you love me, and because
I love you, Mother, I have woven a wreath
Of rhymes wherewith to crown your honoured name:
In you not fourscore years can dim the flame
Of love, whose blessed glow transcends the laws
Of time and change and mortal life and death.

Being Scottish

Marilyn was the second of three children born to an English mother and a Scots father. Her father built his own home in Markinch just after the Second World War, on the side of a hill overlooking the fields of Fife, the railway line and the Haig's whisky plant where he worked as an electrical engineer. His ancestors are all buried in the family plot in the cemetery close by. He was an amateur radio enthusiast, a keen golfer, and the treasurer of the local kirk; a fair-minded and tolerant Protestant without pretension who thought and expected the best of people. Marilyn inherited her sense of duty, justice and fair play from him, and her creativity, musicianship and daffiness from her mother, a Yorkshirewoman who had worked as a nurse in the war and was a splendid baker, singer and jazz pianist. The couple had both been married before. Her mother's first husband was an airman who had gone missing over France, and she had broken off with her family for dark and secret reasons that were never explained. Her father had been married and divorced but this was not discussed either. No one even knew the woman's name. The family mantra was that 'you should always tell the truth, but the truth need not always be spoken'; a belief that led to considerable trouble over the years.

I was born in Cambridge, but my father was a Liverpudlian Scot who fought in the Scots Guards and my branch of the Runcie family originates from Kilmarnock in Ayrshire. Throughout the nineteenth century our family had a draper's shop in the High Street selling suits, overcoats, workwear and even 'little-boy sailor suits for value *extraordinaire*'. I could, if I had the ability, play football or even rugby for Scotland, but my English public-school voice means that I can never pass myself off as a Scot: not even a posh one. I once read out the winning lottery numbers at half-time during a Raith Rovers game in Kirkcaldy but no one came forward because they could not understand what they called 'yer Cambridge accent'. I am a Scot by choice, an 'elected Scot', who still feels a bit of a fraud in the country; and yet I also feel enraged by some English assumptions about Scottish identity.

Two years after Marilyn and I married we moved south so that we could both continue to work for the BBC. I always felt guilty about taking her and Rosie away from their homeland. Neither of them could understand why the English liked imitating their accents as if this was something to be amused by, or how they thought Scots were tight-fisted, or why they refused to accept Scottish money when we were a supposedly 'United Kingdom'. Marilyn was infuriated when her English boss described one of her productions as 'remorselessly Scottish' and how so few people were able to see beyond the haggis, kilts and tartan, quoting P. G. Wodehouse's famous line 'it is never difficult to distinguish between a Scotsman with a grievance and a ray of sunshine.' In Paris, one friend offered Marilyn a glass of champagne assuming that she did not know what it was and had never had it before.

We lived in St Albans and commuted into London on crowded trains for twenty years until we finally couldn't stand it any more and went freelance and moved back to Edinburgh. During our exile, we would return to Scotland as often as we could, not least to see Marilyn's parents and get some proper fresh air. Then, we would drive on up from Fife to Skye and, as soon as we passed through either Glencoe or Crianlarich and saw the smooth roads narrow and the passing places begin, and the grandeur of the landscape open up in front of us, we felt a sense of expansive freedom. We played music very loudly, Big Country, Runrig's 'Once in a Lifetime', 'Letter from America', Barbara Dickson's 'Caravans' and my father's favourite:

Keep right on to the end of the road,
Keep right on to the end,
If the way be long, let your heart be strong,
Keep right on round the bend.

We rented the same house every year, just outside Elgol, with wonderful sunsets and a spectacular view of the Cuillins. It rained often, and there was a fierce wind, but we didn't care. There was always a view and books to read and walks to go on and wild flowers to collect and paint. We read Robert Louis Stevenson and Scottish poetry and the latest novels together with eccentricities such as *The Derk Isle*, a Tintin adventure translated into Scots. We delighted in the incongruity of a Belgian tale peppered with phrases like 'it's luikin dreich', 'dinna staund like a stookie', 'lat's sort oot this clanjamfrie' and 'Scunneration! It's Tintin.'

We found local fish and made soups and shortbread and took boat trips into Loch Coruisk, where Turner painted, and we bought whisky in the bay which Sorley MacLean described in his poem 'Shores':

If we were in Talisker on the shore
Where the great white foaming mouth of water
Opens between two jaws as hard as flint –
the Headland of Stones and the Red Point –
I'd stand forever by the waves
Renewing love out of their crumpling graves …

Dr Johnson came to Skye on his *Journey to Scotland and the Hebrides*, and on one of these holidays we developed the idea to make a play about his dictionary, his travels and his provocations about the country:

'What enemy would invade Scotland, where there is nothing to be got?'

'The noblest prospect which a Scotchman ever sees, is the high road that leads him to England!'

'Much may be made of a Scotchman – *if he be caught young.*'

And there is the famous dictionary definition of the word 'oats': 'a grain which in England is generally given to horses, but in Scotland supports the people'.

In the end, I wrote two plays, *A Word with Dr Johnson* and *Dr Johnson Goes to Scotland*, both performed at Òran Mór in Glasgow and the Traverse Theatre in Edinburgh. Marilyn directed them. They were, in effect, my love letter to Scotland and also a tribute to her, and a thank you for helping me to understand the country better and appreciate what it was like to live here.

Moving back was both a way of hoping for a better life and bringing Marilyn home after too long an exile. We were returning to our roots. In Fife, there was an Imrie who skippered a ship out of St Monans in the seventeenth century, there are Imries who still sail today, and there is a fish and chip shop in nearby Leven called Imries. A 'rouncie' is an old Scots word for horse, and a 'rouncieman' would be a 'keeper of horses'. (A 'runcie' is also old Scots for 'a crease or wrinkle' and 'a coarse woman of foul language, manners and appearance' but I'll let that go.)

Marilyn was so much happier whenever she was in Scotland. Her lungs seemed to open up, her shoulders broadened, her accent strengthened and she smiled and sang and laughed. She had so much more poise and ease and confidence away from the pressures of London. We loved the sea and the landscape and the mad everyday humour of a DIY store called Screw It, an Italian-owned chippy called The Codfather, and a gambling shop called Macbet. Marilyn was home again and came to be more carefree. Whenever she drove me through 'The Kingdom' and seemed to be going completely the wrong way, I would ask her if she was sure of the directions, and she would say, 'You can't go wrong in Fife. Every road takes you home in the end.' And I would reply, 'I suppose it just depends on how quickly you want to get there.' And she would smile and say, 'Are you not enjoying my company? Isn't this beautiful? Look at that view.'

I found it strange, having been brought up in the Oxfordshire countryside where I knew every road and lane, to find myself adapting to this increasingly familiar landscape; to become less English and more Scottish because of my marriage and heritage. I belonged and

I did not belong, but Marilyn was forging a new world for both of us.

It's not always easy. I was as tired as Nicola Sturgeon was after she had spoken at Holyrood and explained that Scotland was 'home to anyone who chooses to live here' only to be heckled with the remark 'except if you're English'. We don't need this kind of nonsense. But Scotland is as lovingly infuriating as any other nation. It can be both aggressive and nostalgic, angry and sentimental, and it sometimes has too fair a conceit of itself. The football is as erratic as the diet – and it must be the only country in the world where you can find a Michelin-starred restaurant next to a methadone clinic. Some people are so angry and drunk and out of it that they want nothing more than 'a square go'. To quote the playwright David Greig in his play *Dunsinane*, the only thing people *can* agree on is that it's cold. But the language and landscape of Scotland, its poetry and song, its enlightenment and its pioneering history, together with its humour and directness, still make it an imaginative and forthright place in which to live. A place of possibility. Marilyn's place. Our place. Home.

She Is Unable to Sing

One of the things I loved best about Marilyn was her voice, and the way she sang in the bathroom and as she walked through the house. It might have been an old folk song, a hymn, some Joni Mitchell or one of Strauss's *Last Songs*. It was a sign that she was happy, full of optimism, ready for whatever the day might bring. I remember saying to Charlotte, before her wedding day and in praise of her future husband, that the one thing I have learned is that it really helps if you marry a cheerful person.

Marilyn started out as a folk singer, playing the guitar and singing solos and duets with her sister in the pubs and clubs of Fife: 'Glasgow Peggy', 'Tarrytown', 'Four Marys', 'The Carls o' Dysart'. It was a way of earning money and having fun and she learned from established performers such as Ray and Archie Fisher, Cyril Tawney, Tom Paxton and the French Occitane singer Jacqueline Conte. She even appeared on television, a recording which is sadly lost, but there is an old reel-to-reel tape that Marilyn cleaned up and had converted into a CD so that it's possible to hear her sing as she did then, when she was nineteen:

Oh sister, sister, come tak a walk
Binnorie, o Binnorie,
And we'll hear the bonnie blackbird whistle ower his note
By the sweet mill dams o Binnorie.

When we began 'courting', that oddly traditional word that politely covers all manner of shenanigans, Marilyn sent me romantic songs about faithless lovers and distant soldiers and sailors, lost love and broken promises. She wrote them out quickly in letters and notes and scraps of paper because she knew them by heart. She used song as another way of talking, expressing her feelings, even saying what she could not say in words. 'Bushes and Briars' became a way of letting me know her fears:

Sometimes I am uneasy and troubled in my mind
Sometimes I think I'll go to my love and tell him my mind ...

She knew that love always involves the dread of losing oneself, of falling so far you can't get back, that it carried such risk, but what was life without risk? We had to chance it all, and laugh and love the moment and so, at other times, she knew that she had to trust that love, or celebrate the fact that it could be absurd and ridiculous as well as fraught with danger and insecurity. She loved to be daft, to riff and to improvise, sending me a card playing on Elvis Presley's 'Are You Lonesome Tonight?':

R you lonesome tonight?
R you thinking of me now?
Rare hearts as one?
R the days when you're not here

Rduous – not fun?
R you lonesome tonight?

Or she crossed Bob Dylan's 'All I Really Want to Do' with a bit of Christopher Marlowe's 'Passionate Shepherd' so that the first letters spelled out my surname:

Really all I want to do, is be
Undressed alone with you
Now I know it's you I love
Come let us all pleasures prove
In bed or out, you're my sweetheart
Every day's a year when we're apart.

When I came back from filming in America, and she was at work, Marilyn left instructions for me to play Joni Mitchell's 'A Case of You'.

'Lined up in the CD player, sweetcakes!'

And I sat on the bed and fell asleep to Joni singing about being in my blood like holy wine and thinking yes, that love was even more than touching souls, it was about being so completely intertwined that you couldn't work out whether any part of you was separate any more; that she had made me whatever I was and would continue to define me and that I could not be described without her.

Marilyn taught a song-writing course at Dartington with her friend Sally Davies where she would draw examples from traditional folk songs such as 'Tom of Bedlam', 'The Outlandish Knight' and 'The Twa' Sisters', and then move on to 'Papa Was a Rollin' Stone' by the Temptations and Joni Mitchell's 'The Last Time I Saw Richard'. Together, we loved to look out for contemporary examples of song as a form of compressed storytelling, whether it was in Eminem's 'Stan', 'A Grand Don't Come for Free' by the Streets or Plan B's 'The Defamation of Strickland Banks'.

She often began her creative-writing classes with 'The Dying Soldier':

When I was on horseback wasn't I pretty?
When I was on horseback wasn't I gay?
O wasn't I pretty when I entered Cork City
When I met with my downfall on the fourteenth of May?

Straight away, you have the place, the date, and the exact moment when the story turns, all in the first verse. Songs show you how to include only what is necessary, and her editing of my novels stressed the need for focus and rhythm and the elimination of excess. Sometimes this meant losing the sections of which I was most proud.

'Do we really need this character?' she would write in the margin, or 'You've done this' or 'Cut!', or an even more brutal 'No! No! No!'

One of her favourite productions was *Dusty Won't Play*, Annie Caulfield's account of Dusty Springfield's tour of apartheid South Africa in 1964 when she refused to perform to segregated audiences. She worked with the singer Frances Thorburn, a blisteringly brilliant actor. It was a show with such bravura and attack, all high-wire, all Frances and all Marilyn, the pleasure of giving it out to a crowd: 'Don't worry, we know how to do this. You're in good hands. Just enjoy it. Just be thrilled.' As soon as it began you could hear the intake of breath from the audience: 'My God, that is Dusty.'

It was a long time after her death before I could listen to the CD of Marilyn singing, hearing the love and joy in her performance, recognising the delight she took in the sheer act of letting her voice run free. I remembered telling people, 'She only sings when she is happy,' and the desperate end of the diagnosis: 'She is unable to sing.'

I waited until she was asleep and listened to her breathing, thinking of 'Every Breath You Take' by the Police and trying to forget that it is actually a song about stalking. Difficulty breathing is a symptom of MND. By a couple of months into the diagnosis, I had become used to the new, terrifying gaps in her erratic breathing, the long pauses when she didn't seem to be breathing at all. I didn't know if her death was going to be tonight or tomorrow night or this week or in a few months. I tried to breathe to the same rhythm so that we could calm each other down. I tried to imagine I WAS her, and what it would be like if I was dying instead of her.

I thought of her carrying voice, her breath control, songs in the shower and as she came out of the bathroom and back into the bedroom:

> *As I walked out one morning in the springtime of the year*
> *I overheard a young sailor or likewise his lady fair*
> *They sang a song together made the valleys for to ring*
> *While the birds on the spray in the meadow gay*
> *Proclaimed the lovely spring.*

Sometimes she would continue drying herself and shake out the talcum powder and sing directly and only to me:

> *Said the sailor to his sweetheart, we soon must sail away*
> *But it's lovely on the water to hear the music play*
> *But if I had my way, my dearest love,*
> *Along with you I'd stay.*

On my desk is the last Valentine card she gave me. It's a red heart placed on a score of music. The heart is outlined by gold wire holding a pearl at its centre. Inside she has written: 'You make my heart sing.'

The One Light We Keep On

Mrs Patrick Campbell observed that 'wedlock is the deep, deep peace of the double bed after the hurly-burly of the chaise longue.' On one holiday in Paris, we went to the Musée d'Orsay and saw Toulouse-Lautrec's famous painting of *The Bed* and Marilyn said, 'Look, it's us, except they're the wrong way round.'

The last Christmas present she gave me was a quilted coverlet for the enormous double bed she had bought for my birthday the previous year. Until then, we had slept in the big brass bed she had kept from her first marriage, and I tried not to mind about this because people tend to hang on to the furniture. I thought of my friend Tom's mother who died in the same bed that she was born in.

But it wasn't long before this new bed and its coverlet had to be moved so the hospital bed could come in. We slept side by side but not in the same bed, neither of us ever saying and both of us knowing that this was the room in which Marilyn was going to die.

We had always found it easy to talk at night. Marilyn called it 'the best part of the day'. It was a way of shutting out the world and being with each other. Now we had to be more careful, time was limited and she was losing the power of speech altogether. Soon there would be no more conversation at all, or I would be talking to her in my head and imagining her replies rather than hearing them directly.

One night, when she could still speak and wanted to share everything, she checked that I was still awake and then said to me in the darkness: 'I don't mind if you marry again, you know.'

And so, just before sleep, I found myself in the middle of a play without a script. I had to be so careful what to say, not just because whatever I said might be wrong, but because she found it hard to speak physically and she must have been gearing up for this, trying to find the right time, wanting the subject aired.

'You do,' I said.

'No, I don't. And I know you will.'

Pause.

'I haven't thought about that at all.'

'Have you imagined it?'

'No, it's ridiculous to think about that now.'

'I know you have.'

This was impossible. I had, of course I had, before I had any knowledge that she was *dying*. Because before then I think, like many middle-aged people (at least I hope I'm right), I had thought about what it might be like to have been married to X instead, if circumstances had been different or life had changed, or if I had never met Marilyn in the first place.

People look back to former loves and mad infatuations and make all kinds of delusional imaginative projections and most of the time they are absurd fantasies. You indulge them to the point of ridiculousness. You even manage to bore yourself. Then you pull yourself together and get on with your life as you should have been doing all along.

But now that Marilyn was still beside me (for how long?) in the dark, and we were together and close and more intimate and fragile and frightened than we had ever been, it was inconceivable to think of being with anyone else, or for anything ever to matter more than this conversation with this person who was so much a part of me lying beside me. *Inconceivable.*

'As long as you're buried with me,' she said.

This was easy to answer.

'I will be.'

'I don't want to be cremated. You know we talked about having our ashes scattered in Venice? I don't want that any more.'

'St Monans?'

'Yes.'

'Burial. I understand.'

Pause – in which I thought, This is too terrible, too mad, I have to think of something to change the mood, to stop her getting too depressed and introverted – although why should she not?

'I could still go first,' I said.

'Don't joke.'

'I will always love you. You know that. You will always be the love of my life.'

'You don't know that.'

Pause.

'I'd have to live to ninety-eight to be with someone longer than you.'

Pause.

'You've worked it out already?'

'I just did it in my head. I wasn't *thinking about it.*'

'I bet you were.'

'I wasn't.' *Pause*. 'You know I love you best. That this is best.'

'I know. I love you best too.'

Pause – in which neither of us knew what to say and I was just about to say 'Night night' again, thinking that all this was finished and she should stop being anxious but why should she not be, she was dying for God's sake, when Marilyn said, 'I think I'd rather you just had a string of affairs with women who can't possibly live up to me.'

This was impossible to predict or answer and it was not helpful to go any further down this route. 'I'll do my best, then,' I said.

'I'm sure you will.'

'None of them will ever come close. You do know that?'

'You say that now.'

'I mean that now.'

This was too raw. But how much time did we have left when she could articulate any of this?

'Let's not argue,' I said. 'You don't have to worry.'

(And I knew that was the wrong thing to say even then but how could I get through one of the last proper conversations we were ever going to have without saying the wrong thing at least once? Never had both of us been so careful of conversation.)

'No, I won't. But I hope I'll be watching over you.'

'You don't need to hope …'

'Like the song …'

'"Someone to watch over me". I'll imagine you watching anyway. You know you'll always be with me.'

'I hope that's true.'

'I know it's true.'

Pause.

Was this the end of the conversation? Could we go to sleep now?

'Night night,' she said. 'And thank you.'

'I love you.'

'I love YOU.'

And I leant over and kissed her on the lips and we both knew her body was failing and I wanted to say to her: 'If I ever love anyone again then *part* of what they love in me, or even *most* of what they love in me, will be *you.*'

But I couldn't say this because I could already hear her saying, 'Well, that is of no comfort to me,' or even her usual response when she knew that I was winning an argument but could not accept it.

'That's true.'

It used to infuriate me. 'That's true? Why can't you just admit that I am right?'

But then we were hopeless at arguments. Every time she was cross with me, I felt so terrible that I was sure my insides were emptying and I wanted to go to the bathroom. This happened so often that she used to shout just as she was getting to her main point: 'Don't wriggle out of it now by pissing off to the lavatory!'

And then there was the time I couldn't stop pressing home my point, I can't remember what it was about, and she said to me, 'Oh, just fuck off and grow up, James Runcie.'

And I said, 'What do you want me to do first? Fuck off and then grow up or grow up and then fuck off?'

She was furious with my pettiness, and I was reminded of being a precocious thirteen-year-old boy, a git really, at my prep school, and the housemaster continually warning us not to talk after lights out and then finally snapping and coming in and turning on all the lights and shouting to a room full of twelve prepubescent boys: 'WHO IS TALKING? WHO IS TALKING?'

And I replied, 'You are, sir,' and got hit with six of the best with a slipper for the cheek of it all.

It was absurd to think of all this now, life in a school dormitory, and I realised that Marilyn's hospital bed was equally so institutional, so resolutely, so practically, so defensively single.

At the Frieze Art Fair in 2018, the Ingleby Gallery showed a group of paintings by Andrew Cranston. They were the size of the spine and cover of a hardback book, unframed and applied directly to the wall, and they were arresting in their eerie directness: a girl and a dog, four heads bobbing in the sea, a baby crawling across a carpet, a semi-nude woman ironing with the steam rising in front of her breasts like a modern Bonnard. They had extraordinary titles: *Loyalty to a Nightmare*, *It Seems So Long Ago*, *In Solace of Dogs*, *If I Were a Carpenter*.

I was particularly drawn to a painting of a couple in bed, because it seemed like a variant on the Toulouse-Lautrec painting Marilyn and I had stood before in Paris. This was all white duvet for two-thirds of the picture, and only the heads of the couple were visible. But they looked like us when we were younger, and again they were the wrong way round. It was called *The Innocents* and I was determined to buy it on a whim. Us in bed. We could hang it in the bedroom. It would be lovely.

'What about this instead?' said Marilyn, standing over to the left and looking at something completely different. 'I think it's more evocative. More mysterious. You have to think about the story behind it.'

It was a dark painting, khaki and sombre green, of a room with a table and three chairs lit by a single Victorian lamp. Painted in enamel oil on the cover of a hardback book by Victor Hugo, it was called *The One Light We Keep On*. It was the artwork the gallery used to advertise the show. They had only just put it up.

'Let's buy it,' I said. Only later did we read the artist's note about it: 'The light maybe of a writer, a night writer. Maybe W. S. Graham, the night–fisherman catching his poems in his nets … The hour is very late or very early or, as my friend Eddie Summerton calls it, "between the late and early". Four in the morning. The hour of the wolf. The hour that most people die and most babies are born.'

It is the time I always wake up, when I wonder if I am still dreaming or not. The painting now hangs in the hall, and every time I pass it to go in or out of the house, I think of that day with Marilyn in the autumn of 2018 before we knew that anything was wrong, and I remember the Smiths song 'There Is a Light That Never Goes Out' and I know beyond all doubt and with all my certainty that her light will be the light that I always keep on.

Goodbye, Old Life!

From: *The Cherry Orchard.*

LUBOV: Let's go!

LOPAKHIN: Are you all here? There's nobody else? There's a lot of things in there. I should lock everything up. Come on!

ANYA: Goodbye, old house! Goodbye, old life!

TROFIMOV: Welcome, new life.

LOPAKHIN: Until the spring, then! Come on ... till we meet again! [*Exit.*]

There are moments of grim humour amidst the dying. 'I am not in pain,' Marilyn told me (although this was not true), 'and I have not lost my mind. At least I have been spared cancer and dementia. I'll leave that to you.'

The nutritionist telephoned to discuss the inevitability of a liquid-only diet and the need for proper vitamins. There were some new flavours of Complan that she thought Marilyn might like.

'I would rather die than eat Complan,' Marilyn replied. 'In fact, I *will* die rather than eat Complan.'

I wrote friends a long and desperate email, letting them know that the end would not be far away. *To imagine it in Chekhovian terms, it's a little like the end of* The Cherry Orchard *— imagine a lit house on a summer evening with no one in it but an elderly servant going round and slowly blowing out all the candles one by one until the darkness comes.*

When Marilyn demanded I show it to her, she was furious, particularly about the reference to Chekhov.

'It's so self-indulgent.'

'But it's the truth. We can't put on a show any more. We have to tell people what's going on.'

Marilyn did not want her friends to know any of the grim and humiliating reality. She hoped that everything would continue to be as right as it possibly could be — even when it wasn't. Although she was a 'patient' patient, she couldn't accept or come to terms with what was happening. She never wanted to die. I couldn't ever persuade her to make her peace or reach a state of resignation and I think that I will always feel a failure for not inspiring any readiness in her. She hated the fact that she was dying until the end.

I once gave a lecture in the National Library of Scotland about David Hume and the exact moment that he realised he was going to die. He was composing a short, handwritten autobiography, twelve and a quarter pages in length, entitled 'My Own Life'. It is dated 18 April 1776 — two months after he had bought his own grave plot for £4, and four months before his death.

At first glance it is not a particularly exciting read; a personal entry, perhaps, for the *Dictionary of National Biography*. But then something extraordinary happens; for this document contains what I believe to be the most telling grammatical change in the history of literature.

After recounting the story of his literary career, his employment in France and his return to Edinburgh, Hume announces the onset of his final illness. 'In spring 1775 I was struck with a disorder in my bowels which at first gave me no alarm, but has since, as I apprehend it, become mortal and incurable. I now reckon on a speedy dissolution.'

The words are specific – mortal, incurable, a dissolution.

This was happening to Hume as he wrote; and yet he was also sanguine: 'I possess the same ardour as ever in study, and the same gaiety in company. I consider besides, that a man of sixty-five, by dying, cuts off only a few years of infirmities; and – though I see many symptoms of my literary reputation's breaking out at last with additional lustre – I know that I had but a few years to enjoy it. It is difficult to be more detached from life than I am at present.'

He had reached a state of acceptance and was ready for death.

Now comes the crucial switch. It occurs right in the middle of the sentence: 'To conclude historically with my own character – I am, or rather *was* (for that is the style I must now use in speaking of myself; which enables me the more to speak my sentiments), I was, I say, a man of mild dispositions, of command of temper, of an open social, and cheerful humour, capable of attachment, but little susceptible of enmity, and of great moderation in all my passions.'

This is one of the great statements of the Enlightenment. David Hume realised the enormity of what he was saying *as he was writing it down*; the fact, and the impact of his death, suddenly hit him – his pen in his hand – and he moved from the present to the past, and from life to death, in the same sentence.

'I am …' he began, and you can sense him stopping. You can almost see the pen in the air above the paper.

You can hear, in that slightest of pauses, Hume correcting himself: '… or rather *was*'.

In my experience authors often do not know what they really think until they write it down. They discover their thoughts in the process of writing. It is the act of writing itself that articulates both thought and emotion.

So in reading this passage you can hear David Hume thinking aloud; and stopping.

Now he must collect himself. He returns the pen to the paper and picks up the pace of the prose with an explanation and a justification ('for that is the style I must now use in speaking of myself; which enables me the more to speak my sentiments').

He realises that this switch of tense makes him free. He does not need to worry about what people will think. When people read this, he will be dead. He can say what he likes; the idea of death liberates his prose.

There then follows a list of his achievements. But these are not *literary* achievements – they are achievements of *character*. He was, he says, 'a man of mild dispositions, of command of temper, of an open social, and cheerful humour, capable of attachment, but little susceptible of enmity, and of great moderation in all my passions … even my love of literary fame, my ruling passion, never soured my humour, notwithstanding my frequent disappointments …'

Cheerfulness, warmth of character and good company are of equivalent, or of even greater benefit, to reputation than literary achievement. 'Mr Hume,' his cousin, the

Reverend John Home, wrote, 'in the latter part of his life, retired to his native country, and devoted the evening of his days to Hospitality, Elegance, Literature and Friendship.'

These were our values. It's what Marilyn and I believed in. Hospitality, Elegance, Literature and Friendship. Now I thought it was my duty to help her come to terms with what was happening and approach the end with the sagacity of David Hume.

Except she wasn't David Hume. She was Marilyn, and she hated everything that was happening. I couldn't foist my opinions and expectations upon her or help her to come to terms with what was happening at all. She had to find her own way of dying, and this was private, almost secret. I never really knew how much she was protecting me from her pain and her feelings or what she thought and feared in her darkest moments because, of course, she could hardly speak. She would listen, and nod, and give little instructions when she could, but she was beginning to be locked in to the intense and devastating loneliness of dying.

We would just have to talk to each other as much as we could and while she was still able to do so. After that, we would have to rely on our mutual love and understanding. The unspoken love. The understood love.

This is now the hardest bit to write.

Because there was no way to predict when the end might come, I said goodbye to her four times. The first two were frightened brevities, 'just in case' farewells, making sure that she knew I loved and would always love her. The third was more urgent, when she could hardly speak at all and I really thought that she might die *that very night*. I hadn't prepared anything. I wasn't David Hume. You don't ever quite think of the last words you might want to say to your beloved, you just have to say them, even if they come out wonky.

So I began to talk to Marilyn as she lay beside me, breathing erratically. I told her that it was all right, I would look after the girls, and we would look after each other, and she had given us so much love that it would sustain all our futures. We would never be without her. Then, just as I was hitting full flight, telling her that I had always loved and adored her and how she would always be a part of me, and that it was impossible to think of myself as a separate person, she said, very quietly: 'Enough.'

I didn't know whether this was editing or because she had got the message or because she couldn't say anything in return. I think it was probably that she couldn't bear to hear all this and to think about what we were both losing. Perhaps it was also to spare me getting upset, even though I had tried not to cry. I wanted to be clear and consoling and full of steadfast love.

I Corinthians 15:58. *Be ye steadfast, immovable, always abounding in the work of the Lord, knowing that your toil in the Lord is not in vain.*

I once staged a non-stop reading of the King James Bible at the Bath Literature Festival. It took ninety-six hours and thirty-eight minutes. I was interviewed about it on Radio 4 and Marilyn recorded the interview on her phone and kept it there because, she said, 'I guessed what they were going to ask and I knew what you were going to say.'

The presenter wondered about my favourite verse and I told him it was from the Book of Ruth and he asked me to read it: *And Ruth said, 'Entreat me not to leave thee, or to return from following after thee: for whither thou goest, I will go; and where thou lodgest, I will lodge: thy people shall be my people, and thy God my God. Where thou diest, will I die, and there will I be buried: the LORD do so to me, and more also, if ought but death part thee and me.'*

But now Marilyn really was leaving me and I tried to tell her that it was all right to let go. She didn't have to keep on fighting. I was 'entreating' her to leave and I had to say this without sounding as if I *wanted* her to die.

I just couldn't believe her suffering, *I could not stand it.* Her breathing became steady and yet desperate. I couldn't take in that she had four or five days of fight still left in her, even when she could no longer eat or drink. But on the last evening I knew that we were approaching the end. We all did, because the carers left in tears.

The girls performed their nightly ritual of rubbing her favourite lavender-scented cream into her sore arms, and Charlotte read her Wordsworth's 'Daffodils'. They lit a candle and kissed her goodnight.

Then Marilyn and I were alone. I had said goodbye three times already and been told that it was 'enough'. What to do? Should I repeat myself? I had said all that I had to say. There were no more words.

But there was music. We listened to the whole of Purcell's *Dido and Aeneas* with the great aria 'When I Am Laid in Earth'. I discovered the recording of Teresa Stich-Randall singing Schubert's 'Ave Maria' that we had listened to together on vinyl just after we had found each other. We were remembering the love we had when we first met and the world was all before us.

In my end is my beginning.

I found Andreas Scholl singing 'Che Faro' from Gluck's *Orfeo*, that great desperate lament as Orpheus sings of his love for Eurydice, and how he cannot bear to live without her, and he looks back to see her because he cannot think of doing anything else, and I promised Marilyn that I would always turn back, I would never not see her, she would always be with me, wherever I was, wherever she was.

I fell asleep. We all did. We couldn't stay awake any longer.

And then, in the darkest hours of the night, as Marilyn slept beside me, with the whole house quiet and at peace, her ragged breathing stopped, and she died.

Son of a Preacher Man

Like doctors, many children of the clergy enter the same profession as their parents; or they go off the rails, reacting violently to the idea of sacrifice and goodness. But I think they also inherit a desire to be heard and to entertain, and so it's no surprise that showbusiness is a strange by-product of a religious upbringing: Laurence Olivier, Alice Cooper, Denzel Washington, David Tennant and Katy Perry are all children of clerics. There is a theatricality to the pulpit, procession and common worship.

I was brought up in the village of Cuddesdon, in the Oxfordshire countryside, where the rituals of birth, marriage and death were marked every day. It was a world where tragedy came to the house. I remember being six years old and answering the door when my father was out. I had to remember a message. 'Kevin Dymock has been knocked off his motorbike. He has internal bleeding. He may not last the night.'

And yet it was also comic. My father's secretary, Mrs Maguire, said that when her husband left her for another woman, it was the mistress who came back to fetch his things. 'What does he like for his tea?' she asked, and the devout Mrs Maguire told my father, 'I was so angry, Vicar, this great red mist descended upon me, and I thought of the rudest thing I could say to her and I just spat it out. *Harpic*, I said.'

Mrs Maguire is the name of the housekeeper in my detective series, *The Grantchester Mysteries*, and the central character, Sidney Chambers, is a tribute both to the maverick eighteenth-century clergyman Sydney Smith and to my father. He is also, naturally, a clerical version of me, imagining a different life I might have led, and Hildegard, his German wife, self-indulgently named after my friend Hildegard Bechtler, is very much Marilyn in disguise.

When I told my father that I wanted to marry her he looked very dubious. My parents had only met her once. Afterwards my mother had said, 'She's very nice but it'll never last.'

'Are you asking for my advice or are you telling me?' my father asked. We were sitting in his study in the middle of Lambeth Palace. There are less intimidating places.

'I'm telling you.'

'Well, then. We'll do everything we can to support you.'

He couldn't marry us in church because Marilyn was a divorcee, but he could still bless us, and rather than reminding us of Dr Johnson's dictum that a second marriage is 'the triumph of hope over experience' he gave us a leather-bound Bible and wrote in the front in big bold handwriting: 'LOVE NEVER FAILS.' He even underlined it.

It was only a few years after he had married Prince Charles and Princess Diana, with the oft-quoted phrase, 'Here is the stuff of which fairy tales are made: the Prince and Princess on their wedding day.' But whenever it is referenced, people fail to remember the warning that follows: 'But fairy tales usually end at this point with the simple phrase, "They lived happily ever after." This may be because fairy stories regard marriage as an anticlimax after the romance of courtship. This is not the Christian view. Our faith sees the wedding day not as the place of arrival but the place where the adventure really begins …'

Marilyn and I married in a registry office in Dunbar, in East Lothian, looking out to sea. The service of blessing was held three days later in Lambeth Palace Chapel with music by Thomas Tallis and William Walton and Harvey and the Wallbangers, with seven-year-old Rosie as the flower girl. It was celebratory and sombre, and my father was determined that we obeyed all the rules and said the prayer of penitence out loud and in front of everyone.

We offer and present to you, Lord, ourselves, our souls and bodies, our thoughts and deeds, our desires and prayers. Forgive what we have been, consecrate what we are, and direct what we shall be, in your mercy and in your love.

He may have been considered 'a wet' by the press at the time, but he was nothing like that when it came to matters of faith:

Let their love for each other be a seal upon their hearts, a mantle about their shoulders, and a crown upon their foreheads. Bless them in their work and in their companionship; in their sleeping and in their waking; in their joys and in their sorrows; in their life and in their death.

I could still preach some of his marriage sermons to this day. He told each congregation that the best present they could give each happy couple was not a food mixer or a set of table napkins but that 'as they pledge themselves to each other before the altar of God, they are surrounded and supported by the sincere affection and genuine prayer of family and friends. That is a present for a lifetime.'

The celebrant then addresses the congregation, saying: 'Will ye who have witnessed these promises do all in your power to uphold these two persons in their marriage?'

People: 'We will.'

Marilyn and I were not regular churchgoers, nor did we pray regularly even though she sometimes wished that we would. I had always been somewhat distrustful of the phrase 'the family that prays together stays together' and, having had an evangelical Christian girlfriend in the past, I am dubious about public demonstrations of belief, preferring to keep my fluctuating attitude to Christianity private.

But I cannot avoid writing about faith, love and death. They are my only subjects, even if I cannot fully trust in the promise that an all-powerful God has an actively benevolent presence in the world. Perhaps I have always been guilty of taking Pascal's wager that it is more prudent to believe than not. It's an insurance policy for eternity. Therefore, whenever I have been asked about it publicly, I have tended to hide behind Thomas Carlyle's idea of a life of doubt enriched by faith.

I came unstuck twice when promoting the prequel to *The Grantchester Mysteries*: once at the Barnes Literary Festival where a woman asked me if I believed, was unsatisfied by my reply and asked, 'Well, do you go to church? Do you pray? You can't be half-hearted about this' – and then again, when I was interviewed for the Salvation Army magazine, *War Cry*. I was expecting the usual cosy little interview, but it began with this question: 'How would you describe your relationship with Jesus?'

'A bit on and off,' I replied, which was hardly satisfactory. I seem to want to have it both ways. I like to be part of the club when I do go to church and can be positively hypocritical with people who take up the option of Christianity *lite*.

I am stroppy, for example, with people in England who pretend to be Christian in order to get their children into a good free Church of England or Catholic school – how they're all eager to help film the nativity play or edit the school magazine but as soon as their kids have got their A levels they're never seen in church again. *Bye!*

And I am unfairly judgemental when people who are, at best, agnostics use historic churches as some kind of drop-in centre for baptisms, weddings and funerals to give their relentlessly secular lives an Instagram-friendly spiritual pit stop.

So, I have sympathy with a vicar at a recent wedding who called a halt to the first hymn when no one was singing it properly. 'Stop, stop, stop – I know you're only here for the architecture – but *make an effort*.'

And there comes a time when you really do have to make up your mind about your faith; and that time is probably when one of you is faced with a terminal illness.

We were sitting looking out to sea in St Monans and I asked Marilyn if she wanted to talk about faith and the funeral and what she thought about God.

'Oh, I'm still quite keen on him,' she said, 'in spite of what he's done to me.'

I had tried to prepare for this moment in my writing. Sidney's wife dies at the end of *The Grantchester Mysteries* and I wrote it in a wild haze of anticipatory grief, long before any diagnosis, just to protect myself, and it had gone down very badly with the rest of the family. ('I hope you're not expecting praise,' said Charlotte.)

But no matter how much you try to imagine what you might feel, to anticipate a situation is by no means to understand it. Everything still comes as a shock and I'm not at all sure if you ever quite get to the stage when 'the readiness is all' or steady yourself for how you are going to feel when you find yourself sitting next to your wife on the bench of desolation.

I asked Marilyn if she'd like to see our friend Neil Gardner, the minister at Canongate Kirk, whom she had mentioned in her plans for the memorial service.

'I would. If he can come. Not on the phone.'

At the peak of Covid the only help being offered was online and on the telephone; but Neil came to the house and kept his social distance and we talked quite naturally and easily about the funeral service as if we were preparing for some kind of party.

We discussed what might be possible under lockdown, not knowing when on earth this was all going to take place, but we had decided on a burial, not a cremation, in St Monans, on the headland looking out to the Firth of Forth. There would be a piper and psalms of the sea. Neil understood. He'd done this before. He is, as we like to say in our family, 'a proper priest', serious and compassionate, kind and funny. He believes that there is a future for our deepest loves and, as he spoke and prayed, I felt the reassurance of centuries of faith.

O Lord, support us all the day long of this troublous life, until the shades lengthen, and the evening comes, and the busy

world is hushed, the fever of life is over, and our work is done.
Then Lord in your mercy grant us safe lodging, a holy rest and
peace at the last; through Jesus Christ our Lord. Amen.

After Marilyn's death, the consolations of Christianity arrived from the most surprising places. Heather, a friend in St Monans, sent me a simple text: *Psalm 34 v 18 God is close to the broken-hearted.*

Our feisty no-nonsense dry-cleaners handed me this card:

Dear Mr Runcie and family
We are so sorry for your loss.
May God's grace enable you to see a future laced with hope,
and may you be given the gift of faith to trust HIM in all
things. As one day gives way to another, so may darkness gives
way to light, sadness yield to joy, and despair surrender to hope
in you.
Thinking of you all at this sad time
Michelle and Marcia

When Marilyn had first taken me to St Monans in 1987, to see Scotland's closest church to the sea, the one with the boat hanging from the centre of the nave, we arrived in the middle of a funeral. It seemed to involve all the men and women in the village, the sexes separated and dressed in black. The only sounds were of a tolling bell, footsteps on gravel, the cawing of the rooks and a distant sea. It was cold and sombre, respectful and strangely unforgiving. *This is what we do here*, the village seemed to be saying, *and this is what we have always done. We keep the faith.*

We moved to the village in 2016, anticipating many years together and a long and happy retirement, and, after

97

we had made some initial adjustments, we decided to re-do the kitchen, asking Alan, the local joiner, if he could organise the refit. He came round, a calm, wise man, who looked like Father Christmas. As is traditional in a Scottish village, he was also the undertaker, and an elder in the kirk, and he was the man you needed to get onside if you were to be a part of the community.

Marilyn quickly made it clear that she had been born in Fife, that she knew the area well, her father worked at Haig's and she had gone to nearby Buckhaven High. Alan immediately started speaking to her as if he had known her all his life.

When I had to tell him that she was terminally ill, he couldn't quite believe what I was saying. There were long pauses. I didn't know if he could still hear me or if the line had gone dead. I told him I was worried that we were in Edinburgh, he was in Fife and we were in the middle of a pandemic. There was a silence and then he said with infinite kindness, as if he were my father or even my grandfather, 'Don't you worry about any of this. Leave it with me. Call when the time comes and we'll be there. You have only one thing to do. Look after her. She's a fine woman.'

After Marilyn died, Alan came within an hour and a half with his son and one other undertaker. He stood at the foot of the bed, and lowered his head, half bowing, as in prayer, acknowledging her death. Then he told me to wait with the girls in another room. We should leave it to him. And then they carried my wife out of the house forever.

We travelled on behind as soon as we were ready. We could not bear to think of Marilyn in St Monans without us. Alan stopped at the house and assured us that all was well, she was in the Chapel of Rest, and he'd give her the funeral he'd hope for himself. I told him that I wanted it to be as traditional as possible, in accordance with all the rites of the Church of Scotland. We decided on a simple oak coffin with rope handles, the kind a sailor might have, with garlands of flowers from the fields and farms of Fife.

The funeral was on 1 September 2020. There were eleven of us when there should have been hundreds. But these were still the days of Covid. Alan arrived and shook my hand and Neil sat with the hearse. It was ten forty-five in the morning, on a bright and clear day. The tide was on the way out, which seemed appropriate. We sat in the cars, and Alan walked ahead of us all with his frock coat and velvet top hat and walking stick – I didn't know it was called *paging* until then – and people in the village stood outside their doors to watch us pass as we travelled through the harbour and up the hill to the kirk and cemetery.

It all took place in the open air and the piper walked us in to 'MacCrimmon's Lament'. Neil stood beside the grave and read from the psalms and prayed. He talked of Marilyn's love of the sea and Christ calming the storm and how the storm of her life had passed and now she could rest. She had no need of her body any more. The coffin was lowered and we threw rose petals and held on to each other, and I couldn't believe that we were doing this now, in a beautiful village, and that this life-force, wife, mother, sister, friend, was no longer with us. Surely this was all a dream, my whole life was a dream, this could not be right, but this calm man was speaking, and it was a magnificent day in an extraordinary place, and it felt as right as it could possibly be. It was everything she had asked for, and we had done it, even though I had never really imagined doing any such thing at all.

The piper played 'The Flooers o' the Forest', and then we were not sure what to do next. He started to lead us away, back home, and we were leaving Marilyn there in the graveyard without us and it seemed so wrong to abandon her. I looked out to sea and remembered my mother and father and their deaths too, and the loss of Marilyn, my greatest love who could never be replaced. Then I thought of the words from the Song of Solomon: *Many waters cannot quench love. Neither can the floods drown it.*

There were gulls swooping low over the far-off water and the light was sharp on the horizon. The day was reaching out for completion: life continuing without her.

After …

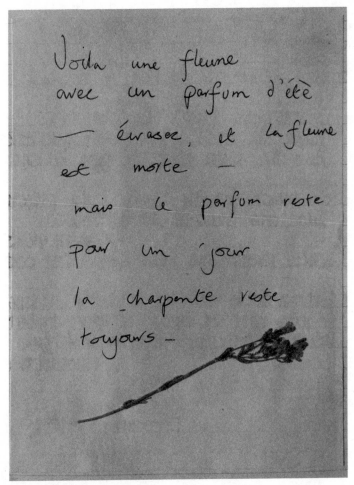

Voila une fleure
avec un parfum d'été
— éwasee, et la fleure
et morte —
mais le parfum reste
pour un jour
la charpente reste
toujours —

Marilyn's notebook, France

Solo

I had never lived on my own before. Everything became strange and dream-like, as if I was inhabiting someone else's life. I couldn't quite believe how any of this had happened. There didn't seem to be any *point* to anything I was doing. I found a card Marilyn had given me, a cut-out of a ship's anchor in blue and white. On the back she had written: 'You are my soul's anchor.' Well, now I was anchorless.

Was this the beginning of old age, I wondered, in which the days feel so long and yet the years are so short?

When we first moved to St Monans, Marilyn was sixty-eight years old and told our friend Hildegard that she was hoping 'for ten good years here'. In the end, we had three and a bit.

My two-year-old granddaughter looked at a picture of Marilyn taken in a garden when she was forty and smiling and had so much life ahead of her: 'Do you want her to come back?'

I said I did.

'But she can't,' Bea told me. 'She died.'

'I know,' I said. 'It's very sad.'

She put her hand to her chest as her mother had taught her and said, 'Grandma in our hearts.'

I read her stories to stop myself crying. I even made one up, about a man who lived his whole life upside down. Then it was time for Bea to go home and I was on my own once more. What to cook and what to remember? What does a widower do with the seemingly endless days ahead?

Time stretched away because there was no urgency. Friends told me that I could do anything I liked. But what did I like? How was I to live now, not so much in the shadow of death but in the darkness of grief?

Sometimes, it was the stupid little things (setting out two cups for coffee in the morning and then realising that I only needed one), receiving her post (Sun Life Assurance guaranteeing a lump sum of £10,000 – *I don't think so*), or remembering that Marilyn always used to accuse me of never putting back the bathmat – *well, I'm certainly putting it back now*. These everyday details were intermingled with the enormous things (not hearing her voice, not having anyone to tell me that they loved me, sleeping alone, imagining her breathing as if she were still alive and beside me in the night).

In the past, whenever anything went wrong in life or at work (an argument with a friend, an impossible television presenter, a bitchy review of one of my books) I would return to her as my strength and shield. *You can say what you like, I don't care, because I've got my wife.*

Marilyn once directed J. M. Barrie's play, *What Every Woman Knows*. First performed in 1908, it's about the feckless son of an aristocrat who only survives as an MP because his wife helps him to write his speeches. She underplays her suggestions, saying that her notes are 'just trifles – things I was to suggest to you – while I was knitting – and then if you liked any of them you could have polished them'. But then, after he ditches her for a trophy girlfriend, he loses his 'neat way of saying things' because his best phrases have all come from his wife. He finally realises that his career cannot survive without her. At the end of the play, she tells him: 'It's nothing unusual I've done, John. Every man who is high up loves to think he has done it all himself; and the wife smiles, and lets it go at that. It's our only joke. Every woman knows that.'

Only occasionally did Marilyn have to remind me of this story, because I freely acknowledged that she was the force behind everything I did. She encouraged me to be more than I ever imagined I could be.

There were times when she ambushed me with ideas. When she went to the BBC for a meeting and heard that they were looking for a history play on a big subject for Easter, she said, 'I'll get James to write a play about Bach.' When a bibliophile told her that five out of the six assistants on Dr Johnson's dictionary were Scottish, Marilyn turned to me and said, 'That's a play.' And when my novel, *East Fortune*, sold badly and I couldn't imagine how I would ever make a living from writing, she said that perhaps we needed to think completely differently about my work.

She was directing John Mortimer's *Rumpole of the Bailey* at the time, and we wondered about the secret of its popularity. What would it mean to write a similar series with a lovable central character, someone like my dad, perhaps? And so, eventually, the clerical detective Sidney Chambers came into being and *The Grantchester Mysteries* began. Originally this was set in Westminster Abbey, but Marilyn said, 'No, no, make it Cambridge, where you were born. You know about that.'

I started to write it, chapter by chapter, and Marilyn would then either pencil notes all over the manuscript, telling me what to cut, clarify or expand, or she would send me an email full of ideas. By Book Three, she would even add passages of her own to give me the notion of where I needed more. This was especially true of the scenes between Sidney and his wife because their marriage was, of course, similar to our own.

One story came back with her suggestions in capital letters:

Hildegard was unimpressed when Sidney returned from his lunch at six o'clock in the evening. She was not jealous of Amanda, she told him yet again, AS SHE POINTED THE COLANDER AT HIM IN WHAT COULD ONLY BE DESCRIBED AS AN AGGRESSIVE MANNER, and it wasn't, SHE ASSURED HIM AS SHE RINSED THE VEGETABLES, that she minded them spending so much time together, but he had completely forgotten that they had arranged to have tea with one of the most boring couples in the village. SHE TOOK THE VEGETABLE KNIFE FROM THE DRAWER AS SHE TOLD HIM HOW she had been stranded with them alone FOR ALMOST AN HOUR BEFORE SHE COULD MAKE HER ESCAPE, and ALSO, SHE REMINDED SIDNEY TESTILY, WAVING THE KNIFE AT HIM EMPHATICALLY, he had still done nothing about finding a new curate to replace Leonard Graham, who would have been able to go in his place. SIDNEY TOOK THE VEGETABLE KNIFE FROM HER, KISSED HER, AND SOLEMNLY PUT THE COLANDER ON HIS HEAD.

It was typical of her to suggest a moment of daffiness to add detail and lighten the mood. She also reminded me that *Rumpole* was based on the idea of a triple narrative and that I could replicate this in *Grantchester*. There should be a crime story that was solved at the end of every episode, a character plot that evolved through the series and a comic diversion to provide light relief. The challenge was to establish an authoritative tone that the reader could trust, keep all the different balls in the air at the same time, and build to a satisfyingly unexpected conclusion.

'Simple,' she said, and laughed. Then she kissed me, lightly, on the lips: a blessing and an encouragement.

We spent so many hours reading, writing and talking through ideas that I came to think of my entire marriage as a process of setting out concepts before editing and revising them. It was not just work, it was everything: plans for a meal or a holiday or when we'd see friends or what we'd say to the children.

Previously I had been irritated when I suggested something to my sister Rebecca and she had replied, 'I'll have to check with Christopher.' Then I realised that I did the same thing. Marriage had made me incapable of independent decision-making.

But now that I was alone, there was no one to refer to in the same way, no *companion* to keep me in check and prevent me doing something bonkers, someone who would understand all and forgive all. I had friends, of course, wonderful friends and fabulous daughters, but I didn't have a *wife*.

I tried to imagine the advice that Marilyn would give me if she was still alive. After all, if my marriage of thirty-five years had been so fantastic, I should at least be able to hear her voice in my head. Perhaps I could go on living by pretending she wasn't dead at all? She was away at work somewhere, in London or Glasgow or staying with friends. But then, after a while, I thought, That's enough of that. Time to get back home now. The joke's over.

I found myself coming out with phrases that I had never imagined saying: 'That was before my wife died … when Marilyn could still talk …'

On being asked about my marital status, with people assuming that I was divorced, I found myself replying: 'No, I'm a widower … I *was* married …'

Then, in a restaurant or at a wedding, I had to find a way of being acceptably single: 'No, it's just me. Don't worry. I'm all right.'

Who was saying these words? They were all emerging from my mouth, but I didn't want to own any of them. Sometimes, I didn't want to talk at all, or even, perhaps, ever again. What could I do about this emptying loneliness?

I didn't want to have to keep going over things, especially the last stages of her illness, or talk about how awful it had all been, but there was nothing else to occupy my thoughts and no way of deviating from her memory because it seemed a betrayal to go on living without her. Happiness was far away but normality was impossible too, particularly at a time when the pandemic meant that there *was* no normality.

I thought about therapy but the last time I had been, only once, a man in a bow tie charged me £360 for a session in which he told me that I reminded him of Stephen Fry.

And so, I decided to concentrate my energies, reduce the number of people I spoke to, and develop an alternative therapy of having one phone call a day at six o'clock with a good friend. I talked to people who were busy and cheerful, theatricals mainly, because they had the ability to make stories, to convert their lives into entertaining anecdotes, to swing between tragedy and farce in the same sentence.

Pip and Siobhán both reported from their television locations, Siobhán telling me that while filming *Midsomer Murders*, 'I've had more Covid tests than I've got lines.' Bill sent me pictures of the 'Bidawee Hand-Knitted Home Studio' he had created in his spare room to record the voice-overs for *The Repair Shop*. 'The commute's a nightmare.'

Julie sent me a cookery book, Signe Johansen's *Solo*, with its subtitle *The Joy of Cooking for One*. I tried out the recipes for 'one-pan wonders' and 'easy week-night suppers'. I concentrated on making simple things with the best ingredients from our local farm shop. Marilyn had always believed in freshness, plenty and simplicity: a bowl of radishes, new asparagus, lemon sole with a tomato salad, the first of the raspberries from Fife.

I remembered praising her when my parents came to dinner, and she said to me: 'I just threw it all together and Bob's your father-in-law.'

On Sunday nights I had scrambled eggs with chives on toast as we had always done. It seemed to mark the end of the week. Now it might as well have been the end of the world. I read the letters of consolation that came after Marilyn's death and couldn't always finish them. One, like this, took several goes to get through, partly because it contains a story I did not know and I felt guilty I had not heard of it. It was from our friend Anna:

Dearest James

How to start? It seems absolutely unfathomable that Marilyn has gone. I can honestly say without qualifications or exaggerations that she was one of the loveliest people I, we, have ever known. Her tremendous, generous warmth just beamed out, like rays from a sun. And her so lightly worn wisdom. I remember her telling me about when one of your children were small and naughty, the key was never to hold annoyance or punishment over them. When they threw the boiled egg on the floor, she said, tick them off soundly, but the next morning make another one and make no reference to the previous day's eggy incident. I have thought of it often – both with babes and grown men – and it has always made me smile and think of Marilyn. How lucky we were to know her, we just a little really, you and your family so profoundly. It is a towering injustice that so many of the best people of all get snatched so soon but then I always think that a day of them, of Marilyn, is worth a decade, a lifetime of so many others, that that is just our lot. Like truffle oil or the loveliest scent, we are treated to only a little, too little of the most wonderful things.

The letters kept on coming. This was from Stuart:

Dearest James

There's a sentence attributed to Ovid. 'Could we see when and where we are to meet again, we would be more tender when we bid our friends goodbye.' One of the most wonderful things about Marilyn was that she always bid goodbye with great tenderness – from the first time of meeting her and you in that curry house in Wantage to the last time of seeing her in the baggage hall of Terminal 5, it was always her way. That was and is miraculously special.

And there was this from George:

All we want is for you to know how much we love you and Marilyn, a woman of oak and of gold. We are here for you always. George.
As I write that I can hear her saying my name in her special way. And it breaks my heart. How I shall miss her. She was a STAR. Her light shall never be extinguished.

Her husband, Crispin, ended his letter very simply:

I so loved and respected Marilyn and will miss her sweetness, perceptiveness and dynamism – such a unique and wonderful combination.
So loved.
Like you are, by me, always.

They were beautiful and saddening letters, written in pen and ink on nice stationery, made all the more moving because they were instinctive and direct. People had set aside time from their daily lives and taken care and trouble to write properly.

Reading them made me want more. I started to go through boxes of old love letters, written before the days of email, when Marilyn and I were first together. I found two hearts that she had drawn and cut out.

The first said: 'J'aime James.'

The other held the words: 'Nous nous aimons.'

Then she continued: 'We need not only to love, and be loved, but to know that we are loved. The realm of silence is large enough beyond the grave.'

Marilyn always wrote straight from the heart: 'I do hope, and now <u>trying</u> to pray again, that our love and faith in one another won't ever wither. I think that it would be the saddest thing ever in my life – I hope I will never disappoint or distress you by anything I might do. You must help me to be more open, braver, to trust myself more. I need you for all these reasons, but most of all I need you because I love you and love you loving me. I'll talk to you tonight …'

How much would I give for one more of those conversations? I thought of all the times I had distressed and disappointed *her* and whether I had ever been a good enough husband. Too late now. All too late.

Dwelling on guilt and misery was not doing me any good but sometimes I could not help but pick away at the scab. Grief became every resting thought.

I looked up the letter the clergyman Sydney Smith wrote to Lady Georgiana Morpeth in February 1820, listing twenty pieces of advice to help his good friend overcome a bout of depression: 'Make the room where you commonly sit, gay and pleasant; be as much as you can in the open air without fatigue; don't be too severe upon yourself, or underrate yourself, but do yourself justice. Short views of human life – not further than dinner or tea.'

I decided to draw up my own version of coping: even thinking of what Marilyn would have done if I had died instead of her.

What would she do, I thought, if she was with me now?

In St Monans we would sit together and watch the light change over the sea and remember holidays in the south of France, Ischia or the Venetian lagoon. On a warm day you could even imagine the Firth of Forth as the Bay of Naples, with Berwick Law as a mini-Vesuvius. There would be the newspapers, or a new novel or a collection of poetry. She might like a glass of cold champagne. We could go to the fishmonger and buy a piece of hake and wrap it in tinfoil with butter, lemon, capers and white wine.

I forced myself to keep the house tidy and engaged in therapeutic cleaning and angry hoovering. I bought nice soap and talc and new cologne and lit scented candles. I polished my shoes and put on my best outfits as Marilyn would have done. I changed the bedlinen and sprayed our bedroom with her perfume. I tried, as my father had always recommended, to 'keep cheerful'. I did this by listening to banging pop anthems or to Bach cantatas, all played very loudly.

Sometimes Bach proved to be too much. I remembered a story about a man weeping uncontrollably in a car park. When asked by a stranger if he was all right, he replied, 'I'm listening to Bach,' and the stranger said, 'That explains it.' I realised the composer's genius was to create a bridge, often in a single piece of music, that stretches from the deepest sorrow to the most exhilarating joy.

I decided I had to work at grief and to keep attacking it even if there were times when I had to submit to its relentless grip and treat it as the price we pay for love. I kept as busy as I could. I tried to imagine Marilyn encouraging me and telling me that it was all right, she was still with me and always would be. We couldn't let a stupid thing like death defeat us. I could do this. I could survive all this pointless emptiness.

Be Marilyn.

That's what I had to do now.

Shouting at Television

I missed watching television together. We often put on cosy crime to escape the strange news agenda of terror and sentimentality. ('The world's going to end, we're all going to die, but, in the meantime, while you're watching, here's a piano-playing kitten.')

Whenever we turned on to *Poirot*, or *Death in Paradise* or *Midsomer Murders*, Marilyn would provide a running commentary on the plot and the actors. She always anticipated the twist, spotted the murderer and called her spoilers out loud. 'The housekeeper's their birth mother … oh God, it'll be the doctor again … it's the cleaner, like the postman in Sherlock Holmes … they're not husband and wife: they're brother and sister. It's Anna Chancellor. It has to be. Otherwise, she wouldn't be in it.'

Sometimes we would already know the criminal because our friends were in the show. Pip was a villain in the ITV series *Heartbeat*, Deborah bumped her patients off in Alan Bennett's *Hallelujah* and Siobhán played twins in *Sea of Souls* which is always a giveaway. It's also a truism that the least famous person is the victim and the most highly paid actor either did it or will be the glamorous red herring. Witness Richard Attenborough in the original production of *The Mousetrap* (the famous actor, even if he's playing the policeman, has to be the murderer). Harriet Walter warned us that she is 'always the red herring' until that proved to be not quite so true in *Killing Eve* in which she trained assassins.

Shouting at the television was not confined to crime. We also liked the ridiculousness of eating ready-meals to watch *MasterChef* and heckling the contestants: 'Life's too short for jewelled Persian rice!' Or 'Not another bloody velouté.' We watched *Gardeners' World* on Friday nights and would shout back at Monty Don as he described his Paradise Gardens or a particularly delicate bit of planting: 'Try doing that in Fife, mate!'

On the night after Marilyn died, I watched the programme with Rosie and Charlotte. It featured an 87-year-old man who was sure he had 'ten more years of gardening still in him' and we all shouted out at exactly the same time: 'Oh fuck off, you bastard.'

On these days of grief and anger, I was filled with fury towards everyone except Rosie and Charlotte. I came to hate smiley photographs of newly engaged couples drinking cocktails on Instagram; text messages that ended with the word 'Hugs'; a perfectly innocent grandmother, the same age as Marilyn, pushing a pram in the street; stick-thin drug addicts outside the methadone clinic refusing to die. Why were they still alive when my wife was not?

When we met the neighbours in the public gardens, they told us they were getting the Covid vaccine 'next week'. The man was going to be eighty on Sunday and so it was 'quite a relief'.

After they had left us, Rosie said, 'Is it just me or did you feel visceral hatred towards them?'

It wasn't just us. I checked with my friend Rachel, who had been widowed two months before me, and she texted back: *Any 'older' couple wandering along holding hands and I'm ready to spit at them.*

I watched David Byrne's *American Utopia* concert and when it came to my favourite song, 'Once in a Lifetime', I found myself no longer wondering how indeed did I get here, and what my life was about, and thought instead: Where has it all gone? How did any of this happen?

I saw a repeat of the sitcom *Mum*, with Lulu and the Lampshades singing the theme tune 'You're Gonna Miss Me When I'm Gone', and shouted out, 'YES I DO.'

I realised that the 'stages of grief' – shock and denial, pain and guilt, anger and bargaining, depression, reconstruction, acceptance and even hope – were not 'stages' at all. They could all happen at the same time, or at least on the same day. They were like the weather. You never quite knew what you were going to get next.

I wondered if I should have done something more to prepare for this, the Johnsonian 'calamity' of the death of a wife. I remembered teaching at the Arvon Foundation and meeting a woman who had just lost her mother. She stood beside her father at the crematorium, and he said to her: 'I've been waiting all my life for this.' The line is pure Chekhov in that it is both comic ('I am rid of my wife at last') and tragic ('I've always dreaded this feeling of loss and abandonment') at the same time.

My friend Beth phoned me from France to ask how I was and said that the longer I talked to her the more dread she felt. Both her parents were still alive. 'I know it's coming for all of us.'

It's not as if we hadn't been warned. Marilyn's father had always told her whenever she complained about anything: 'Life's tough and then you die.' When she was a little girl, Siobhán's mother said to her: 'You die alone, so you have to learn to live alone.' And I was brought up in a vicarage where the Book of Common Prayer provided a constant reminder that death could come at any time.

I wasn't christened by my father, but by his friend Lancelot Fleming, who was known for his saintly absent-mindedness. He began my service of baptism thus: 'Man that is born of a woman hath but a short time to live and is full of misery. He cometh up and is cut down like a flower; he fleeth as if it were a shadow, and never continueth in one stay.'

'Lancelot,' my father interrupted, 'that's the funeral service.'

Perhaps this is why I came to write detective fiction. My life began with a funeral. And I have a theory that crime writing has displaced religion in the West to become the secular space in which we address our deepest fears and anxieties.

A hundred years ago, in the United Kingdom, people used to recite the Book of Common Prayer at least twice a day, at morning and night: 'Good Lord, deliver us from lightning and tempest, from plague, pestilence and famine; from battle and murder, *and from sudden death*.'

Now, in a less Christian world, perhaps the most frequent way we think about the human condition is through crime fiction and drama. It allows us to think safely about death and look for the consolation, justice and closure that is found wanting in real life.

Death is, of course, the great subject. Mortality fires our search for meaning. In February 2021, the BBC repeated a film about Keats's final journey to Italy that I had made in 1995 with Andrew Motion. It had marked the 200th anniversary of the poet's birth. Now, twenty-five years later, it was the 200th anniversary of his death. We hired an old Lowestoft fishing smack, the *Excelsior*, seventy-seven feet long with dusty red sails, and Andrew read from Keats's letter to his friend Brown about his great love for Fanny Brawne, written aboard ship in 1820: 'The thought of leaving Miss Brawne is beyond everything horrible – the sense of darkness coming over me – I eternally see her figure eternally vanishing. Some of the phrases she was in the habit of using during my last nursing at Wentworth Place ring in my ears – Is there another Life? Shall I awake and find all this a dream? There must be. We cannot be created for this sort of suffering.'

When we got to the house in Rome where he died, I sat on his bed and looked at the daisies carved on the ceiling and remembered how Keats had said that he thought they were the flowers growing over his grave. The curator of the Keats–Shelley Association asked me if I would like to see Keats's death mask. She took it out of its case and gave it to me. She let me hold his head in my hands. It was cold and small and white. I thought of the lines from *Hyperion*:

> Then saw I a wan face,
> Not pin'd by human sorrows, but bright blanch'd
> By an immortal sickness which kills not;
> It works a constant change, which happy death
> Can put no end to; deathwards progressing
> To no death was that visage; it had pass'd
> The lily and the snow ...

I held the face of Keats and I did not want to give it back. But I had to. I had to wake from the dream – but even then, I was filled with that most Keatsian of sensations, the feeling that transient, fleeting, poetic and transcendental moments are but glimpses of eternal rest – and that, in Wallace Stevens's famous phrase, 'death is the mother of beauty'.

I watched the film again and could hardly believe I had made it. It was slow and elegant and overproduced. Any television executive now would have told me to get a move on; but I was proud of its grace and beauty, its music and photography, its confidence to take its time and be poetic. It asked viewers to stop their hurrying lives. After I had seen it once more, this evidence of a former life, I stepped into the street and couldn't believe the noise and the bustle, even in lockdown, and what seemed to be nothing less than the sheer banality of everyday existence. I looked at people going about their business, putting on their masks at the bus stops, calling out random greetings and farewells, and wanted to shout and swear at them all over again: 'What are you doing *shopping*, for God's sake?'

I remembered the Book of Lamentation from the funeral service and sent the verse to Rosie. *Is it nothing to you, all ye that pass by? Behold, and see if there be any sorrow like unto my sorrow, which is done unto me, wherewith the LORD hath afflicted me in the day of his fierce anger.*

This was the strange paradox of grief. We think it is unique to us and yet it is common to all.

I looked at a little black notebook Marilyn had given me with 'Inspirations and Ideas' gilded on the cover. Inside she had written 'For my beloved James' and quoted from Raymond Carver's 'Late Fragment'. I started it in Istanbul, on our last holiday together, with our friends Bill and Hildegard, Jo and Stuart, and it contains notes from exhibitions and ideas for novels. It begins with what

Henry James called a *donnée*, the germ of an idea, based on the fact that we were there on St Andrew's Day, the patron saint of Scotland. With the town of St Andrews being just by our home in Fife, Bill and Marilyn had the notion to go on a series of holidays that would collect his scattered relics until we had seen the whole body – his main relics in Amalfi, Italy; his skull and a finger in Patras, Greece; his shoulder in Edinburgh; his arm in Cologne; and another 'small relic' in Kiev.

Then there were notes for a series of stories concentrating on human anatomy – the pianist's hand, the actor's voice, the alcoholic's liver; the lover's lips, the raised eyebrow, the fingerprint. I planned a novel based on different parts of the human body and had the idea to structure it around Rembrandt's painting of *The Anatomy Lesson of Dr Nicolaes Tulp* until a quick internet search informed me that Nina Siegal had already spent six years doing this.

'Never mind,' Marilyn told me. 'You'll have more ideas. You just have to keep thinking them up.'

And then the notebook changed: gone were the ideas and instead came the hastily written reminders of problems, phone calls, things I had to do: 'Choking, thick saliva, nebuliser unit, community nutrition team, key info summary, oral antibiotics. Call Duncan Reekie re St Monans grave. Fife Council burial plot.'

After that it ran out. There were only blank pages.

I was going to have to think how to fill them again.

With this.

We're Not Really Here

Halloween.

There was a fierce wind off the sea in St Monans, the lightweight table I should never have ordered was thrown across the garden, its base broken and the chairs scattered. The plants were scorched by wind and sea salt. It was as if the local poltergeist had been at it again.

A blue moon hung low in the sky. Marilyn's brother was born on a similar night and it is the defining anthem of the football club I support, Manchester City, a team that played attractive free-flowing football in the sixties when I was growing up. We even had 'Blue Moon' sung at our wedding.

The children gave me a Manchester City shirt for my fiftieth birthday, with RUNCIE 10 on the back. In 1968, when I was nine years old, my parents put blue-and-white icing on my birthday cake and gave me the away kit so I could imagine playing for them when I did a kickabout in the back yard.

'It's Corrigan, he throws the ball out to Book, Book passes inside to Doyle, Doyle to Bell who finds Summerbee. It's back inside to Lee, and now Runcie's making a run. Runcie has the ball, it's 1–1 in the last minute of the cup final, he cuts inside, he goes past Bremner, he goes past

Hunter, it's on to his right foot, he shoots, AND RUNCIE SCORES, what a goal!'

No one can quite understand this passion for a team for whom I have no natural affiliation. I had never lived in Manchester. My father supported Liverpool. I should have been a fan of Oxford United when I was a boy, or Watford as a teenager, because that was where we lived. But it was always City, for all their glamour and their failings, their champagne swagger and their inability to defend. I also love them for their sense of humour, joshing the well-dressed José Mourinho with a chant of 'Your coat's from Matalan' or commemorating one of the Manchester United player Wayne Rooney's latest conquests with 'He's fat, he's red, he'll take your gran to bed.'

In the dark days of the early nineties and the early noughties they ended up, temporarily, in what was technically Division 3. This was also when one of their most iconic songs, sung to the tune of 'We Shall Not Be Moved', came to the fore. It's 'We're Not Really Here'.

We are not, we're not really here
We are not, we're not really here
Just like the fans of the Invisible Man
We're not really here.

It was considered unbelievable that a team with such a trophied history should be forced to play at York City, Chesterfield and Lincoln, where the chant may have been first heard after a shock defeat in 1996. The team really were, at times, very bad indeed. (I watched a particularly grim 0–0 draw with Crewe Alexandra and so yes, to quote another chant, 'I was there, I was there, I was there when we were shit.')

At home in St Monans, I watched City played Olympiacos on television. It was 3 November 2020, the night of the American election. The Etihad stadium was empty of fans due to Covid and the banners across the seats read 'We're not really here'. So, this was a kind of reverse. The people were absent, they were not there, but they were watching on television and were being quoted as if they were both there and not there at the same time.

This existential freefall is, perhaps, the nature of what it is to be a writer or, like Marilyn, a director. You have to be inside a scene, watching and observant, and at the same time you have to be anonymous. You can't intrude or make it part of your ego. The characters should appear to play each scene independent of direction but be natural and unpredictable as if everything is happening live every night. As a writer and a director, you are part of the process but have to pull back. You are both there and not there. 'We're not really here.'

Henry James wrote about this; how writers need to be both present and absent at the same time; how they must dominate their material and yet let go to give the characters room to inhabit the story. In *The Private Life*, the playwright Clare Vawdrey only truly exists when he is alone, sending out a doppelgänger when he is in company; while the gregarious socialite Lord Mellifont completely disappears when he has no one to talk to. There are times when neither of them is really present, creating different versions of themselves in the theatre of everyday life. Lord Mellifont 'was all public and had no corresponding private life, just as Clare Vawdrey was all private and had no corresponding public one'.

There is a gulf between privacy and performance, the private and the public self, and Henry James is asking: 'Which is real?' And there are times when I wonder when I am most myself and if the person showing off at a literary festival is really me or even a person I'd like to be. Even writing this memoir, rather than a novel, I have to think if I am really being honest and truthful. Sometimes I am embarrassed to be the 'James' I show to the world, a public version that, like everyone, has an underlying nervousness and anxiety. I know that I only really feel at home not so much in a physical space, but when I am alone with Marilyn in bed at the end of the day, and I don't have to worry about anything any more because she is there and we can talk and nothing matters apart from each other.

Except now she isn't.

Or is she?

Perhaps I have disappeared too. Like Lord Mellifont in the Henry James story, I have 'no corresponding private life' or at least no love life except in memory and the imagination.

My sister used to say to me: 'It's so hard to know what Marilyn really thinks.' There were times when she would, indeed, put on a social performance or be excessively 'polite' to someone she disliked. But it *was* easy to tell what she thought when you learned to read the signs, though she hated confrontation. She would always try to deflect it, or put it off, or hope it would go away if she left it long enough (whereas I always like a bit of a barney).

In more tedious situations, she would keep on asking questions in the hope that the person speaking would be so unusually boring that they would paradoxically become interesting: a dinner-party guest explaining how a fax machine worked, a plane-spotter at a wedding talking through the technical details of Gatwick Airport's departure board, a woman insisting that a suitcase could only be used eighteen times before it wore out. These people didn't always come out the other side to be worthy of anecdote and, when they didn't make the cut, there were post-mortems on the way home when Marilyn would rant at me and shout that 'they were confusing me with someone who gives a fuck'.

She always was what her friend Georgia calls 'a champion swearer'. On our twentieth wedding anniversary, Marilyn gave me two prints modelled on Penguin book covers. The first dustjacket reads: 'Fuck Art, Let's Dance.' The second says: 'Fuck Dancing, Let's Fuck.'

But, in company, she wanted to be kind and for the party to be gay, and to bring out the best in people; in me, her family and those she worked with. She was always pushing people to think creatively and to do more than they thought they could.

This social wondrousness could be hard to keep up, even exhausting at times, but I think this was one of Marilyn's greatest professional achievements – to be entirely responsible for a show and yet *to appear absent*. It's a bit like parenting. You parent a child, you parent a show, and eventually you have to let go of them both.

We're not really here.

But you are, of course, and perhaps it's enough that you know and, in reality, they know too.

When the City fans sing 'We're Not Really Here' they are defiantly asserting that they *are*, in fact, present. They are bloody well there. Another possible origin of the song comes from the idea that City fans managed to infiltrate the infamous Den at Millwall when away fans were banned and sang it there – but this seems unlikely bravado. However, I quote this now because Marilyn was a great admirer of the chant 'We are Millwall Super-Millwall. No one likes us. We don't care' because it is sung to the tune of Rod Stewart's 'Sailing' and Rod Stewart albums are what everyone's Scottish dad used to get for Christmas.

Although Marilyn never quite got the point of football, she understood the idea that it was unscripted theatre, that a manager such as Pep Guardiola, like a drama director, would have to wrangle a cast including stars and egos, make individuals play as a team, and be responsive to setbacks, weaknesses and unexpected defeats.

And she always 'got' the drama of cup runs, minnows versus giants, and the grim humour of the sign in the back of the bus in 1975 when Scots fans returned from Wembley after a 5–1 defeat to England with the taunt: 'You couldnae make it six.'

One of her favourite stories was to tell of the infamous exchange between the radio commentator David Francey and television's Archie Macpherson at a Scotland away game in Hungary. Francey knew that he wouldn't be able to remember every Hungarian footballer and so asked his colleague to let him know the correct name if any of them scored.

They did.

In the midst of the chaos, panic and excitement, Francey asked Macpherson who had hit the back of the net.

'Fucked if I know,' came the reply.

So Francey picked up his microphone and uttered the immortal words 'Yes, it's that man, FUCTIVANO' to his startled listeners.

She loved this story and its opportunity for more 'champion swearing'. She was thrilled by the theatrical heat of improvising on the spot to disastrous effect, but the idea of giving it a go, throwing yourself into things and being an enthusiast lay at the heart of her personality. The idea of delight, of being in the moment, and a *true supporter*, lay behind Marilyn's idea of parenting, friendship, direction and love.

One of the writers she worked with most frequently was Michael Chaplin and their last production together was *For the Love of Leo*, a radio drama series about a widower in Edinburgh searching for love after the death of his wife and her funeral in Canongate Kirk. The ghost of the wife, played by Beth Marshall, even talks him through the future candidates and the memories of their marriage.

Listening, or rather trying to pay attention without quite being able to face up to it, I couldn't help but feel: 'For God's sake, this is ridiculous. Marilyn does know I'm listening to this, doesn't she?'

For this to be Marilyn's last production and for a third series to be made after her death and from beyond the grave? I wondered what I was supposed to think. Was this her chance to talk back to me, her way of dealing with anticipatory grief, of going first, even a kind of revenge for the anticipatory grief in my fiction in which loving, generous women with beautiful voices are either redeeming the hero (me) or dying to leave them bereft (also me)?

But then, I had to remember, this series on Radio 4 was not actually about me. It was a drama by Michael Chaplin who, presumably and amazingly, didn't think about *me* at all when he wrote it. And despite all the attention it got, and the love for Marilyn that was shared on Twitter about the production after she died, I couldn't help but feel disorientated. *My wife*, if you don't mind. And yet, and yet, it also became a haunting and a comfort. She was both present and absent, like the characters in the Henry James story, a friendly ghost.

I thought of all those films with the guiding presence of the dead over those left behind: Patrick Swayze in *Ghost*, Alan Rickman in *Truly, Madly, Deeply*, and, perhaps more accurately, Elvira in Coward's *Blithe Spirit*, blowing in through the French windows and wrecking any chance of a second happiness.

I think I'd rather you just had a string of affairs with women who can't possibly live up to me.

I thought of this business of absence and presence, of Halloween and ghosts and hauntings. At Halloween I imagined I was living in a ghost story that everyone else had read and that no one had told me about.

I watched football without her and was intrigued by the collapse in form of the champions, Liverpool, deprived by Covid of the Anfield crowd to roar them on and 'suck in' the extra goals. There was an article about their manager, Jürgen Klopp, and how he surely wanted to tell everyone: 'You do know that this isn't real football?' It's a pale imitation. It's not the same game without the supporters, and I started to think that this was an exact metaphor of my life because all its special atmosphere had been removed too: *You do know that this isn't real life?*

There is, at times, a giddiness to grief. You feel a recklessness after the worst has happened. The house can burn down, you don't care about personal ambition and 'nothing really matters', to quote 'Bohemian Rhapsody'. You have been given a bizarre freedom.

To continue with the football analogy, it's as if you're in an existential version of extra time; or it's as if you've already been relegated and can play as attacking a game as you like because you have no defence and the result doesn't count. I watched West Bromwich Albion, doomed to the championship, beat the mighty Chelsea 5–2 because they had abandoned all hope and played with all the brilliance of 'having a laugh'.

I planted daffodils and had to go back to the garden centre for more earth. 'I don't know why I'm doing this,' I told Phyllis, Fife's blue-eyed queen of bulbs and bedding. 'Sometimes, I can't see the point if it's just for me.'

'It's for her too,' she said. 'She's watching you. She'll know.'

But is she? I wanted to ask.

We take comfort in the idea that the dead are watching over us. You can just about see our house from the graveyard, and I know she's facing in the right direction. That's what Alan, the undertaker, told me.

'She can see you. Don't you worry about that. You think I'm joking?'

So, I thought of what it might be like not to be haunted, but to be accompanied. To have a happy ghost as it were, a blessed ghost, someone who was there and not there.

'I'm not *really* here.'

But you are.

May Her Memory Be a Blessing

Working in the media is often hypocritical nonsense. It never ceases to amaze me how people responsible for the most sensitive programmes about art, love, joy and beauty can still be total bastards. My friend Jamie was made redundant at the BBC in the days between his mother's death and her funeral. The Head of Music and Arts acknowledged: 'I know it's not a good time for you, but we can't wait. Sometimes these things have to be done.' His main aim ('we can't wait') was to get it all over and done with as quickly as possible. At another time, my friend Joanna, a pianist, had to cancel a day of filming after her mother-in-law's death and was told: 'Why can't you just move the funeral?'

We live in an age where the unbereaved have little awareness of what loss is like. Only a month after Marilyn died, I received a text from a colleague hoping I was feeling 'a bit better'. Rosie told a friend she had been depressed and was asked: 'Oh, have you had a bad week?'

Then a very kind woman I don't know well wrote to say: 'You must feel you have lost half of yourself.'

Must? Half? No. *All sense of myself. All of it.* I do not know who I am any more without her.

In the past, grief was more visible. There were mourning practices, customs, rules. Cassell's *Household Guide* from the 1880s takes the reader through four sections of 'Death in the Household', including instructions for the most ostentatious of ceremonies: 'Funeral costing £53: hearse and four horses, two mourning coaches with fours, twenty-three plumes of rich ostrich-feathers, complete velvet covering for carriages and horses, and an esquire's plume of best feathers; stout outside lead coffin, with inscription plate and solder complete; two mutes with gowns, silk hat-bands and gloves; fourteen men as pages, feathermen, and coachmen, with truncheons and wands …'

There was a sumptuary aspect to lamentation. Queen Victoria had black tears stitched into her handkerchiefs and helped Courtaulds to a fortune in the manufacture of black crêpe. If I had been grieving in Victorian times, people would have been able to tell just by looking at my hat-band: 'The width of the hat-bands worn differs according to the degree of relationship. When worn by the husband for the wife they are usually at the present time about seven inches wide. Those worn by fathers for sons, and sons for fathers, are about five inches wide. For other degrees of relationship, the width of the hat-band varies from two and a half inches to four inches.'

The consolation of religion is strangely absent. Instead, this is an advertisement for grief, a shopping opportunity, a chance to go to Jay's Mourning House (founded in 1841) for nineteenth-century retail therapy and stock up on all kinds of clobber: veils of crêpe and dresses of parramatta, mourning caps lined with white lace, plastrons edged with rows of dull black beads, all to show – well, exactly what? That you are respectable, that you know how to behave, that you feel deeply. You love and have suffered and are behaving well and in accordance with decency. A modern pin simply says 'Please be kind to me, I'm grieving' which is a more minimalist way of doing things.

The Victorians viewed mourning with dramatic inevitability. You have been warned. Now, it's here. You have arrived in death's waiting room at last. It reminds me of my father telling me that one of his parishioners was 'in the departure lounge'. When it came for his own turn to die, he said to me: 'I know I'm at the gate. The best we can hope for is that the flight's delayed.'

We no longer live in the Victorian era and so we have to find a modern manner of mourning. How can we acknowledge death, talk about it and be kind to each other? What will be most helpful? There is bereavement counselling, therapy, faith, routine and memorialising (this book). There are visits to the grave, a favourite place, letter writing, conversations on the telephone, walks with friends. There is Time, *the great healer*. Time, with a capital letter. Time, that, we are told, makes everything more bearable: *This too shall pass*. But it doesn't look like passing.

There is no formality to grief. Some days pass well enough apart from the odd *bouleversement*, the half-hour gusts of inexplicable melancholy and the bursting into tears when a song comes on the radio (Bastille's 'Good Grief', Adele's 'Hello', Bob Dylan's 'I Want You', the Script's 'If You Could See Me Now', Paloma Faith's 'Only Love Can Hurt Like This').

Picking up a book by Susan Stewart, *On Longing* (it seemed appropriate), I found a note Marilyn had left for me:

Tuesday before leaving –
My own darling –

Ways to feel better soon –
Have a long deep sandalwood-scented bath
Sip peppermint tea
Listen to Bach
Look at the lilies
Read Charlotte's note to the tooth fairy by her bed
Remember I love you
M

This was hopeless. I went to see Charlotte, foolishly thinking that because she had a husband and a daughter she would somehow be better adjusted to this; that she might be further down some kind of 'road to recovery', rather than the 'road to nowhere'. But one of her closest friends had died in her sleep at the age of thirty-one, and another had lost a baby when twenty-three weeks pregnant. She told me that she was living in 'a plague of grief', that the Book of Job had nothing on this. I realised that there was absolutely no right way of getting through all the things that the family were feeling. There was no magic cure or best way forward or 'road map back to normality'. There was never going to be any normality again.

Grief is a virus. It keeps mutating.

There was also the problem of insomnia. In bed, and without Marilyn, I was constantly turning to my left and finding no one there. Sometimes, when I woke up in the middle of the night, I tried to pretend that she had gone to the bathroom or was making a cup of tea. She'll be back in a minute, I thought. But she never did come back. I tried to sleep and then dreamt that her death was all my fault and woke again just before five, the exact time she stopped breathing.

I dreamt that she was ill, and we were in St Monans and Andrew Motion came to see us (it must have been the repeat of the Keats film). He asked for some red wine, but we didn't have any. I went out to buy some and the whole landscape changed. I was on the coast, but it was a steep and rocky escarpment. I couldn't get off it. There were some children and I asked them the way to the village shop because nothing was familiar. They told me there wasn't one. I turned back to go home but there were fields in front of me and no sign of any buildings apart from the St Monans Windmill. I thought, Well, that's all right, but our house had disappeared. I asked an old man where it had gone but I couldn't speak, no words came out of my mouth. There was no way I could get back to Marilyn. I was lost. She was with someone else. I was not there. And I was to blame for her dying.

In another dream, I bought an open-topped sports car but it was so low that I couldn't see ahead and shouldn't have been driving. Then the bottom fell off. I was next to a church but, when I tried to call for help, I dropped the phone and that broke too. When a mechanic came, it was Grayson Perry. I asked if I could use his phone to call Marilyn but all the instructions were in Chinese and there was no response to any button I pressed. Then I dropped that phone as well.

I was going mad.

Bizarrely, I wondered if this was perfectly normal. Grief makes you crazy. In the aftermath of Joe Biden's victory in the American presidential election, I looked up all that a man acquainted with sorrow had thought after the death of his wife and daughter: 'For the first time in my life, I understood how someone could consciously decide to commit suicide ... not because they were deranged, not because they were nuts. Because they'd been to the top of the mountain, and they just knew in their heart they'd never get there again, that it was never going to get – never going to be that way ever again.'

After the death of his son, Biden spoke of how you had to get through a year of anniversaries before you could start to recover. I thought of Marilyn's birthday, and our wedding anniversary, and Christmas, and New Year, and Valentine's Day, and Easter, and my birthday, and Charlotte and Rosie's birthdays, and everything that we had been doing in the previous year and how we had to live through all the reminders of the diagnosis, the disease and her death before we could ever think about anything else.

And contemplating 'a year of anniversaries', I picked up Leon Wieseltier's book *Kaddish*, in which he writes about saying the same prayer three times a day, morning, afternoon and evening, in shul, for the year after the death of his father.

He examined the teaching of Nahmanides, the thirteenth-century philosopher whose reflections on mortality were compiled into his *Torat Ha'Adam* or *The Law of Man*, a book that begins with 'a perplexity': 'Since man is destined to die, and deserves to lie down in the shadow of death, why should we torture ourselves over somebody's death, and weep for the dead, and bemoan him? After all, the living know that they will die. It is puzzling that those who know what will come to pass should then mourn, and call others to lamentation.'

Wieseltier learned that sorrow is a form of remorse. Mourning is an act of repentance, a duty to attend to the cares of the world. It is a process of prayer and ritual that leads one to pay more attention in memory than one did in life, to understand that love is strong as death, and to be grateful for the blessed lives that have been lived.

After the twelve months of saying the kaddish every time a mother or father is mentioned, the mourner adds the words: 'May his memory be a blessing for life in the world to come.' Modern Jews have made this simpler: 'May his memory be a blessing' here, upon us.

I thought of Marilyn, and what a gift it was to know her, and I planned to use the phrase every time I spoke her name: *May her memory be a blessing.*

But in the narcissism of grief, this wasn't enough. I wanted to think about her and acknowledge her and pray for her *all the time.* In the midst of the Covid lockdown, I spent so much time alone that I even began to enjoy and depend upon it; a separation from the world.

My life was grief.

Sometimes I worried I was over-remembering the last year to the detriment of previous years. So much suffering, so much pain.

I tried to think positively, that Marilyn's life was about far more than its final year, and that I shouldn't let her memory be defined by disease.

But I couldn't stop remembering how awful it was. And I could no longer hear her beautiful voice as it was. I was obsessed by the end, by her not being able to say anything clearly. What did she mean by 'esh' – was it 'fresh'? But fresh what? And then spelling out letters and not being able to guess what she was saying and then realising there was nothing I could do anyway: 'B–R–E–A–T–H–L … *breathless.'* How could I help with that?

I started to garden furiously, wearing all my best clothes because I didn't really care about anything any more. I bought some horticultural grit which was nice and some ice-white pebbles which were not. I was about to put them down by the front of the house when I could imagine Marilyn mouthing the word 'vile' as if the word itself was too horrible to say out loud.

The insomnia persisted and in the middle of the night I found myself shopping online for things I didn't need: a set of sushi knives, two Eazi Kleen ear-wax removers, and a shiny silver jacket made out of copper wiring that could only be worn by a grime DJ in East London. I convinced myself Marilyn would say 'Why not?' even though I couldn't hear her saying it.

Then, after I had left St Monans for Edinburgh, ten minutes into the journey I was caught up by traffic and roadworks and was stuck behind a van advertising mobility scooters – *The Best a Gran Can Get!*

For God's sake, I thought.

I let out this sigh, as I often did when this kind of thing happened, and suddenly there she was, sitting beside me again, saying what she always said when she could see that I was tense even though a journey had only just begun.

'Would you like a Softmint?'

Her voice had come back, clear and true, and she was with me once more. Perhaps this was the beginning of some kind of recovery?

Her voice came out of nowhere, in a traffic jam at the bottom of a hill. It wasn't anything profound. It was completely mundane and yet it was also overwhelmingly beautiful and consoling, a practical everyday love, normality returning.

'Would you like a Softmint?'

May her memory be a blessing.

Dr Johnson's Sermon

After the death of his wife on 17 March 1752, Dr Johnson wrote a sermon in her honour which he asked his friend John Taylor to preach. It was composed in the heat of grief, just as he had written *Rasselas* in a week to pay for his mother's funeral. The sermon has an extraordinary fluency, praising his wife's inestimable virtues. But Taylor refused to preach it, finding the celebration of Tetty Johnson's virtues excessive and untrue, telling friends that, far from being a saint, the woman 'was the plague of Johnson's life, was abominably drunken and despicable … Johnson had frequently complained to him of the wretchedness of his situation with such a wife.'

So, what was going on here? Why do the living want to make saints of those they have lost?

The Johnsons' marriage had lasted seventeen years. Elizabeth Jervis Porter was the widow of a mercer and woollen draper with a dowry of £600 a year and three children of eighteen, sixteen and ten. She was forty-six years old when they married (although she wiped six years off on the marriage certificate) and Johnson was twenty-five. Her family could not understand why she would throw away her life, and her dowry, on a penniless man who was more than twenty years younger with few realistic prospects save his literary ambition. He was tall, lean and lank, wore his natural hair rather than a wig, had scrofula scars on his face and according to Lucy Porter, his future stepdaughter, was 'hideously striking to the eye'. He spoke with 'convulsive starts and odd gesticulations' and was prone to introspection and depression. But her mother pronounced: 'This is the most sensible man that I ever saw in my life.'

People could not understand it. The actor David Garrick described Tetty to Boswell as 'very fat, with a bosom of more than ordinary protuberance, with swelled cheeks, of a florid red, produced by thick painting, and increased by the liberal use of cordials; flaring and fantastic in her dress, and affected both in her speech and general behaviour' and she was said to have come from a hard-drinking family. Johnson insisted that it was 'a love marriage upon both sides'.

By her late fifties, however, Tetty avoided his sexual advances, moved out to Hampstead and turned to laudanum, gin and books of romances. She was described by various contemporaries as frail, fearful, drunken and neurotic.

But, in his sermon, Johnson was having none of this: 'Let it be remembered that her wit was never employed to scoff at reason, nor her reason to dispute against truth. In this age of wild opinions, she was as free from scepticism as the cloistered virgin.'

This seems unlikely, but Johnson continued with a defence of his wife that is so bold that any refutation would seem churlish. 'She was extensively charitable in her judgments and opinions, grateful for every kindness that she received, and willing to impart assistance of every kind to all whom her little power enabled her to benefit. She passed through many months of languor, weakness and decay, without a single murmur of impatience ...'

This is also improbable ...

'... and often expressed her adoration of that mercy which granted her so long time for recollection and penitence.'

I just do not believe this – just as I do not believe the gravestones that say: 'After a long illness, patiently borne.'

But Johnson was determined to define his wife's lasting reputation before anyone else did, ideally as some kind of latter-day saint. He wanted the world to know that she was wonderful, and I realised I had been trying to do this too.

With Marilyn, MND was not exactly 'patiently borne' but she tried even though she was also, by turns, angry and depressed. It may have been *seen* to have been 'patiently borne' when the professional carers came in and she was wheeled to the shower and hoisted from room to room because it made the process easier and she had no choice. But that did not mean she accepted or ever came to terms with the death knell of disease.

She only did not want her character to be corrupted by it. Just as she was determined to be clean and sweet-smelling and well dressed, she wanted her graciousness, kindness and thoughtfulness towards other people to be preserved; and although she could not reply to all the messages of love and goodwill that came to our home, she did send this to her former colleague Gordon House. It was one of the last emails that she was able to write herself:

Dearest Gordon,
Thank you for your lovely card and the very kind words and thoughts within it. It means so much to me. Being thought of

and remembered is everything in this life; it's all we have and all we take with us.

I always remember and often think of your generous and appreciative words and wise and kindly advice over the many years we have known one another.

Thank you for all of that.

With warmest affection,

Marilyn

She wanted to be her best self for as long as possible even though the family found this quite hard to live with. Catherine, her friend and colleague, wrote to me to say that she was not fooled, and she knew what Marilyn was doing, but please could I tell her the truth? So, the girls and I found ourselves keeping up appearances, following what Marilyn wanted, while sometimes betraying her by telling our friends the facts.

At the same time, she would still send out extraordinary responses. Here is one:

Beloved Tom,

What a moving and heart-warming letter … with many thoughts which I have never heard you speak, and which mean so much to me, hearing them so beautifully expressed by you now. This pandemic makes my own health seem not so important in the global scheme of things. I don't feel alone in my predicament and even the prospect of dying is less important; I have had a wonderful life and am blessed in so many ways.

Speaking of blessings, I must tell you how very much your garden videos mean to me. I know, love and remember every inch of your garden, and walking through it with you, hearing the swish of your broad measured strides through the grass, I

am there, and can smell the fresh leaves after rain and the scent
of Sue's cooking from the kitchen, as you and I and James
walk through the prairie with you before lunch. Please keep
them coming; they are balm for the soul; more than ever now.
My enduring love to you and Sue.
Always,
Mxxxxxxxxxxx

Because of these letters some people would tell us that
they were pleased she was still working. They assumed the
progress of the disease was quite slow and that she might
last another couple of years and perhaps they could come
and see her after all? And the girls and I would have to say,
no, it's impossible.

Some friends thought that we were being difficult, surely
the rules of 'not seeing anyone' did not apply to them?
And we would say, yes, it really is the same for everyone,
Marilyn is not at all well, she does not want to be seen in
this state. We would even get annoyed with her when she
was publicly brave because we said it was unrealistic. We
couldn't keep up the pretence and she would, in turn, be
infuriated by us. None of us knew what we were doing. We
had had no training for any of this: but we all understood
that she wanted her memory preserved at its best.

It reminded me of all the times when I had been most
exasperated with her bountiful-hostess saintliness and she
would turn to me and say: 'I know, I know. I am impossible.
It must be so difficult to be married to me. I don't know
why you put up with me. It must be so hard for you.
SO hard. God, I can't IMAGINE how hard it must be.
Poor you. Poor, poor you, to have a wife like me. I'm just
TOO kind, I have too MANY FRIENDS, I am just TOO
CHEERFUL, I should be more depressed, more neurotic,

more impossible and then I'd be SO MUCH MORE INTERESTING TO LIVE WITH …'

And she would go on and on and on until I had to say: 'Just stop it.'

There were times when the girls complained and she would stand back with her hands on her hips, as if impersonating Tammy Wynette, and quote from the song 'No Charge' in which a mother refutes her little girl's bill for mowing the yard and making her own bed by citing all that she has done for free: giving birth, nurturing her, caring for her when she was ill, loving steadfastly through every setback – *no charge*.

And Rosie and Charlotte would be as infuriated by that as by people saying 'I wish she was my mother' and we would all want to shout: 'SHE IS NOT A SAINT.'

Even Dr Johnson realised that he might have gone too far in the pursuit of his wife's canonisation. 'That she had no failings, cannot be supposed; but she has now appeared before the Almighty Judge; and it would ill become beings like us, weak and sinful as herself, to remember those faults which, we trust, Eternal Purity has pardoned. Let us therefore preserve her memory for no other end but to imitate her virtues …'

And leave the rest to God.

But what is going on here? Why this urge to canonise your late wife? In literature, it's quite common. Milton wrote the sonnet 'Methought I saw my late espoused saint', 'vested all in white, pure as her mind', and Elizabeth Barrett Browning in her *Sonnets from the Portuguese* replaced religious with secular adoration:

I love thee with a love I seemed to lose
With my lost saints – I love thee with the breath

148

Smiles, tears, of all my life! and, if God choose,
I shall but love thee better after death.

Thomas Hardy, whose first wife Emma Gifford died at the same age as Marilyn, seventy-two, also converted death into divinity. He rewrote the history of their relationship in the famous *Poems of 1912–1913*, going back to the beginning 'as at first, when our day was fair'. Emma was dressed in her 'air-blue gown' and Hardy was trying to relive his relationship all over again, making up for all his mistakes and neglect, appreciating all the best qualities of his wife that he had failed to cherish when she was alive.

Claire Tomalin described the death of Emma as 'the moment when Thomas Hardy became a great poet'. Some eighty poems belong to her. Reading some that were less familiar to me, I found that they could just as well have been about Marilyn.

How she would have loved
A party to-day!
Bright hatted and gloved,
With table and tray
And chairs on the lawn
Her smiles would have shone
With welcomings …

I can see Marilyn now with her extravagant greetings: 'Hello Gorgeousness!', 'Now heaven walks on earth!', 'Tell me good things!'

Yet Hardy's second wife Florence, like Johnson's preacher, was having none of this. 'All the poems about her are a fiction,' she observed, 'but a fiction in which their author has now come to believe.'

Florence Hardy is clearly a stickler for literal rather than fictional or emotional truth. But then if Hardy had been after that, perhaps he would have stuck to prose. What both he and Johnson were creating were acts of reconstruction, mixtures of memory, remorse and creative hope.

It's still a mistake to canonise the dead because it turns them into something they are not, something less human, an idealised apparition. We have to acknowledge that however marvellous our partner may have been in real life, they were no Mother Teresa. Even Mother Teresa wasn't 'Mother Teresa'.

In real life, supposed saints, an ersatz saint, your common or garden saint, is quite difficult to share a home with. Ask their partners. They need to be loved. They are not the ones who cancel the dinner party or give out home truths. They are too preoccupied by being saints. (Like a friend's brother who was 'too busy with the Church' to attend the bedside of his dying mother.) Your duty, if you live with a saint, is to preserve their sainthood. And it can be bloody annoying.

Perhaps if you can't live up to the job the only way of coping is to behave badly and enhance their sainthood. 'I can't help being difficult. I'm married to a saint.'

At one point I decided to talk to my friend Pip about the difficulty of having a 'publicly perfect' wife, because I was convinced that he had one too. 'Of course, it's infuriating,' he told me. 'But that's part of the attraction. If your wife was faultless, life would be boring. Never forget the importance of exasperation in a marriage.'

In his biography of Johnson, Walter Jackson Bate argues the push for his wife's sainthood is eventually due to gratitude. Johnson was forever grateful that, in his youth, she had saved him from penury and madness. She supported him in a way that allowed him to become the man he was. Nothing about her subsequent behaviour could ever erase her initial act of helping him discover his identity.

When a friend asked Marilyn how she put up with me, she smiled and said, 'I just let him get on with it. We both know we'd be lost without each other.'

Well, here I am: lost.

Dr Johnson's way of coping was to hold up his hands, or rather, put them together, and give everything up to God. He then reverts to a kind of blessing: 'Let all remember, that the day of life is short, and that the day of grace may be much shorter; that this may be the last warning which God will grant us, and that, perhaps, he who looks on this grave unalarmed, may sink unreformed into his own!'

It's the traditional Christian conclusion and it has a wonderful rhythm to it, Johnson the lonely cellist playing away at the back of the church when everyone else has gone home.

So why did Taylor not preach this sermon? Possibly to resist hagiography, but also probably because he thought he should say something himself rather than read out a husband's words — or rather the last words.

If you want 'top billing' on a shared gravestone then you die first. If you would prefer to have the last word, then you should organise events so that you die second (and it's probably best not to marry a writer. They always want the last word).

But perhaps we, the living, must continue to honour the dead without making saints of those we have loved. It is an extreme form of humblebragging, a dark and petty thought: 'I may be a bit crap, but my wife wasn't, so that counts in my favour. And by the way, if she was a saint, why do you think she chose me? My wife's a saint and yours is a bit normal and boring. I've loved the most and I've lost the most – so I WIN.'

This rush to saintliness is dishonest regret and I really can't be doing with it. But what is honest regret? What is loving someone and remembering them truly and faithfully? Can you love again, albeit in a different way?

My father once told me that 'it's good to grieve but a sin to hug your grief'. A sin? Or a self-indulgence, an inability to move on – or a desire to protect yourself?

Because, having gone through all this, I worry that if there is 'a next time' or 'a new love', then I will inevitably think: What if she gets MND too? Or Parkinson's disease? Or cancer? Can I really go through all this with someone else?

Then the thought comes: What if I get it? Who will look after me? Will Rosie and Charlotte have to care for me too?

And the answer is: 'Probably, yes.'

For this is what it means to confront the next stage of grief and the inevitability of mortality: 'Do I really want to drag a new love into such desolation? Wouldn't it be easier just to dwell in this one loss, rather than take on the possibility of it happening all over again?'

A friend, who was keen on a widower in the south of France, was rejected with this brutal sentence: 'Anyone who thinks I'm going to love anyone ever again will have to take this ring off my cold dead finger.'

He could, perhaps, have expressed himself more gently. But then grief can be violent as well as quiet and frightened and inward and depressed. It can be used both as defensive armour and as a weapon, an unexploded grenade in a future relationship when you have forgotten that you have already taken the pin out.

I remember a priest once telling me that the key to bereavement was 'time and tears' and it came out so pat that I wanted to kill him, even then, before Marilyn died. Surely, it's more complicated than that? But then again, perhaps it isn't, and time is another kind of privilege.

Rather than being the devourer of our lessening days, perhaps grief is the opportunity to let things fall.

It allows us to acknowledge that while emotions may not falter, and while our feelings may deepen and darken, and the engulfing sadness will inevitably come back to overwhelm us again and again, often when we are least expecting it (seeing a child run excitedly towards her mother in the park, hearing the snatch of an old song), we are reminded that this too will pass; that the dread of transience, the inability to hold on to all that which is good and all that which is lovely also enables us to let go of the pain – if only fleetingly.

We can perhaps take holidays from grief, allow simple pleasures, 'be kind to ourselves' and acknowledge that while those we have loved were not saints, they were people just like us, and we loved them for all of their flaws and all of their glories.

We loved them for their transience, their smile, their laughter, the sound of their voice, the memories we made. We carry them with us through the darkest days, and learn to be honest about the past, realistic about the future and grateful for all that we have known.

That's the aim. But it's still hard.

A Fine and Private Place

On the first Saturday in August 2017, I travelled to Grantchester to open the summer fete. I was very touched to be asked to do this, as I was never quite sure whether they approved of my series of novels set in the village or of the television series that followed. They had enough tourists because of the setting, the proximity to Cambridge and Rupert Brooke's poem 'The Old Vicarage, Grantchester'. The only problem was that I had double-booked myself. I was supposed to be at the Dartington Summer School of Music, in Devon, for the first day of a week's residence. I was not overly worried, as my teaching did not begin until the Sunday, but was alarmed when Marilyn rang me on the train down:

'Did it go well?'

'It went brilliantly, darling. I was introduced as "the hero of our village".'

'And are you drinking white wine after your triumph?'

'I am.'

'Then you need to slow down. You're onstage tonight.'

'WHAT?'

'There's a late-night concert at ten. It's seventeenth-century lute music. You know what lute players are like?

They spend more time tuning than they do playing. Anyway, the performer says he needs eight minutes to tune. Joanna said you would read some appropriate metaphysical poetry to fill for him. She says she'd told you.'

This was my friend Joanna MacGregor, the artistic director. I recalled that she had mentioned it, but I didn't remember that I had actually been 'told'.

'Anyway, you'd better get on the internet and choose some poems. I won't keep you. See you later, darling.'

I started my search. Marvell, Herbert, Donne. I decided to begin with the belter that is Marvell's 'To His Coy Mistress'. I continued to down the white wine for courage and arrived in only just enough time to greet an anxious and serious performer before the concert began. I was ushered on to the side of the stage and looked out to see an audience of some 300 people wondering who on earth I was and what I was doing onstage with a master lutenist.

By the time came for me to 'fill' I thought the only option was, as the Scots in the theatre say, to 'gie it laldy' so I pronounced in my best booming, amused, theatrical, flirtatious voice:

Had we but WORLD enough … and TIME,
This COYNESS … LADY, were no CRIME …

There was a bit of a titter, which I took as encouragement to overact further. Let's have fun, I thought. I can really go to town on this:

My vegetable love should grow
Vaster than empires and more slow;
An hundred years should go to praise

Thine eyes, and on thy forehead gaze;
Two hundred to adore EACH BREAST,
But THIRTY THOUSAND to the rest …

And build to the end:

Let us roll ALL OUR STRENGTH AND ALL
OUR SWEETNESS up into one ball,
And TEAR OUR PLEASURES WITH ROUGH
STRIFE
<u>*Through*</u> *THE IRON GATES OF LIFE …*

Dramatic pause:

Thus …

Further dramatic pause:

though we cannot make our sun
STAND STILL,

Knowing smile, increase in volume:

Yet

Last dramatic pause – bring the audience in:

WE WILL MAKE HIM RUN.

Hold position. Smile. Shy little bow. Await applause.
It came.
Afterwards I asked Marilyn if I had got away with it.
'Not too over the top?'

'A bit pissed, but yes, good fun. They loved you.'

'Marvellous.'

'Not as much as I do, though.'

'I know that.'

'My turn, now. That's enough nonsense.'

Two years later we talked about having a sundial in the garden in St Monans. Our friend Lida, a letter-cutter, could perhaps design one for us and we could incorporate the end of the Marvell poem.

> *Though we cannot make our sun stand still*
> *Yet we will make him run.*

It was a symbol of Marilyn's attack on life, the desire to make the best of everything, to appreciate every minute of every day. It was a theatrical determination, a refusal to be bored, a desire to intensify all that we experience, to let nothing pass us by.

I remembered copying out Walter Pater's admonition at the end of his book *The Renaissance*. 'A counted number of pulses only is given to us of a variegated, dramatic life. How may we see in them all that is to be seen in them by the finest senses? How shall we pass most swiftly from point to point, and be present always at the focus where the greatest number of vital forces unite in their purest energy? To burn always with this hard, gemlike flame, to maintain this ecstasy, is success in life.'

But, by the time we approached Lida we already had the death sentence and so we talked to her not just about the sundial but also about the gravestone, and what that too might say. We were reminded of the earlier lines in the poem:

The grave's a fine and private place,
But none, I think, do there embrace.

Lida sent us her designs for the sundial and then for the gravestone, with wild flowers growing around its base. Because it was going to be a shared grave, we decided on our joint profession: *Storytellers.*

Looking at the flowers shown around the foot I remembered Marilyn's love of drawing plants, dating back to botany at school. Whenever we were on holiday she preferred to stop and draw rather than take photographs, even if it was just something in pen and ink that she would fill with watercolour later. The image could be impressionistic, or it could be quite detailed, but she was convinced that this act of observation would help her remember a place far better than if she took a photograph or made notes or kept a diary.

As a result, our home is full of her notebooks and sketchbooks:

Foxgloves at the window, Cuillins beyond, Elgol, July 2012.

Just one of the many seashore plants that grow in the sea walls in Ischia, thick, rounded robust leaves designed to resist salt-water.

July wild flowers, Port Isaac clifftops: coltsfoot, thorn-stemmed bramble, stately cream cowslips, convolvulus, brown dock, marram grass.

Vivid pink alpine flowers growing in the rocks by Loch Coruisk; the plantain, clover and campion meadow at Beauville.

Sometimes, when we stayed with friends, she would paint still lives of the vase of daffodils on the kitchen table, or the pot of geraniums outside the back door. Before and after she died, some of these friends arranged small shrines of the paintings and gifts she had given them. Corners of rooms were dedicated to her memory. They sent me photographs to show how much they were thinking of her. They would always love her, they said. Attention was a kind of prayer.

When Marilyn was alive (there's a phrase I never thought I would write), she took great care and delight in leaving little vases of flowers in the guest bedroom when people came to stay. These were not big formal displays but takings and mementoes from the garden. Now I vowed that I would try and do the same for her. I decided to make 'a graveyard garden' so there would be something fresh and different to bring to the cemetery every week. It would be a task in which I might even find joy, just as she delighted in making her floral arrangements. It would be creative and apposite, a different way of remembering her, constructive and forward-looking, a memorial that mixed hope with beauty.

I started to plan the garden in September, only a few weeks after the funeral, when there was still plenty of colour: pale and rich pink cosmos, deep blue agapanthus, white roses, long-lasting Cape daisies. The Japanese anemones were at their fullest and highest and yet to be toppled by the wind. (For this is a windy garden, right by the sea, not prone to frost but biting winters when an afternoon gale can turn everything brown and destroy all hope and promise until the first snowdrops.)

In October I looked to pink nerines and yellow alstroemeria (even though Marilyn hated yellow flowers she allowed the paler kind along with daffodils in the spring). I picked asters and the last of the white roses and in November there was still some pink flowering hebe, lavatera and rosemary to tie into little sprays.

December was more of a challenge but there were hellebores and cyclamen, red-berried holly and skimmia, cotoneaster and snowberry.

In January there were pink and white heathers, and greenery for Burns Night tied with a tartan ribbon, but it was hard to find arrangements on the days of wind and darkness. I was still waiting for crocus and snowdrop. I planted a mimosa tree because I remembered us going to a New Year's Day concert in Venice and listening to John Eliot Gardiner conduct a series of the great opera arias. But there was no chance of mimosa prospering in Fife in January. The wind shredded all hope off the tree. It had been a ridiculous idea. So I went to the Co-op instead and bought hyacinths and a white orchid.

In March I planned *Iris reticulata* and *Muscari* 'Cupido', and *Senecio* and *Scilla* and white 'Thalia' daffodils. Then there would be the first of the tulips, *orphanidea* or *hageri*, and by April there were her favourite fritillaries, *michailovsky* and *persica*, and pink lily of the valley and the first anemones, *coronaria* 'De Caen'.

I remembered her painting a posy of them that we bought once in France and her saying in our hotel room: 'I love anemones. They die so beautifully.'

Once the bluebells and the peonies and the tulips were up in May, it was going to be a home run for a summer with 'Spring Green' and 'Prinses Irene' and 'Brown Sugar' and 'Queen of the Night'. Then, in June, there were the first white roses, lavender and lilies, honesty and *Ammi majus*; and by July there would be white lupins and foxgloves and 'Ivory Castle' poppies. I tried to grow the same red poppies that we saw in the *Creation* exhibition in 1984, before we were married, the poppies that reminded her of her childhood. There were going to be so many flowers that I thought I could probably take a different posy and lay it on the grave every day. By August there could be sunflowers and sweet peas, freesias and the marguerites. Then it would be the anniversary of her death and another September and another year to think and to plan and learn from my mistakes and appreciate that gardening is about hope.

There was the apple tree she gave me for my last birthday that I shared with her. It is called 'Marilyn' and I thought of the carol, 'Jesus Christ the Apple Tree', that we sang at my father's funeral. My friend Carolyn sent me a link to a concert that she was singing in the Wigmore Hall and without thinking I turned it on and heard her first words and burst into tears:

I will give my love an apple without any core
I will give my love a house without any door
I will give my love a palace wherein he may be
And he may unlock it without any key.

I told Neil, the minister, that there were times when I could not believe that Marilyn had been buried, that those were her mortal remains below ground. He reminded me of what he had said before the funeral: 'She doesn't need her body any more.'

I planted more snowdrops and daffodils and, as I dug and scooped back the earth, getting the soil under my fingernails, I could not help but think: She is in the ground too. And the thought was both unbearable and ridiculous. I found that, when I had finished, I had to go back to the grave and talk to her or be silent, I didn't know which. I hadn't yet learned what you were supposed to do at a grave apart from just stand there and stare into the distance and let the grief come. And so, I gathered up a little bouquet of hebe and pink mallow and rosemary, *that's for remembrance*, and I stood there in our fine and private place and thought of her and the flowers I had planted and the graveyard garden I had planned and all the times that I was going to be with her in the future on this high headland. And then, as I turned to leave on a calm and strangely windless day, with the cold still a long way off, I didn't say goodbye because, I decided, there's no point any more. There is no goodbye, and there never will be. She will always be with me. There will always be a future for a love such as this.

Mindless Tidying

My godmother was a lovely woman called Celia, a hoarder who threw nothing away. I was her lodger for two years at a relatively early stage of her obsession but, even then, the path up the stairs was filled with piles of paper and her bedroom floor was obscured by mounds of clothes and files and notebooks hidden under Indian dustsheets. I used to wonder how she ever found her way to her own bed without slipping or tripping. But I did understand why she never brought any of her romantic interests back home. In the end she did slip, just at the age where the distinction between 'falling over' and 'having a fall' becomes clear. Yet that didn't stop her. One evening we asked the new upstairs neighbour round for drinks. When he went home, we didn't spot that he had left the front door open. Half an hour later the police were round, thinking that something suspicious had occurred. They told us very solemnly that we had been burgled.

'I don't think we have,' said Celia.

The policeman was amazed. 'But can't you see your flat's been ransacked?'

After explaining that our flat was always like this, Celia smiled and confessed to me: 'I'm afraid that's not the first time it's happened.'

It was the spring of 1983 when the Eurythmics had just released 'Who's That Girl?' and I was keen on an appropriate Sloane who was otherwise involved with the minimalist architect John Pawson. Obeying his instructions, she had stripped her flat so that the wooden table at its centre held only a vase of daffodils and a soft Italian leather notebook that was too precious to write in.

It was no way to live a practical life but, when I met Marilyn, I found she was, at least in theory, a great believer in the William Morris idea: 'Have nothing in your house that you do not know to be useful or believe to be beautiful.' And so, when we came to share our lives, we had a joint purge of our possessions in anticipation of Marie Kondo's advice that we should only keep items that 'spark joy'. Unfortunately, this provoked argument rather than delight since, on seeing that we had duplicates, I sent the wrong things to the school sale, most notably a first edition of the Penguin Mersey Poets with its pop-art cover and the vinyl of the Beatles' *Revolver* because I had it on CD and considered that it took up less space.

I was forgiven, just, but it was always brought up in the subsequent years whenever I wanted to throw anything away (I am a great chucker-out). Then, later on in our marriage, we found inspiration and extremity in Michael Landy's Artangel show *Break Down* in which he took over a London store and destroyed everything he owned: all 7,227 of his possessions.

It was February 2001. Charlotte was twelve at the time and we both thought that she should witness this contemporary art 'happening', a literal and philosophical erasure of property, gifts, identity and memory. Michael Landy was at the centre wearing welder's glasses, surrounded by men and women in blue boiler suits breaking down objects into manageable chunks and placing them on a great winding conveyor belt of destruction. And the irony was that it was all taking place in the United Kingdom's Capital of Acquisition: Oxford Street. This was John Lennon's 'imagine no possessions' being enacted. All of Landy's worldly goods were split into ten categories: Artworks, Clothing, Electrical Items, Furniture, Kitchen, Leisure, Perishables, Reading, Studio, Vehicle (his car).

Even the presents that people had given him were there: a Damien Hirst spot paperweight, a Tracey Emin 'Be Faithful to Your Dreams' handkerchief, an Anya Gallaccio mirror, all his memories and photographs. Everything was catalogued, even stuff that should have gone to the dump:

E921: Philips HD4575 – broken cream-coloured plastic toaster with burnt crumbs in catchment tray

E927: Kenwood Cassette Receiver KRC-150L – car stereo with missing detachable face off control panel from Volkswagen Golf CL

E954: Ikea broken white plastic kettle with white electrical flex and moulded three-pin plug

We watched a white T-shirt from Scrapheap Services, with a faded black Jelly Tots sweet wrapper screenprint on the front, pass us on the conveyor belt. His father's old coat. Even his car was broken down. All he had left were the clothes he stood up in.

Now, after Marilyn's death, I was faced with another clear-out, another breakdown.

But what to keep and what to throw away?

First to go were the medicines that had to be returned. Then the medical equipment (all the things that we had only just acquired that had become redundant within weeks: bath chairs, walking frames, commodes, wheelchairs, slings and hoist). The hallway was filled until it resembled a hospital storeroom.

Then, after a few days, underwear, stockings – but it was far too soon for shoes, clothes, dresses, make-up or perfume.

It was the reverse of collecting, this removal. I wanted to de-hospitalise the house and make it normal, but what was normal after a death? How could a house ever be the same again?

Possessions were replaced by absence. The objects that remained had to work harder. Marilyn's treasures had to be brought out and displayed. They might not spark joy, but they were memories, and they could be beautiful once more.

She liked to tidy and make arrangements. It was her way of relaxing, putting things right, placing items *just so*. Perhaps it was a way of exercising control in at least one area of her life when she found everything else chaotic. Start small and work up from there. Most of the time she did it without thinking, as if she was in a kind of dream. The family came to refer to it as her 'mindless tidying'.

We noticed that our friend Hildegard, the designer, did it too, hiding a stray cable, moving a wooden bowl an inch to the left on a table, picking up a glass and putting it next to something else, tutting at the mantelpiece or despairing at a stray sock left on the floor. Marilyn and she were the same – and this abstract and dreamy control-freakery was adopted by her friend Deborah for a performance in Sam Holcroft's *Rules for Living* at the National Theatre. When Marilyn went to see the play, she thought, 'Hang on a minute, that's what I do.' She asked the actress afterwards if she had nicked her mindless tidying. Deborah just smiled and said she couldn't think what her friend could possibly mean.

So, in turn and in tribute, I started to make little displays of flowers and vases and I arranged white china on a shelf as if it was a Hammershøi painting. I looked at interior design magazines which never ever show a television or a computer or a cable and tried replicating their impossible minimalism. Then I looked at one of Marilyn's last arrangements. It was a small collection of leatherbound books, special editions and miniatures, grouped on the chest of drawers in the bedroom: Rossetti's *Goblin Market*, *The Story of Tennyson's 'In Memoriam'*, the Book of Common Prayer, Matthew Arnold's *Selected Poems*, Elizabeth Barrett Browning's *Sonnets from the Portuguese*, Ruskin's *Mornings in Florence*. The pile of books had a simple elegance which I knew she would have found pleasing. I thought of her doing it, I could imagine it all, and there was something indefinably moving about it.

I remembered a letter that Proust had written to a friend in 1913: 'We think we no longer love the dead but then we catch sight of an old glove and burst into tears.'

I became distracted. I found myself carrying socks around the house, looking for the shoes I had worn the previous day. By the time I discovered the shoes, I had put the socks down somewhere else. I couldn't remember where they were and couldn't be bothered to find them. In any case, I couldn't see the point of putting on shoes any more because that might mean going out and facing the world and I didn't want to do that or make another decision.

Then I realised my feet were cold. I needed the bloody socks after all. But should I just put the shoes down again to go and find them because, if I did, would I know where I had left them?

I remembered my mother telling me, 'They're where you left them,' and finding it so irritating.

Then I heard Marilyn's voice, bright and clear, saying, 'Here they are.' She always had a way of walking into a room and finding things that had been staring me straight in the face. I hadn't noticed, and I almost wanted to accuse her of having only just put them there, or of carrying them with her all along, or of deliberately confusing me. But she would just smile and say, 'Look. Here,' and maybe even give me a little kiss and tell me not to get in a state. Everything was going to be all right. There was no need to make a fuss.

Now I remembered all this, I couldn't move. I just wanted her back. All I could do was sit down and cry and think what it was like when she was in the world every day.

This tidying was not sparking any joy at all.

But then I managed to get up and start again and find things that I had forgotten we had given each other. Pens and pencils and notebooks; pillboxes, brooches and compact mirrors; a china plate with a bluebird, a tray for asparagus to be brought out every May, a sugar sifting spoon, a miniature glass vase for floral arrangements. I remembered the look of horror on her face when I gave her a pair of tights as part of her Christmas present one year (I still don't know why I did this) and I tried to get away with it by saying: 'At least it wasn't an iron or a Hoover.'

After her death I found that I was reconfiguring an idea that I had put into one of the *Grantchester* novels, where Sidney and Hildegard wrap up possessions they already had but had forgotten about in order to appreciate them all over again, bringing objects back out into the light.

I moved a picture into the bedroom. It was by Audrey Grant from an exhibition of paintings based on a study of the dancers in Scottish Ballet. Marilyn had chosen an image that wasn't of the dancers but their instructor, observing them like a theatre director, entitled *Standing Figure*. She thought the woman looked a bit like her and she gave it to me for our wedding anniversary in 2014. Now, as I was handling the picture once more, I remembered that she had stuck an observation on the back of the frame:

> *This woman is waiting for the man she loves.*
> *She knows he will be with her soon*
> *She can't wait to see him because she knows that when he appears*
> *Everything will suddenly seem right again, everything possible,*
> *Hope restored; all calm and bright.*
> *She is happy to wait, because he will always return,*
> *Whatever comes between them when they are parted one from the other.*

And then I remembered we had had a bit of an argument about it. I had complained that I was always with her and that all this 'happy to wait' was nonsense because I was the one that did the waiting. She was always so busy that she was never waiting for anything apart from delayed planes and trains.

I remembered going to Istanbul, before the diagnosis, in 2019. We went to see Orhan Pamuk's Museum of

Innocence only to find that it was closed. But we took the novel with us, the story of Kemal's obsessive collecting throughout his romance with Füsun and his creation of a series of exhibits in a museum to her memory. It was filled with his girlfriend's clothes, restaurant menus and old postcards; soda bottle caps, a whisky glass, a sugar bowl, an ashtray, 4,213 cigarette stubs.

At the same time, we remembered Leanne Shapton's intriguing and adventurous photographic novel of evidence, *Important Artifacts and Personal Property from the Collection of Lenore Doolan and Harold Morris*, the story of a love affair told through its memorabilia, catalogued as if everything was up for sale. The reader has to unravel the story of a relationship through the potency of its imagery: an invitation to a Halloween party, the menu for a Valentine's dinner, a photograph of the couple dressed as Benjamin and Mrs Robinson from *The Graduate*, duplicate paperbacks, handwritten notes, photobooth pictures, and then, towards the end, the bill for a restaurant meal where the main course is cancelled and it's all over.

And so, after Marilyn's death, I wanted to do something similar but *in real life* and more focused, to make the kind of arrangements she would have made, to place little objects in the window and create small shrines, keeping everything tidy and seeing if everything out and 'on display' was meant, our home becoming a cross between an art installation and a Museum of Marilyn.

But as I started what might be called *mindful* tidying, I went through crammed and overcrowded drawers and found so much stuff that was hers and hers alone and nothing to do with me. What, for example, should I do with the photograph album of my wife's first wedding when both of them are dead and they had no children?

What do I do about her letters from people other than me? What do I do about my own letters that I have hung on to that I would rather my children did not read? When is the right time to throw things away? How do you curate the life of the one you have lost: and how do you protect and preserve your own personal archive?

I found the tiniest notebook at the back of a drawer with a watercolour of a rose that Rosie had given her and a little inscription she wrote on the day Charlotte was born: 'She is mine to be with and I hope to be what she needs and I can think of no reason why I could ever desert her.'

There was a little pen-and-ink drawing of a statue in Notre-Dame, a watercolour of a Christmas tree and of a couple of dark red poppies with buds she painted at Sissinghurst in 1992. Then there was this:

Two of the many things I love about James Runcie:

The index and middle fingers of his right hand have two small hillocks where pens and pencils over forty years have hollowed out spaces – where all the words he's written have first left their mark on his hand and then the page

Just before James lies down to sleep, he takes off his glasses, with his back towards me, and there are two small clicks – click, click – and the small sound signals his leaving the world of sharp focus and clarity for the world of dreams and me.

I looked out the presents she had given me over the years: a gold chain with a heart and charm initials: M, R, C; the four little Calvados glasses that were my first Christmas present; a brass Mizpah 'sweetheart' brooch dating from the First World War, engraved with the phrase,

'The Lord watch between me and thee, when we are absent one from another.'

I remembered the long yellow scarf that she had given me and bought another as if she were still alive and it was our first Christmas all over again.

I found the Montblanc 'Noblesse Oblige' pen her mother had given her and I thought it would be nice to use it to write about her. Perhaps it might help the words come, there could be consolation and reassurance as I wrote, with her voice at my shoulder rather than the usual demon of doubt.

But I couldn't quite work out if I needed a spare cartridge in the barrel and ended up jamming it in so that I couldn't close the pen properly or write with it all. Looking up potential solutions on the internet, and employing my incompetent DIY (which had once seen a shelf collapse and me throwing a Hoover down the stairs when I couldn't find a way of opening the bag), I used a screw to try and pull it out and that got stuck too and so I had to send it to a pen repairer, and after I had done so, and while thinking about rewriting one of the Dr Johnson plays that we had done, I turned to his dictionary and looked up the definition of the word 'repair':

Repair: To restore after injury or dilapidation … to fill up anew, by putting something in place of what is lost.

I looked up other words:

Restore: To bring back, to retrieve.
Resuscitate: To stir up anew, to revive.
Resurrection: Revival from the dead; return from the grave. *He triumphs in his agonies whilst the soul springs*

forward to the great object which she has always had in view and leaves the body with an expectation of being remitted to her in a glorious and joyful resurrection. Spectator.

And I realised, on receiving the restored pen, that writing this with her nib was a way of her guiding me. The flow of ink and prose was a different kind of bloodstream, of both memory and inspiration. This was an act of recovery, where recollection, art and beauty could be the greatest consolation. These were small steps, word by word, sentence by sentence, page by page, in the new grammar of righting oneself, regaining balance, moving towards a way of making sense of all that had happened without entirely thinking about it. The unselfconscious flow was its own form of mindless tidying.

Dressing and Undressing

But what to do with the clothes that were left behind, in the wardrobe, by the bed and under the stairs, in the spare room and in St Monans: the frocks, the shoes, the jewellery, the outfits for special dinners and celebrations and ... her wedding gown?

At our service of blessing in Lambeth Palace Chapel, Marilyn wore a full-length cotton needlecord dress in pillar-box red from the theatrical costumier Droopy and Browns. My father's press officer was appalled.

'The scarlet woman. What will the papers say?'

'They're not here,' he replied, thinking the whole thing rather amusing.

'Someone will tell them,' she said. 'No one's going to keep this quiet.'

But they did.

Marilyn liked to dress well and theatrically. Her wardrobe was full of spectacular garments that she never saved for 'best'. She wore them every day: an antique Japanese kimono that she 'borrowed' from the back of a costume store at a provincial theatre; a deep purple long-sleeved Issy Miyake blouse; a crew-neck Ralston dress in black and Prince of Wales check with a full-length curtain-ring zip; a cream cotton summer dress with a Japanese sunray pattern in red, black and sand; a black Lagenlook jacket with a fabulous wide collar that fastens with two large shiny buttons.

She loved vintage and was proud that she still had the Biba jacket she had bought in the late sixties. She was specific about colour, avoiding yellow and green, insisting they made her skin look gaunt, and generally wore clothes as boldly as those old Soviet posters in red, black and white, with accents of silver, pink and blue. We were amused when we went to an exhibition at the Ingleby Gallery only to find that Marilyn's dress was in the same blocks of colour as a Callum Innes painting. 'You must let me take a photograph of you in front of that,' I said. 'It's the perfect match. Woman as work of art.'

'Trying my best,' she said. 'You can send it to the girls.'

When she finished dressing and thought she was ready to go out she would turn to me and ask the same question her mother had always asked her father: 'Will I do?'

And I would say, of course, yes, you look marvellous, splendid, but we were never actually 'ready'. There was still the business of perfume and lipstick and finding the right handkerchief and checking her handbag. We were a good fifteen minutes away from leaving the house and all of this was before the whole business of considering the weather and deciding on the right kind of coat.

There was a duster in splattered black and silver; a high-collared ruched coat with contrasting horizontal stripes in black and burnt sienna; a white wool and polyester Moyuru coat-dress with a photocopied winter woodland design; a black and white Yiannis Karitsiotis woollen coat with two bright red front buttons; and a 'when I am old I shall wear purple' coat, a full-length lilac hooded foldaway mac in nylon and polyester.

She wore this to a memorial service in Southwark Cathedral. We were just about the last to arrive and were shown to our seats by a worried-looking steward in a tweed jacket and a battered straw bowler decorated with fake flowers. She had little pebble-rimmed glasses and looked like the kind of woman who would get bumped off in the first act of *Midsomer Murders*. Then I realised.

'My God, it's Alice.' (This was the woman before Marilyn that I nearly married.)

'Hello, James.'

'Darling, this is Alice.'

Marilyn looked at her and smiled. 'Well, I'm very pleased to meet you, Alice.'

The organ started up for the processional hymn and my 'near miss' made her way back to her seat. Just before the first words were sung, Marilyn turned to me and said, as brightly as possible, 'Any regrets?'

Sometimes, like the actress Beryl Reid, Marilyn started her outfit with the shoes. Even though Marilyn Monroe almost certainly did not say the words, she liked the quotation: 'Give a girl the right shoes and she can conquer the world.'

There were red suede ankle boots and pink leopard-skin court shoes and black etched-leather lace-ups. On our visits to London, she would buy reflective grey cycle sneakers, or neon-orange patent-leather derbies, or Gatsby black-and-gold peep-toes. They were flashes of style but also conversational starter-points. She thought it was good to give people something to talk about and, after she died, the women from the cleaning company we employed to keep the house going told me that they used to have a game of 'Guess which shoes Marilyn will be wearing today?'

There were twelve of these women, who cleaned from a rota in pairs. On the day of the funeral, they held a two-minute silence for her, wherever they were working. They all stopped whatever they were doing to remember her. I can't really write these words without crying.

Marilyn could never pass a jewellery stall in a holiday market, often looking for the gaudiest and kitschiest items they had: glass that caught the light, bright earrings in geometric shapes, clacking necklaces and statement brooches. One of her signature pieces of costume jewellery was a series of liquid-glass rings in the shape of a cube with different-coloured inks inside. People always asked where she got them (they are available online and cost £17) but she told them not to worry, she would send them one; and she did.

Her dress sense meant that she was always noticed, which meant that she was frequently robbed. On a long weekend in Prague someone tried to steal from her handbag every single day that we were there. When I suggested that perhaps, possibly, she might want to dress down a bit she said: 'What do you want me to do? Wear a fleece?'

One Christmas I gave her a red leather double-zipped handbag. Both girls agreed that it just said: 'Rob me now.'

After our friend Bridget from the BBC had all *her* jewellery stolen, she sat down and drew each item from memory for the purposes of police and insurance. Marilyn was so taken with the idea of drawing her own jewellery that she started to do the same, often noting when and where she had bought a piece:

A pair of vintage 1950s clasp earrings. Two perfectly shaped star fish. Three pearls set in each leaf – gold stud balls texturing the skin of the fish. I wore them on holidays to Crete and Skye. Bought London. £55 in 2002.

A pair of pearl and mother-of-pearl cascade earrings bought in Ischia.

A shell bracelet from Kate, 2001. A Christmas gift.

Turquoise blue glass earrings from Ischia.

Cream soapstone earrings strung on small wooden beads. Bought in Mallorca.

A giant shell pendant from Girona, Spain, iridescent opalesque strung on small wooden beads. Charlotte wore it in a school play.

The amber James brought back from Poland.

In the summer she always carried a Japanese paper fan in her handbag. Because she was so pale, she disliked the heat (which makes us wonder all the more about vitamin D deficiency as a possible cause of MND and its higher levels in Scotland). She enjoyed the dramatic flick of a fan, and knew how to rock the look, using it as a gestural punctuation point when closed, waving it like a Restoration actress when open, and even holding it just below her eyes as if she was Scotland's first geisha.

We once went to a High Table dinner at an Oxford college. She sat between two dons who didn't ask her a single question for the whole night. This is quite common in such situations, but Marilyn wasn't used to it. At first, she was delighted that the woman next to her was an expert in late-eighteenth-century fans, but then realised that her fellow-guest could talk about nothing else. On the way home, she was furious.

'I tried my best, darling, my absolute best, but it was USELESS. I asked her about seventeenth-century fans and nineteenth-century fans, but she said, no, she only knew about the eighteenth-century fans. I wanted to know about her favourite fans. She didn't have any. I asked her if she had any fans at home, if she collected fans herself, and she said she did not. I wondered if she had ever been asked to advise actors on how to hold a fan, but she said no, she hadn't. I asked her every possible question I could think of until I ran out. There was a silence and, *even then*, she didn't think to ask: "And what do you do?" Not even "Do you have a fan yourself?" I gave her two hours of opportunity to talk about her bloody fans. What are these people like? And by the way, she had absolutely no sense of style, no sense of humour and no imagination. She couldn't have been more dull, *even on the subject of fans, which should be fascinating.* We're never going to one of those bloody things again. Next time, you can go on your own. Unbelievable. Unforgivable. Really. Ridiculous.'

Even at the end of her disease and her life, there was a refusal to dress down. She wore a twisted turquoise-and-coral rope necklace with a magnetic clasp that was easy to put on and take off; Salvador Dalí earrings with a lobster and a telephone; and the room was filled with the scent of English Oak and Hazelnut.

Rosie helped her to decide what to wear from a selection of five or six outfits that were easy to manage and made her comfortable. I was seldom involved in this after Marilyn had a food spill at lunch and insisted that I change her dress. I made a bit of a hash of it with the sleeves and the back and the pulling it down and the checking that it was straight across the shoulders. When I had quite finished, she said, 'You've always been hopeless at putting on and taking off women's clothes. I blame myself. But I'm not going to start teaching you now.'

I remembered walking into a hotel restaurant on the day of our arrival for a short holiday in France. We were straight off the plane and the last to arrive and the dining room was full of the restrained chic of silent and judgemental Saturday diners on their day off. It was the kind of place where if you do talk then your only conversation is about the food and the white wine is stored in an ice bucket half a kilometre away to prevent you pouring it yourself.

Marilyn was wearing a peach-coloured floaty linen top. She had her neon-orange patent-leather derbies on her feet. Our fellow-guests gave her the twice-over. We ate and chatted away but the sophisticated locals kept on looking across as if warning us that, if we enjoyed ourselves too much, we wouldn't be able to appreciate the food.

We had the first asparagus of the season, lemon sole with French beans and a lavender crème brûlée. Although we had been the last to arrive, we appeared to be the first to finish. Marilyn pushed back her chair and stood up to leave. She smiled, put her hand to her lips and walked towards the door. Then she turned, made sure that all the sombre diners were looking at her and said to me very sternly: 'Now we go fucky fuck.'

She always had a great sense of timing. After she died, Susannah, a theatre critic, wrote to me saying that she wished she had known Marilyn better. 'Almost weekly on the radio I am caught up in a play, wait to hear the producer's name and find yet again it is Marilyn. She must constantly have made people listen differently and respond better: what a gift. Her style, too, comes back to me. I remember at a Bloomsbury party a few years ago, she was in blue-and-white swirls with a big collar. Alexandra

[Editor-in-Chief] commented on how washed-out some of the young were, and said: "Look at Marilyn – that's how it's done."'

One of her last productions was *A Portrait of a Gentleman* by Peter Ansorge. It was inspired by an account of Henry James clearing out the Venetian lodgings of his 'intimate friend' the 53-year-old novelist Constance Fenimore Woolson, who had committed suicide by throwing herself out of a second-storey window on 24 January 1894. In April, James opened the closed-up Casa Semitecolo with his friend's sister and was given responsibility for the author's literary remains. In them, he found sketches and ideas for novels, one of which was to inspire his short story 'The Beast in the Jungle'.

The story is about a man called John Marcher who is convinced that he has been marked out for something rich and strange, and that he will know the moment because it will be when the metaphorical 'beast in the jungle' pounces. But he fails to realise that his defining moment is not literary achievement but the love that is standing right in front of him: May Bartram. This character is modelled on Constance, a woman who was now dead and lost to him. James had missed his defining moment, caught up by distracted vanity, and was now faced with nothing but his own arid end for 'no passion had ever touched him'. Only after her death did he realise what he had missed.

According to his biographer Lyndall Gordon, as they finished clearing out the lodgings, James hired a gondolier to take Constance's dresses and throw them into the lagoon. 'But the dresses refused to drown. One by one they rose to the surface, their busts and sleeves swelling like black balloons. Purposefully, the gentleman pushed them under, but silent, irreproachful, they rose before his eyes.'

Marilyn was always taken with this idea: of the Venetian lagoon which we had often discussed as the place where we would like our ashes to be scattered, and of the stylish ballgowns in silk and taffeta that refuse to sink, even at the end of a gondolier's pole.

Style cannot be sunk.

Looking at her full wardrobe, I decided I was going to keep some of her clothes. The girls could have a rummage, but I would not separate them out or sell them or even take them to the Venetian lagoon and sink them myself. So, I have decided to leave them alone. I can even imagine the clothes talking to each other, with their own memories, telling of their adventures and their last outings and what it was like to be picked out and worn by Marilyn.

I went back to my desk and found a letter written to me by our friend Tom: 'Sitting here in the barn I can almost reach out and touch Marilyn across the table, no doubt with large bright buttons, red shoes, lots of rustling black silk. Marrying her was the best thing you ever did, wasn't it?'

It was.

The Kite

Marilyn hated having her photograph taken. She wanted it over and done with as quickly as possible even when I explained that the more trouble I took, the better the final image would be. She never trusted the camera, preferring to draw, and was useless at taking photographs herself. It just didn't interest her. Sometimes I thought she was deliberately bad at it, just as some men are hopeless with household tasks so they don't have to do them. The first photograph I ever took of her, outside her back door in Edinburgh, in red coat and black-and-white cotton gingham dress, carries a patient but suspicious look as if she is saying: 'Do you have to carry on with this? What are you going to do with it? I'm not at my best.'

At her best was always how she wanted to be.

She did allow photographs at our wedding. I took a picture of her turning round and smiling from a bench in Venice on our honeymoon that came to be used in her obituaries. I wanted people to use an image from when she was happy rather than sick. She was picky about who she allowed to take the photographs and was best when she was photographed unobserved. She hated being arranged into a photo-opportunity (someone else directing) or being asked to stare into bright sunlight on holiday with other people who didn't know how to take a decent picture. I had to keep explaining why she didn't like it and sometimes even ask people not to insist on photographing her as she really did absolutely hate it.

The more I worked in film and television, the more I began to understand lighting. Then I was given a bit more latitude and permission to sneak the odd photograph of Marilyn, especially when I told her the lessons I had learned from cameramen: how it was far better to shoot into the sun (the exact opposite to the childhood use of the Instamatic on summer holidays) and then use reflectors to provide most of the key and fill light; how Philip Bonham-Carter, who shot Delia Smith and the Queen, preferred to keep the cheek on a woman's face nearest the camera darker, so there was foreground shadow and the viewer would look into the frame and into the light; how the great Remi Adefarasin (*Truly, Madly, Deeply*; *About a Boy*; *Elizabeth*) employed a single light source behind Susan Wooldridge reading in bed in my film *Miss Pym's Day Out*, using the open book to bounce the light back into her face like Rembrandt's *An Old Woman Reading*.

Marilyn was amused by my account of filming the most famous woman I had ever met, the legendary Lauren Bacall, who didn't charge a fee but insisted on a suite at the Algonquin in New York together with her own driver, make-up and hairstylist, as well as approval of the lighting, the camera angle and a longer-than-usual portrait lens. No wide-angle nonsense, no shooting from below the eyeline, no direct light, and everything bounced apart from a soft 'butterfly light' for the eyes, as used by Josef von Sternberg for Marlene Dietrich. The cameraman was my friend Jeremy Pollard and it took two and a half hours to get right. When Marilyn saw the final film (it was a documentary about Henry Moore) she said, 'Well, that's it, then. You just have to photograph me like I'm Lauren Bacall.'

And from then on, we had no overhead lights in the house, just reading lamps, wall-lights and candles. Everything had to be softly beautiful. We had to live, even though we were in a terraced house at the end of a cul-de-sac in St Albans at the time, as if we only existed in a Vermeer painting with a Chardin still life on the kitchen table and a Rembrandt on the wall.

Fortunately, Charlotte has become a very good photographer and so when we decided to renew our vows for our twenty-fifth wedding anniversary, she offered to take all the pictures as her present to us. It was an incredibly moving occasion, a mixture of thankfulness, celebration and showing off. 'We might as well do this properly,' said Marilyn, 'we're not going to have another chance.' Pip Torrens read the Shakespeare sonnet 'When forty winters shall besiege thy brow', Siobhán Redmond had learned 'My love is like a red, red rose' and Bill Paterson read the Gospel account of the wedding at Cana in the Scots translation by William Lorimer. He performed it as if he had just come from the scene and was telling the story as an anecdote to his friends in the pub.

'TWA DAYS EFTERHIN there wis a waddin at Cana in Galilee. Jesus's mither was there, an Jesus an his disciples wis amang the friends bidden til it. Efter a while the wine was aa dune, an his mither said til him, "They hae nae mair wine."

'"Ye can lae that tae me," said Jesus; "my hour isna come."'

Charlotte's photographs of the occasion are nearly all observational rather than posed and they focus on the details: the silver rings on our hands; Marilyn rehearsing the singers and listening attentively to her friends, unobserved and at her best. It is this sense of her being involved in life that shines out most strongly. Perhaps her distrust of photography came from the fact she had to stop for it. It was posed. It didn't feel real. It took time out of the business of living, of getting things done. 'He who binds himself to a joy,' I can hear her beginning and me interrupting and finishing the Blake quotation, 'DOES THE WINGÈD LIFE DESTROY. Just as long as you don't mind being "binded" to me.'

'Always binded. You know that. Too late to get out of it now.'

When she was ill, I had to take her photograph for her Blue Badge, not that we were going out much. 'Don't show me,' she said, 'I can't bear to see it,' and her look in the photograph was the first time I ever saw her defeated by illness. It says, 'I told you I hated having my photograph taken. I know you have to, but I still hate it and now it has come to this and there is nothing either of us can do about it.'

But this wasn't the last image. There is one of her in St Monans in a red bobble hat on that last Midsummer Day, of her smiling back at me, tender and full of thirty-five years of love, patience, tenderness and acknowledgement. There is also a final blurred and accidental image of the inside of her hand, with its last strange baby-like softness, taken by accident on my phone.

Then, just before she died, her friend Eileen sent us a black-and-white photograph. It is of Marilyn flying a kite on the beach, looking up, full of delight and glee and joy.

She is excited and happy and it became one of the images we chose to send out and remember her by. It is at the front of this book.

Two weeks later, Gerda Stevenson gave us this poem.

Old Photograph of a Young Woman

(in memoriam Marilyn Imrie, 1947–2020)

I didn't know you then,
wind-blown lass, happed
in your winter coat –
time was all ahead,
like the kite you guide
on a single gossamer thread
and only you can see,
its flight path beyond the frame;

everything is light
in this faded black and white –
your skin, your smile, the sky,
the bright sand of a Fife shore,
your future flying before.

White Tulips

On Valentine's Day 1985, the year in which we married, I gave Marilyn a bunch of forty white tulips. I didn't want to do the cliché of twelve red roses, or twenty-five, or fifty of anything. I wanted something simple and different and wrapped in brown paper. I never realised this would become a tradition, but I soon came to know that if I ever failed to do this over the next thirty-five years it would be an unforgivable black mark. She told me of a line from a sequence of poems, dedicated to her, that she had directed before we met, by another Marilyn, the Canadian writer Marilyn Bowering, about the most famous Marilyn of all time, Marilyn Monroe. It was called 'Anyone Can See I Love You'.

If ever you can walk into a room
And not come first to me:
whatever your reasons are,
they are not enough.

This became the number-one rule of our marriage and white tulips became the floral signature of my devotion. We would stop whenever we saw them. I sought out references to them in art and literature: in Elizabeth Blackadder's watercolours, in the photographer John Blakemore's *The Stilled Gaze*, where they lie post-coitally on a table, in Deborah Moggach's novel *Tulip Fever* and in Sylvia Plath's poem featuring tulips that open 'like the mouth of some great African cat'.

Marilyn loved the way tulips stood proud in a glass vase and then fell away, relaxed and unashamed in the coming days. I found myself giving her other presents that were also simple, minimalist and white, perhaps because they provided a sense of cleanliness, erasure and starting again. Looking back over these memories, I found another reference to the colour in a message I had placed in *The Times* on our very first Valentine's Day, full of adolescent admiration: 'Oh white giraffe, see how the happy thrush loves you!'

I should have been chucked on the spot. What on earth was this nonsense? It's only one step away from couples who speak baby-talk. But I remembered how Marilyn had told me how peaceful and elegant she thought white giraffes were, identifying with their oddity and difference. That's why I must have referred to her in the same way, as something magical, rare and beautiful, as mythical as a unicorn, but real, and here on earth.

And this is how our relationship seems now, as something out of dream and myth, as ghostly as the sight of white giraffes standing and staring back at the camera before walking elegantly away. I can't quite believe either that it happened at all or that it is over: or, at least, 'over' in the physical, earthly sense.

I can't look at white tulips without thinking of her and wanting to take them to the grave. I discovered there was a tulip called *Tulipa* 'Marilyn' and even though it wasn't one she would have particularly liked, in red and white (she preferred single colours), I ordered a hundred and planted them as soon as they arrived because I was impatient.

I thought of us coming over from Edinburgh, at the height of the first lockdown when it wasn't allowed but the doctor told us, 'For God's sake just go,' so that she could see the tulips in our garden in St Monans for the last time, and I remembered, when we finally had to leave, wheeling her away in the wheelchair she hated and her crying out the line from Walter de la Mare's poem 'Fare Well': 'Look thy last on all things lovely …'

I wondered if I would ever get used to the sadness of this loss. When I first wanted to be a writer, I copied out a passage from *Next Time I'll Sing to You*, a play by James Saunders, in which a character talks about the way in which grief is a kind of universal undercurrent beneath all our behaviour, and I reread my O level copy of Wordsworth's 'Tintern Abbey' in which I had underlined the passage about 'the still sad music of humanity' as if I had known what this was like and what it meant. I was seventeen at the time and didn't have a clue.

At the end of our friend Shelagh Stephenson's play, *The Memory of Water*, written shortly after the death of her mother, the character of Mary leaves the family home for a funeral in the freezing winter snow and is asked about her future: 'What are you going to do?'

And she replies: 'Learn to love the cold.'

So this is what I found myself doing, living with the memory of my wife in the middle of a pandemic Scottish winter, picking up tips on how to live on my own for the first time in my life. I was advised to do nothing irreversible in the first year of mourning; to make sure I took exercise;

to phone a friend every day and be kind to myself. Rosie reminded me: 'You have no skin.'

I was told to eat properly and follow a routine and not drink too much alcohol, preferably none at all. Batch cooking helped, apparently. Then I could just 'take things out of the freezer' and I wouldn't have to 'waste time' cooking again and again. But I quite wanted to waste that time, and watch football, and read and write and talk to friends. I had plenty of time to waste, and then later, after I had thought about this, a song came on the radio, a hit from the eighties, Owen Paul singing 'You're My Favourite Waste of Time'. I told Rosie that I thought I had given it to one of my old girlfriends.

'You did,' she replied. 'You gave it to my mother. On vinyl.'

Julie sent me exotic Ottolenghi recipes that might as well begin: 'First fly to Tel Aviv.' I watched cookery programmes on television, but I was brought short when I saw Nigella Lawson wearing the same Venetian dressing gown that Charlotte had given Marilyn two Christmases ago: a cream and pale blue map of the city in the lightest silk. It was surreal to see Nigella wearing it. I watched her creating a dish that called for Aleppo pepper, and it seemed so incongruous to be making something with pepper from Syria that I phoned Pip and ranted at him and he said, 'I know, what next? White Helmet risotto?'

I read other people's memoirs for comfort: Joan Didion's *The Year of Magical Thinking*, Alison Light's *A Radical Romance*, C. S. Lewis's *A Grief Observed*, Gillian Rose's *Love's Work*, Ian Ridley's *The Breath of Sadness*; all those harrowing accounts of widows and widowers so stunned by loss that their only way back was to try and write their way out of it.

It's inevitable for any writer to want to do this because there can be no other subject. How can you concentrate on making up stuff for some stupid novel when you've just lost the love of your life?

Despite the company, I questioned why I, too, was writing a memoir and if this book was really for anyone other than me? What could I add, not so much to the gaiety of nations but to the community of sorrow?

But then I thought that this book was about *Marilyn*. That would make it different, because there was no one like her and never would be and she was going to see me through all this. It was almost as if we were writing it together, as had been the case with all my writing in the past. But this had to be true and like us and so, as well as being sad and serious, it had to be larky and daffy and full of life: a reversal of 'in the midst of life we are in death', becoming instead 'in the midst of death we are in life'. Reading it, I thought, should be like meeting her for the first time, or her walking into a room, smiling and perfumed and fabulously dressed and people thinking: Thank God, she's here. I don't have to worry. I can relax now.

It used to annoy me whenever I went to parties on my own. People would immediately say, 'Where's Marilyn?' as if my presence alone was not good enough. But now I realise it was because they could not imagine me without her.

Well, they can now.

I read in the *New York Times* of a couple who had only just met when the pandemic began, and how they had to sustain their love when they were apart. One of them told the reporter: 'I think the reason we have lasted was because we always tried to be thankful for having met, instead of questioning that we were separated.'

Gratitude is part of love. I remembered my father's bold assertion in the Bible he gave us that 'Love never fails' with its confident underlining. I looked up the promises of Christ in St Paul's Letter to the Romans: *For I am persuaded, that neither death, nor life, nor angels, nor principalities, nor powers, nor things present, nor things to come, nor height, nor depth, nor any other creature, shall be able to separate us from the love of God, which is in Christ Jesus our Lord.*

Sometimes this is hard to hold on to. There's a grave near Marilyn's in St Monans which has the inscription: 'If love could have saved you, you would have lived forever.'

Most of the tombstones talk of eternal rest and are appropriate for a fishing village: 'Life's storms are passed for evermore' and 'After storms safe harbour'. There is Protestant modesty too: 'Worthy of remembrance' as if some people are NOT worthy. Other inscriptions are uncompromisingly straightforward: 'No time left'. Several compare the transience of life with the promises of Jesus: 'With Christ – which is better'.

Rosie joked that they should have added a question mark and then we had a blasphemous laugh and I asked: 'Which is better? Christ? Or Marilyn?'

'That's a tough one …'

'I think I'd rather have Marilyn.'

We shared this grave humour and I was struck by how cheerful some of the other inscriptions were and how they quoted from the favourite phrases of their beloved dead. 'Man up!' Another had the invocation: 'Smile, smile, smile'.

Joint graves talked of couples being 'reunited' and 'together at last'. But I did not think it needed my death to join me with my wife because I did not feel separated from her at all. Broken but not separated.

I held on to a perfect palm-fit pebble that I asked Lida to carve for me before she did the gravestone, with the 'M' on one side, the 'J' on the other, a portable memento. It was and is like carrying a piece of the grave.

Sometimes, I take it out and pass it from hand to hand. I put it on the table by my side when I am writing. It says: 'Marilyn is here.'

When I wrote to people to thank them for their condolences, I had a card designed to make it easier and special. It was based on the definitions of the word 'Marilyn' as 'wished-for child', 'beloved' and 'star of the sea'. It read:

In the darkest of skies
A sea of starlight

Despite the convenience of the card, I still took trouble over what I wrote inside – after all, what else was I going to do to fill the time and what could be more important than this?

I said that all recognition was a gift of grace, and that grief was unpredictable. We know people can't live forever but, as with all that is awful, we hope to be spared, or at least for the inevitable to be delayed. And now there is the loss, but also the grace and privilege of knowing Marilyn, a woman as rare as a white giraffe, and for a love to be known and experienced and remembered and lived with and comforted by. Perhaps the boundaries between life and death are more permeable than we think.

On the first Valentine's Day without her, I laid white tulips on the graveyard grass, on the spot where I knew her heart should be. I looked down and I didn't know what to think or say; but I did recall the end of Henry James's story 'The Beast in the Jungle', when Marcher visits the tomb of his dead love: 'What it all amounted to, oddly enough, was that in his finally so simplified world this garden of death gave him the few square feet of earth on which he could still most live.'

I wondered what it might be like to throw myself down on to the ground, just as Marcher does. I could lie down on Marilyn's grave, on *our* grave, and wait for the wind and the rain and the darkness. It would certainly make it easier for the undertaker, who could simply move me to one side, summon the gravedigger and tip me in.

Hypothermia. It would be one way to go.

I remembered Siobhán telling me her plan, when the time came and she thought she had really had enough of life, to drink a bottle of vodka and crawl under 'the hedge of doom'; and of my friend Sarah telling me that when she nearly died of hypothermia, while swimming in the sea, 'it was rather lovely'.

But this is an indulgence and a fantasy. I must keep on living with grief and possibility and the hope of adventure. Friends tell me: 'It's what she'd want you to do.'

But is it? Really? Marilyn didn't seem that keen on my future life without her. She did her best but I think – no, I know – she *hated* the idea of her life without me and my life without her. She was furious about not being able to spend more time as a grandmother (she had less than three years), or as a mother, or as a friend and even as a wife. She was unspeakably depressed, *literally unspeakably*, by the inevitability of death. There was nothing I could do, *absolutely nothing*, to make her accept it, or ready herself for it. The greatest tragedy was to see someone so optimistic, so cheerful and such a force for good in the world, a woman who could change the mood of a room just by walking into it and saying, 'Hello Gorgeousness', brought low and into such despair.

What I do know is that my task now is to live for her, to try to continue a love that is both real and imaginary; to incorporate her velocity of character and all that was best in her, celebrating the fact that we knew and loved each other for as long as we did.

This is my duty, I think, as I lay the white tulips on her grave. It is my calling, my task, and my great good fortune, to have been given the grace of such a love.

Not the End

Honeymoon, Venice, November 1985

Acknowledgements

Thank you to Gerda Stevenson for her poem 'The Kite', to Marilyn Bowering for 'Anyone Can See I Love You', to Shelagh Stephenson for allowing a quotation from *The Memory of Water*, and to the Ingleby Gallery and Andrew Cranston for use of their exhibition catalogue *But the Dream Had No Sound*. Sorley MacLean's poem 'Shores' from *Poems to Eimhir* is reprinted by kind permission of Carcanet Press, Manchester, UK and the poet's daughter, Ishbel MacLean.

Thank you to Hildegard Bechtler, Georgina Brown, Susannah Clapp, Michelle Green, Marcia Haig, Anna Keay, Stuart Rock, Crispin Simon and Tom Stuart-Smith for permission to cite their letters. Thank you to John Butt, Louise Dobbin, Deborah Findlay, Rachel Foster, Rachel Fox, Neil Gardner, Beth Holgate, Florence and Richard Ingleby, Bridget Kendall, Lida Kindersley, Anna Ledgard, Allan Little, Liz Lochhead, Joanna MacGregor, Juliette Mead, Teresa Monachino, Marion Nancarrow, Bill Paterson, Sarah Power, Jane Raven, Siobhán Redmond, Heather Smith, Alan Stephen, Pip Torrens, Harriet Walter, Jo Willett and Richard Williams for stories included here and for their sustaining friendship.

Thank you to everyone at MND Scotland and Eidyn Care and to all the district nurses at NHS Scotland. Thank you to Dr Ali Joy, Dr Anne-Louise Jennings, Dr Sue Stuart-Smith, Dr Graham Russell, Dr Jane Wilson and St Columba's Hospice.

Thank you to Marilyn's fellow producers: Catherine Bailey, Eoin O'Callaghan and Gordon Kennedy.

Thank you to everyone at Bloomsbury: my adored editor Alexandra Pringle, Allegra Le Fanu, Sarah-Jane Forder and Philippa Cotton.

Thank you to my agent David Godwin for unswerving loyalty, steadfast wisdom and unerring immediacy.

Thank you to all my friends, both mentioned and not mentioned.

Thank you to my beloved sister Rebecca and her family, and to Rosie and Charlotte, Sean and Bea for everything. And welcome, Anwen, whom Marilyn would have adored.

Thank you to you, the reader, for reading this. Seize the day, remember well, love fiercely.

A Note on the Author

James Runcie is an award-winning film-maker, playwright and literary curator. He is the author of twelve novels that have been translated into twelve languages, including the seven books in the Grantchester Mysteries series. He has been Artistic Director of the Bath Literature Festival, Head of Literature and Spoken Word at the Southbank Centre, London, and Commissioning Editor for Arts on BBC Radio 4. He is a Fellow of the Royal Society of Literature. He lives in Scotland and London.

A Note on the Type

The text of this book is set in Bembo, which was first used in 1495 by the Venetian printer Aldus Manutius for Cardinal Bembo's *De Aetna*. The original types were cut for Manutius by Francesco Griffo. Bembo was one of the types used by Claude Garamond (1480–1561) as a model for his Romain de l'Université, and so it was a forerunner of what became the standard European type for the following two centuries. Its modern form follows the original types and was designed for Monotype in 1929.

CARLOS SANTANA

Also by Marc Shapiro

My Rules:
The Lauryn Hill Story

James Cameron:
An Unauthorized Biography

CARLOS

MARC SHAPIRO

BACK ON TOP

SANTANA

ST. MARTIN'S PRESS  NEW YORK

www.stmartins.com

Designed by Kathryn Parise

LIBRARY OF CONGRESS CATALOGING-IN-PUBLICATION DATA
Shapiro, Marc.
    Carlos Santana: back on top/Marc Shapiro.
        p.   cm.
    Discography: p.
    ISBN 0-312-26904-8
    1. Santana, Carlos. 2. Rock musicians—United States—
Biography. I. Title.

ML419.S22 S53   2000
787.87'164'092—dc21
[B]

                                                        00-040514

                    First Edition: November 2000

            10 9 8 7 6 5 4 3 2 1

This Book Is Dedicated to

My wife, Nancy, and daughter, Rachael, who have given me a lifetime of wonderful moments. Bennie and Freda. Superagent Lori Perkins. Selma Howe—supermom. Glenda Howard at St. Martin's Press. The rock gods at Poo Bah Records. Cool writers: Stephen King, Clive Barker, Charles Bukowski. Cool bands: KISS, Black Sabbath, Blue Oyster Cult, Cirith Ungol, Booker T. and the MGs, Jefferson Airplane, the Doors, Mountain. And finally many thanks to Carlos Santana: You've lived a life worth writing about.

Contents

Contents

Introduction

No-Brainer

Ah yes, the introduction. That point in every celebrity biography where the author does a mental 180 and a triple lutz as he or she attempts to explain why the subject of their tome is worthy of sainthood. Well, you won't get that kind of song and dance from this author. I'm not interested in preaching to the choir.

Because most of us know Carlos Santana like a book. This is just an opportunity to revisit the man, get a little deeper into his life and his music and discover all the neat stuff we thought we knew about this master guitar slinger . . . but really did not

Let's face it, the music of Carlos Santana has threaded through the lives of many baby-boomers, and now a newer generation is enriching it with great memories. There's probably a whole lot of us who lost our virginity, or were conceived, to the sounds of "Evil Ways" and "Black Magic Woman" playing on the stereo or on the eight-track. And who does not remember bopping down the highway, in what passed for cool wheels at the time, with "Jingo" or "Soul Sacrifice" blaring out of your tiny-ass speakers? Oh yeah, the *Woodstock* movie. It was not as good as being there, but we sure got a better view of the Santana band, stoned out of their minds, burning up the stage. And what about you twenty-first-century kids? I'm sure you're making your own life and history to the sounds of *Supernatural.* In the best sense of the word, we've always been riding with Carlos at our back.

I was in the army in 1968 so I missed what must have been those legendary days on the streets of Haight-Ashbury and those way-cool nights at the Fillmore West when cultural history and great music were made. But thanks to *Rolling Stone* magazine, I had seen all the pictures and read all the stories of this wild-haired Mexican with this equally wild sound. He had the look. He had to know how to play.

I missed Woodstock and the opportunity to see a stoned Carlos Santana make his ax cry like nobody's business on that showstopper of all showstoppers, "Soul Sacrifice." But I did not really need to be there. Because I had heard the buzz and when the first album, *Santana*, hit the bricks in Europe, I quickly wore out a first copy and was working on a second when my orders came down, setting me free.

I had never seen the man in the flesh. But I already felt like I knew him.

It would be a few years before I finally got to see Santana perform his magic live. The first time was at Cal Jam, that monster of a rock fest. Carlos played like a madman, his face contorted in ecstasy; the power of his music moved people like they had never been moved before. The next time I saw him was at the U.S. Festival in 1983, a largely corporate last gasp of great outdoor rock shows in the U.S.A. Yeah, Carlos was making big bucks that day. But he was playing like he was hungry and the music riddled the audience like a volley of automatic-weapons fire.

Previously I had seen him indoors in the support role for David Bowie's Thin White Duke tour. I was high all three times but slipping through the haze each time was the power of the music and the fact that when Carlos Santana plugged in his guitar and turned it up to ten, you knew you were in for a wild ride.

Like I said, for most of you, this probably sounds like old news. If you're anywhere between forty-five and death, you were probably at those same gigs. Hell, we probably shared a joint. And you probably played *Abraxas, Caravanserai,* and, yes, even *Live Carlos Santana* (surely you remember that outrageous Hawaiian volcano gig with Buddy Miles) until the grooves spit blood.

If you're anywhere between birth and, say, twenty-five, you probably have had Santana stories up to your ears. But hey, the brainwashing must have worked, because you dug out your parent's old slabs of vinyl or maybe snuck a CD home inside your jacket so your friends who live and breath Snoop Doggy Dogg and The Cure wouldn't rag your ass . . . and liked what you heard.

But let's be honest, Santana has not always been a slam dunk. Even his most ardent supporters have occasionally been put through the wringer by this musician of many faces and facets.

Yeah, he was right on when he was playing that hot Latin shit that got girls to dance nasty. But, when he found God . . . well, that was a whole other story. Sorry, Carlos, I didn't dig the short hair and the white duds. And even when your guitar raged, a lot of that stuff in the 1970s sounded more like a sermon on the mount than a call to party down.

However, Carlos was smart. He figured out how to have it both ways. He would play cosmic cowboy on his

Devadip stuff. Carlos Santana actually took on the name "Devadip" when he converted to Hinduism under the leadership of Sri Chinmoy. He actually rocked hard in a jazzy, New Age sort of way, and then pulled together a Santana album that would drive you to . . . well, you get the picture.

In the final analysis, Carlos Santana has always been as good as his word, as good as his music, and, most importantly, true to his soul. Face it, handling any one of those aspirations would be a tall order for most mortals. Santana has been keeping these balls in the air for thirty years.

Carlos Santana is not the perfect beast. He's often been out of step with the rest of the music world. He's had demons, personal and chemical, which he's done battle with over the years, and, yes, finally conquered. And when he starts with that spiritual rap, you know that somewhere, somebody's eyes are glazing over. But in the end, all of this adds up to one pretty interesting picture.

Personally and professionally, this cat's real. When he's not entertaining millions of people with that wailing mother of an ax, he's taking his turn driving the kids in the neighborhood car pool or hanging out at the local vegetarian restaurant. He's never taken any great pains to hide away. You want an autograph? Sure. Want to tell him he's great? No problem. Tell him he was out of tune at his last gig? He may not agree with you but he'll listen. It does not get any more human than that.

Carlos Santana: Back on Top tells the whole story. It's cool to like Carlos Santana. You could see yourself hanging with him. No matter what your age.

—MARC SHAPIRO

1

Back Through the Front Door

Carlos Santana had plans for the Grammys. And it was not going to be a rushed thirty seconds where he would read off a hastily scribbled list of names.

"A Grammy Award would mean that I get an opportunity to thank the people who made it all possible. But it would also be an opportunity to invite the audience to meditate in silence for ten seconds to visualize equality, justice, beauty, grace, excellence, and compassion."

That kind of sentiment on a night made to order for honoring commercial success and corporate plunder would seem pretentious in the extreme coming from just about anyone else on the planet. But coming from Carlos Santana, it all sounds real . . . and possible.

Because Carlos Santana is more than a virtuoso guitarist. Of course, there's that, too. Exploring the endless possibilities of world music on the strength of a soaring, individual style of playing that incorporates a dizzying mixture of Latin and Afro-Cuban rhythms with screaming leads. There's his ax, the most secret and sacred of weapons, that mixes the intensity of rock with the sheer emotion of blues, soul, and jazz, and which he has often described as "the cry." The sounds of Carlos Santana come from a place most musicians never reach—the heart and the soul.

"Playing guitar is both a physical and a metaphysical experience," Santana has said. "It's a beautiful way to touch yourself and to touch other people. My goal is to always play the guitar from the heart."

This statement is part and parcel of the Carlos Santana mystique. If there is an arrogant bone in his body, he keeps it well hidden. Yes, he is prone to what would be best described as spiritual New Age raps that often leave the listener dazed, confused, and fighting a snicker. But the reason you don't laugh is that one is not prone to risk hurting the feelings of one who truly believes what he is saying and has the spiritual and creative chops to back it up.

The result of his conviction to musical and spiritual truth has been one of the most supportive and loyal fan bases in the history of popular music. Since 1969, more than forty million copies of his albums have been sold throughout the world. Santana has managed a consistent performing career that has seen numerous incarnations of the Santana band and his star-studded solo outings play in more than fifty countries in front of more than twenty million devoted fans.

And it is a fan base that has spanned the generations. It is not uncommon for Santana shows to be filled with families. Fathers and mothers whose right of passage was often a tune off of the first Santana album, passing their music down to their kids who have just come upon the guitarist as a hip find on the strength of the album *Supernatural.* Teenage girls now scream Santana's name much like their mothers did years earlier.

Santana thinks he knows the reason why he has—even through the years when he did not have hit records—continued to be a shining star in the musical universe. One reason is the resurgence of classic-rock radio which, he points to with some pride, continues to play the finer moments of his more-than-thirty-year career. But, for Carlos, there is also a bottom line.

"There are so few musicians with passion out there

and passion is something the kids can feel. The kids know when something is happening."

Carlos Santana is on a never-ending journey toward inner peace and perfection. In his hands he is doing much more than merely playing notes, chords, and melodies. Santana's soaring, knife-sharp leads and muted, introspective riffs are the guides to something much bigger than the popular-music world he walks. His is a world of music, mixed liberally with spirituality and driven by a singular worldview of social injustice and the power of prayer and religious fervor to set things right. It would not be a stretch to describe the introspective, soft-spoken guitar player, with the soft eyes, slight frame, and curly ringlets of hair, as the musical reincarnation of Gandhi. It is a trait that has not been lost on his musical contemporaries.

"Carlos Santana is the sweetest man I know," guitar great Eric Clapton once acknowledged, looking back on his many decades' association with the man. Blues legend John Lee Hooker was likewise impressed with Santana. "He's one of the greatest men I've ever worked with. He's a perfect gentleman."

Dave Matthews, one of the current generation's rock royalty who worked with Santana on *Supernatural*, was quick to jump on the guitarist's bandwagon. "Hanging out with Carlos was really enlightening. Even though he's such a heavyweight, he's an incredibly kind man. Recording with him was like being away at a retreat as opposed to going to work."

Carlos Santana is a gentle man; an often private and distant man who, arguably, functions on a different spiritual plane than most of us. He admits to not getting out as much as he used to. Watching television, reading a good book, and attending to his myriad of good works is where this former rock bad boy is at these days.

However, being in a spiritual place does not mean that Carlos Santana has lost the eye of the tiger. The man has not gone soft. His stance is far from passive. He's uncompromising when it matters, and can slip into open defiance at a moment's notice. There are few in celebrity circles who can touch Carlos Santana when it comes to integrity and honesty. And he has no patience when it comes to those who cross that line.

"I don't subscribe to the three *p*'s," offered the musician. "Pimps, politicians, and the pope. They all lie."

Comments like those arise often in Carlos Santana's world. He is not afraid to speak his mind. He is not afraid to offend. These traits are part and parcel of the reason why his most consistent detractors—and, yes, there are a few—often refer to the guitarist as somebody who, philosophically, is still stuck in the 1960s. But while Carlos has often expressed his admiration for a lot of what came out of that whole San Francisco/Haight-Ashbury period, his beliefs are very much of modern times.

"Some people think I'm full of mumbo jumbo," he once said, acknowledging his detractors. "But I feel I've learned about responsibility and about two things that many people lack . . . focus and determination."

And, because of that, Carlos Santana is not afraid to walk the walk.

Over the years, Santana's convictions have been regularly tested. Twice in the 1990s, Santana was invited to the White House to perform by President Bill Clinton. While he was in tune with much of Clinton's social and political works, and had a good feeling about the man personally, he turned down both invitations on the grounds that the Latin American dignitaries who would be present represented countries who were soft on civil rights. And when the political climate in Vietnam was not to his liking, the performer backed out of the opportunity to be the first U.S. rock performer to perform in the country since the end of the war.

"My lips don't smell like anybody's behind," he once remarked in a moment of open rebellion against the establishment.

His defiance of the things he feels in his soul are wrong has also extended to the social ills of this country. He willingly jumped at the chance to do the music for Norman Lear's Hispanic-themed television series,

Aka Pablo. But once he took a look at the pilot script, Santana backed out, for what he felt was a good reason.

"Would you believe that on the second page of the script they had a Mexican character taking a siesta at two P.M.?" he remarked. "I decided then that I could not be involved with that project."

Nor could he, in all good conscience, return to the stage at Woodstock in 1994 when he found out the performers were almost all white. Santana would not be involved in anything that was not in the spirit of the original Woodstock "with people of all colors coming together in a hopeful spirit." The promoters wanted Santana's blessing and presence so much that they ultimately added four black performers to the bill to get him to participate.

And it is his overriding faith and innate ambition that has served Santana well in a career that has spanned more than thirty years and thirty albums, that has allowed him to survive the temptations of stardom as a superstar Latin-blues rocker, on the strength of such raw musical visions as *Santana* and *Abraxas,* the wasted drug-induced triumphs of nights at the Fillmore and a breakout performance at Woodstock, and the often turbulent attempts to find himself in the arms of a God he could attach his musical and personal visions to.

There was the successful marriage of music and

spirituality that resulted in the progressive grooves of *Caravanserai* and *Love Devotion Surrender.* A religious falling-out with his once beloved spiritual leader led to the wide-ranging decade of the 1980s, in which *Zebop!* once again found the guitarist having fun with his music. Carlos Santana arrived at the end of the millennium healthy, happy, and in a state of grace. But, as always, inevitably at odds with musical conformity.

For, you see, Carlos could not sit still. No sooner had he found a form that he was comfortable with, than he was on to something else. Rarely coming up for a breath of air commercially, his career has been counted out more times than Rocky's.

"There have been a lot of times when people told me, 'You're committing commercial suicide.' And a lot of times they were right. That's a lot of suicides, man. But I'm still here."

A big reason for his continued survival has been his instinctive approach to avoiding the pitfalls of stardom. Santana learned a lot about surviving the excesses of the 1960s when his band emerged from the streets of San Francisco and onto the top of the charts. He remembered "being slapped hard" by the abundance of drugs, sex, and other self-destructive perks of the rock-and-roll game. But he saw that way meant disaster and, by the early 1970s, he was happily married, in tune with his religious side, and, by his own laughing estimation, "pretty boring."

A position he happily maintains to this day. "I'm invisible," he quietly boasted. "I don't have the tabloids and people like that in my face. They stay away from me because my life is very boring to them. There's no, 'We found Carlos with a goat' kind of thing. My wife and I have been together for twenty-six years. So there's nothing for people to go after. And I love it this way."

Santana had emerged in the mid-1990s as a world-music icon, revered as a rock god by millions but also considered a literal dinosaur in the reigning days of grunge, rap, and alternative music. He had continued to be a popular concert attraction throughout the world and his increasingly ultraprogressive recorded forays into jazz, blues, and all influences in between, continued to sell at a consistent clip. The hits were not there like they used to be, but you could always count on the latest Santana album to at least sell its weight in gold and produce some mighty arresting sounds in the process. But the ability of his music to reach millions through the speakers of radio had, largely by design, continued to elude him.

You had to go all the way back to 1977 and his cover of the Zombies' hit "She's Not There" to see Santana's name on the high end of the commercial Top 40. And while his albums regularly made the *Billboard* charts, they never hit number one. Nor did Santana really care. Until the day his personal frustration with the world led Santana to a very private and personal conversation with an angel named Metatron. Where, in a sense, he made a pact with the devil to once again be commercially viable.

Long a deep and philosophical thinker, Santana had become disheartened at what he perceived as "the cynicism, the violence, and the other negative crap that young people were absorbing from the media today." In his tortured vision of hell he saw children selling their bodies to get high and escape from a world that offered no hope. In private dreams and meditations, Santana offered up his dreams of making a record that would carry the message of love, peace, joy, and light to combat the evil in the land. Even if it meant going in a commercial direction that he had not actively pursued in years.

"I got told by the angel, in my dreams and meditations, that 'We're gonna help you get back into the ring, because we want you to utilize your sound and vibration and resonance to hook up with a lot of new people.'"

Santana took up the cause with his typical fervor and, along the way, discovered a new level of musical spirituality. Contrary to his early fears, the collaborations with this new crop of singer-songwriters did not feel forced. In terms of his own creative being, Carlos Santana felt reinvented. Initially, his insecurities about this latest venture had him ready to call the new album *Mumbo Jumbo*. By the time it was finished, he had christened the effort *Supernatural*—because that's how it felt to him.

The result of Carlos's willingness to step into a brave new musical world was that *Supernatural*, a tough mixture of 1990s musical sensibilities and his signature soaring and melodic playing, raced to the number one slot on the *Billboard* charts, his first number one album since 1971. The first single off the album, "Smooth," a duet with Matchbox 20 singer Rob Thomas, became Santana's first number one single in more than twenty years. Carlos Santana's prayers had been answered. But even the normally unflappable guitarist was shocked by his return to the commercial world.

"I'm more shocked than surprised," sighed Santana, late in 1999 as he watched *Supernatural* reach to the sky. "I had no idea that the album would take on this configuration. I'm very grateful."

And he was more than a little bit excited when *Supernatural* received eleven Grammy nominations. It was not Santana's first shot at the gold ring, however. In 1989 he received a Grammy for Best Instrumental for the composition "Blues for Salvador." But he sees this current crop of honors as something completely different.

"Back in 1989, that was kind of coming in through the back door," he maintained. "This one feels like it might be going through the front door."

But whatever happens at the Grammys, Carlos Santana feels the creative and life experiences that brought him into the new millennium on top have already made him a winner.

"To me it's all been grace," he recently said, with no small amount of humility. "Tonight I could be hiding in the bushes across the border in Tijuana, trying to get into America."

2

Street Smarts

If you blink you'll miss Autlán de Navarro.

Located on the semitropical, rugged Mexican coast-line, a speck on the map between Guadalajara and Puerto Vallarta, Autlán de Navarro is like a village out of time. The moon sets easily and unobstructed most nights, forming an almost mystic connection between sky, water, and rolling hills. It is a town where tradition, especially as it pertains to religion and family, is strong, and where houses are still made of dried mud and stone.

"They don't have any lights," explained Santana of

his birthplace. "They don't have any running water, fences, and chickens run all over the unpaved, dirt roads. It is a simple, beautiful, and unpolluted land."

It was in these primitive and yet quite mystical environs that José Santana and Josefina Barrigan grew up, courted, married, and settled in the first of a series of primitive brick-and-mud shanties and began raising a large, traditional Mexican family in much the same way that their families and their families' families had done before them. José Santana had been quick to pick up the occupation of his father, Antonio, who had eked out a living in the 1920s and 1930s as a French horn player in a local municipal band. Antonio had been introduced to music at an early age and had felt obligated to pass the family tradition down to his son José.

José had learned his lesson well and, as he grew to manhood, was very much in demand in the small village as a violinist and bandleader of his own group, a traditional swing–oriented group called Los Cardinales, which played elegant interpretations of Duke Ellington and Cole Porter songs. When the mariachi craze hit Mexico in the late 1940s, José donned the traditional sombrero and serape and was soon plying his trade with the traditional music of his homeland.

Carlos would later recall that his father and his band were very much a focal point of their small town. José and Los Cardinales would often entertain at town weddings, baptisms, and social and political functions. Carlos recalled that when Los Cardinales struck up a fiery tango or a traditional mariachi-style waltz, the townsfolk flooded the dance floor.

It was into this world of peace and simplicity that Carlos Santana, the middle child of seven Santana children—four girls and three boys—was born on July 20, 1947. José Santana was proud of all his children and loved them all dearly. But there was a near-psychic bond that formed instantly between the father and his middle son. As he watched Carlos wiggle and coo in his crib just days after his birth, José felt in his heart of hearts that Carlos was destined for bigger things than the dusty roads and simple lives lived by the people in Autlán de Navarro.

Young Santana's early memories were, not surprisingly, simple ones. There was the constant moving from house to house as the Santana family fortunes rose and fell. There was the simple joy he found in playing with his siblings and the neighborhood children. There were those cold and cloudy days when he would cover his face and race inside ahead of a big wind or the onset of rain.

The youngster grew up in a close-knit, devoutly religious home where his loving parents taught him everything he would need to know to survive in the world. "From my mother, I learned that everything in life is borrowed from the Lord. From my father, I learned that life is service. From both parents, I learned good manners."

In looking back on those early years, Carlos instinctively felt that the bond between his father and himself was something special.

"All of my sisters and brothers were special but, for some reason, I felt I was the apple of his eye. I felt like I could get away with more. I don't know if it was because I was lighter in skin or he knew I was going to be a musician. All I know was that he was less tolerant with everyone else."

Which was not to say that Carlos and his brothers and sisters ran wild. José and Josefina set definite limits. A certain amount of childish acting-out was allowed, but it only took a stern look or a curt warning to let the Santana brood know they had stepped over the line. Rarely did any of the Santana children make the same mistake twice.

Carlos, out of necessity, learned the reality of sharing everything from living space to hand-me-down clothes and toys with his siblings. Carlos, even at that early age, had a natural instinct for generosity and did not have to be prodded into sharing with others. Also not surprising were the early childhood memories of his father performing at various village functions, and of learning to love music and the roving bands of musicians who often pulled into town as part of their regular tour of the outlying areas. In looking back, he likened his earliest musical memories to being struck by Cupid's arrow for the first time.

"There was this Mexican band that played in our village, that dressed up with bows and arrows who played this funky weird music," Santana reflected. "There was also this group called Los Indios Tabajara that played more traditional folk-music songs."

Everything about the art of music seemed to mesmerize Carlos. He would watch wide-eyed as these costumed troubadours made beautiful sounds that drove people to dance and be loving and friendly with one another. It was a power that young Carlos Santana wanted to possess someday.

But what really drove home the power of music to young Carlos was watching his father play. "As a kid I remember watching how people's eyes would light up when my father played his violin. At that point, I knew he had the power to validate people's existence."

The Santana family was far from typical. The reality of having to support a large family often required José to go where the jobs were, which translated into long periods on the road, playing in other cities in Mexico and, occasionally, in California, where a thriving multicultural music scene had sprung up on the other side of the border in San Diego. José and Josefina had an understanding that was typical of the times: She would stay home and raise the children and he would go out and make the money.

But, for Josefina, this arrangement always held some trepidation. She sensed that her husband—who was cut from the same traditional, macho cloth as most Mexican males—had a roving eye when it came to the ladies and, although she had never found proof that he had been with other women while he was on the road, there was always a sense of uneasiness when she kissed her husband good-bye.

Absences of anywhere from six weeks, to six months, to a year, were not uncommon in the life of the Santana family. The Santana children missed their father, but had been taught early on that this was what their father did to keep a roof over their head, and so they adjusted to the idea that José would not always be around. However, with Carlos, there was a particularly acute sense of longing when his father was on the road. It was not only that Carlos missed his father; he also missed what his father and his talents represented in his childlike dreams and desires.

When the road trips were over and he was home, José soon realized that Carlos, unlike his other children, was captivated by the sound of music in a much more personal and spiritual way than most. And so José made the decision—much as his father had done with him—to teach his son how to play. When Carlos turned five years old, he began learning theory and the technique of the violin from his father.

José was patient in teaching Carlos. He felt that his young son needed the nuts and bolts of music. But he was not overly strict and allowed the love of the instrument and the music to set his young son free. Carlos recalled that although he spent seven years trying to master the instrument, it was ultimately a losing battle, punctuated by fits of temper on his part, and his father's disappointment and frustration.

"My dad taught me the violin for seven years and I could never get anything out of it," chuckled Santana at the memory of those tortured lessons. "I always sounded like Jack Benny no matter how hard I tried. Only Jack Benny could really play. But I sounded like Jack Benny when he was fooling around. Finally I told my dad I hate the way it (the violin) smells, the way it looks, and the way it sounds."

Santana's sense of family was disrupted anew in 1954 when his father left once again, this time for Tijuana, in search of work in that city's booming mariachi music scene. José would occasionally send letters and some money back to the family, but by 1955 Josefina was living in fear that her husband, whose fidelity on those long periods away from home she continued to doubt, had found a new life and would not be coming back to them. And so she made the fateful decision to sell their furniture for gas money and piled her children into an old Nash Rambler station wagon. As Carlos recalled, "She wanted to go looking for my dad, and so, one day, we just took off."

The trip from Autlán de Navarro to Tijuana was an eye-opener for Carlos. It was the first time he had ever been out of his birthplace. His eyes were glued to the car window, gazing out in wonderment at the small towns, smaller than his own, and the miles of desert that raced past him.

The Santana family pulled into Tijuana days later—hot, tired, and anxious to find José. They went to the address on the last letter José had sent his family and Josefina knocked on the door. Years later, Carlos would painfully recall what happened when the door opened.

"This woman who opened the door said, 'No, I don't know what you're talking about. He doesn't live here. You've got the wrong place.' So, of course, my mother's heart sank to her feet. My mom broke down. We didn't have any money and we didn't know what to do. Suddenly this old wino came over to us and asked who we were looking for. My mother showed him a picture of my father. He said, 'Oh he's in there. Knock again. He'll come out.' "

Josefina knocked again.

"This lady came out again and started screaming, 'What do you want? I told you he's not here.' Just then, my dad poked his head through the door, saw us and the car, and his face became like the NBC Peacock rainbow, turning all the different colors of surprise, anger, frustration, and fear."

José and Josefina got into a loud and ugly argument right in the middle of that Tijuana street. Finally José, feeling very much responsible for his family, moved them to a run-down shanty called the Colonial Hotel. For the next two months the Santana family lived in a room that had no furniture, doors, or windows. Carlos recalled that his parents, who remained separated, were barely speaking during that time in the Colonial, but his father would stop by occasionally with bags of groceries and, for the kids, a dose of reality.

"One day he came by with a bunch of Chiclets gum, broke the gum in half, gave half to me and half to my older brother and said, 'Don't come back until you've sold them all.' And I thought, 'Oh, so that's my reality now.' "

The truth of the matter was that Carlos had already realized the reality of life in Tijuana. The city, alive with strip bars, prostitutes, cheap liquor, and a thriving criminal element, was constantly on the make. Little kids would peddle parking spaces for cash. American soldiers and students would regularly scamper across the border into Tijuana in search of cheap thrills and carnal knowledge. The neighborhood young Carlos lived in was so rough that the police would rarely go there and, when they did, they were often sent scampering by a hail of rocks.

There was no hiding the smell of poverty that permeated the air and rattled down the dusty streets. Everybody grew up quickly in Tijuana—especially Carlos, who sensed, early on, that survival was the name of the game in this garish nightmare of a city and, when it came to his family, money was the all-important commodity.

Relations between Carlos's father and mother eventually improved to the point where his father's visits became more frequent. The guitarist, in looking back upon those dark days, felt that the improvement in his parents' relationship had a lot to do with "the fact that we had something in common between us, the music."

Eventually José moved the family to a better part of town, ended his relationship with the mystery woman, and moved back into the family home. To this day, Carlos is not sure if his mother actually forgave his father for his infidelities, but she had decided a cordial family life was better for the children than a totally fragmented one.

The next few years would see Carlos grow up to the ways of the world and the street. The Santana children began attending Catholic school in Tijuana, but Carlos found the educational experience as meted out by old school nuns and priests was not to his liking.

Years later he would wince at the mere mention of his Tijuana schooldays. Typical of the strict Catholic approach to education, a big part of Carlos's education consisted of being screamed at or hit. He would often report the treatment to his parents who insisted that that was how Catholic school was, and that he should get used to it. Carlos grew defiant in the face of such extreme treatment and found himself thinking of leaving school at the first opportunity.

José Santana recalled, years later, that he and his wife continued to hammer home the importance of education to their rebellious son. And they sweetened the pot with the carrot young Carlos preferred.

"He studied in a school of music, after he went to his regular primary school every day. In that music school they wanted Carlos to learn to play the clarinet. He did not like the clarinet."

In the meantime, José Santana, convinced that his son would follow the musical path of himself and his father before him continued to fill Carlos's head with musical theory. At an early age Carlos could read music, and his father would regularly drill him on various European styles of playing while continuing what seemed to be a losing battle to get his son to adopt the violin as his instrument of choice. But for Carlos, the violin continued to be a losing proposition. "I just couldn't get a feeling for it. My playing was no good. I used to say, 'Man this is sad. I don't like this.' "

Carlos persisted, however, eventually reaching the point where he was coaxing a semblance of melody out of the instrument. José, encouraged by his son's progress, insisted that his son begin contributing to the family income, and so it was not long before Carlos, still struggling to maintain interest in formal education, began learning his street smarts with his first professional music job.

"After a while I started playing out on the street with two other guys with guitars and it was like, 'Song, mister? Fifty cents.' We played all the stereotypical Mexican shit for the tourists and I was dressed in this cowboy outfit. For me, it was like, 'I hate this stuff!' "

The reason for Carlos's musical rebellion was fueled by Tijuana's close proximity to the United States border and, consequently, to American radio. It was those countless hours spent listening to radio stations that straddled the U.S.–Mexican border, and in particular such blues greats as Muddy Waters, Jimmy Reed, John

Lee Hooker, and Lightnin' Hopkins, that succeeded in turning the impressionable young Carlos Santana's head around.

"Blues was my first love," he revealed. "It was the first thing where I said, 'Oh man! This is the stuff.' It was so raw, so honest. From then on I started rebelling."

Rebellion hit the preteen Santana like the proverbial ton of bricks. He began to take in the sights and sounds of the world in which he lived and found that, literally and figuratively, it smelled of piss and puke. His attitude only worsened when he began playing with his father in dirt-floored bars where corrupt cops would paw prostitutes because they could, and tabletops were black from the heat of stubbed-out cigarettes and soggy from spilled beer. He did not like the idea that the music his father's band played was largely ignored by the drunk customers. He felt his father and the music deserved more respect.

Things did not improve when Americans came across the border. Carlos would watch as they became drunk and began shouting lewd things at the working women who would laugh and ignore their rude advances. Not a night went by when the impressionable youngster would not watch as somebody vomited all over a table or passed out on the floor, usually to awaken minus his wallet or anything else that could be turned into cash.

Carlos learned quickly about "class." "I learned in Tijuana that you can't buy class. Prostitutes had more class than a lot of the people I would go on to meet. They did what they did to support their children because there were no secretary jobs down there."

Adding to the degradation was the inevitable point in the evening when some drunk would pull out a fat wad of bills, give it to his father and tell him to play his favorite song fifteen times in a row. Degradation turned into humiliation when his father took the money and began to play. Carlos made a major life decision at that point. "I said, 'When I grow up, I'm going to play what I want to play and they're still going to pay me or I'll be doing something else.' "

It also did not help Carlos's state of mind that José's band was paid to play old-style Mexican standards with limited chord changes and little inspiration. On several occasions Carlos, his youthful enthusiasm racing, would attempt to liven things up with an unusual progression, only to have José silence his efforts with an onstage scolding. The stifling of his music only made Carlos angrier with the whole Tijuana music scene.

"I'm watching all this as a kid and thinking, 'Damn! This planet is funky,' " recalled Santana of his youthful defiance. "My father would look at me and say, 'What's the matter with you?' I told him, 'I don't wanna be here. I don't want to live this kind of scene. Look at where we are, just smell it! Do you think this scene is better than anything else?' That was the first time I ever spoke back to my dad and I thought he was going to slap me. But he didn't. It was like I opened his eyes."

Years later, Carlos would also offer that his father had passed down a bit of advice that would stay with him forever.

"He told me when you're onstage, you have to put away your anger and pain to make people happy. Once you go home, you could kick and curse, but he was adamant about presenting yourself with kindness and softness."

Once again José Santana was forced to leave his family in search of work, across the border up in San Francisco—in 1960. Although Josefina suffered sleepless nights at the prospect of her husband cheating on her again with other women, she had a more immediate concern: Following the departure of his father, Carlos had begun finding excuses to avoid practicing the violin, and when he did practice, his mother noticed that his heart was no longer in it.

Feeling her husband had invested too much time and effort in Carlos's musical education to have it go to waste, Josefina began encouraging her son's interest in nontraditional Mexican music by allowing him to experience different kinds of music in a live setting. Palacio de Municipal Park in Tijuana had long been a gathering place for working bands to come and jam, and to try out different styles of music. On a good day, the casual listener could experience rock, soul, blues, and a form of music his father detested, *pachuco* (a mixture of traditional Mexican music, doo-wop, and blues), played by the top musicians in the city.

Carlos Santana's eyes went wide the first time he went to Palacio de Municipal Park and heard the outrageous sounds of Xavier Batiz and his band, the TJ's, as they blasted out "Last Night," "Green Onions," and the other rock and blues songs regularly heard on the radio. He marveled at his first look at a band whose members sported pompadours like Little Richard, and he flipped at their way-out costumes that featured khaki pants with razor-sharp creases.

But not surprisingly, what struck deepest in the young Santana's soul, was the music.

"The sound of electric guitars, amps and everything, for me it was like watching a flying saucer for the first time," remembered Santana of his first encounter with the TJ's. "Once I heard the guitarist hit an amplified note, for me it was something magnificent."

And, for the first time, Carlos was embracing a performer who was playing a style of music he truly loved.

28

"Xavier was playing music specifically by B.B. King, Little Richard, Bobby Bland, and Ray Charles. He had those four guys down. The way Xavier was playing with the beautiful twang and tone really hit me."

Carlos remembered becoming like a puppy dog, following the TJ's to every gig, including the band's regular Friday-night performance at Club Latino-American. Carlos was a sponge, soaking up the band's style and, in particular, Xavier Batiz's technique—his guitar playing had an almost hypnotic effect on the youngster.

Carlos recalled that he would often follow the band's moves like a guided missile. His eyes would focus on Batiz and mentally catalog all his moves: where he placed his fingers on the fretboard and the way he touched the strings to get those magic sounds. It was a classic case of putting the cart before the horse. He did not even own a guitar but he already, in a sense, knew how to play it.

Xavier Batiz soon became aware of the fact that this youngster with the curly hair and wide eyes was showing up at just about every show the band played. And he quickly became aware that Carlos was paying a little bit too much attention to how Batiz was playing.

"I wanted to join his band," Carlos said. "That was really what was happening at the time. He inspired me to get into my instrument but he didn't really teach me as much as people say. He was sort of stingy. If I was looking where he was playing, he would turn the other way so I could not see the chords he was playing."

Josefina would delight in her son's tales of how cool the TJ's were and how great Batiz's playing was. She would, in turn, write her husband enthusiastic letters about how Carlos was interested in music again. José responded by sending back a beat-up electric guitar. Carlos happily took the offering as a sign that his father would not fight him on his choice of instrument anymore, and immediately began learning how to play. "Because of all the training that my dad gave me on the violin, learning the guitar seemed pretty easy."

One of the first songs Carlos mastered was the rock instrumental classic "Apache," by the Shadows. He would also learn to play "Peppermint Twist" by Joey Dee and the Starliters, Jimmy Smith's "Walk on the Wild Side," and, in the process of trying to master Xavier Batiz's licks, he discovered B.B. King.

Carlos spent all his waking hours learning the guitar. Eventually he began to coax chunky blues chords out of the instrument. It was raw and not perfect, but the first time he played something that sounded kind of like what he had heard on the radio, he knew his lot in life: He would not be an accountant or an English teacher—he would be a guitar player.

By the time Carlos Santana turned twelve, his reputation had spread throughout the streets of Tijuana and so, despite his young age, the reigning bands on the dance club–strip club circuit were more than willing to listen when the young guitar-slinger would approach them for a job. Carlos, with the blessing and support of his mother, eventually landed his first job in a band called the Strangers.

"With the Strangers I started out playing electric bass because the leader of the band owned all the equipment and told us who would play what," recalled Carlos. "But after a while people told him that I played too many notes for bass and he should let me play guitar."

Carlos played with the Strangers for four months—long enough to get the feel of the rush of playing in front of a large, appreciative crowd, and to further immerse himself in the idea of playing in a band and how the instruments combined to create an energetic whole. Carlos eventually left the Strangers and, in search of a more prestigious gig, landed a job in a house band for a strip club called the Convoy. For Carlos, this first job in a house of ill repute had its ironies.

"On Sunday afternoons, I would play the violin in the park while the priest held Mass and then, at night, I would play in the strip joints. To me, it was all one."

Ever the vigilant mother, Josefina had some initial concerns about her very underage son playing in a club where women took off their clothes, men often settled their differences with broken beer bottles and knives, and the police looked the other way as drugs flowed freely. But she knew her son was too far into the music for her to deny him and, besides, the nine dollars a week he made would go a long way toward helping the Santana family keep their heads above water.

Carlos had little trouble fitting in at the Convoy. The club owner and the other musicians were impressed by this youngster with the adult musical vocabulary. In the twilight world of Tijuana bars and strip clubs, Santana being underage was never an issue; nor was the fact that he would be seeing prostitutes and strippers earning their livelihood. The law had been bent and pretty much broken in Tijuana long before Carlos Santana walked through the doors of the Convoy for the first time.

"I would start playing at four o'clock in the afternoon and we would finish our last set at six o'clock the next morning," said a bemused Santana, looking back on his days at the Convoy. "We'd play one hour and then watch the hookers strip for another hour. Then you'd play for another hour."

Through the darkly-lit, smoke-filled club, young

Carlos Santana continued to soak up the subtle elements of rhythm, timing, and expression. He made no bones about the fact that he wanted to learn, and the grizzled musicians marking time on the tiny stage were more than willing to teach him. He was overjoyed at the parade of black musicians, who often crossed the border to pick up extra money playing at the Convoy and would embellish the basic bump-and-grind strip soundtrack with large dollops of the blues.

"I got a big education at places like the Convoy," related the guitarist. "It was tough but I ended up learning a lot."

Especially about the power music could have over the fairer sex. "I learned how to strip a woman just by using my guitar. The older band members would notice when a woman would get drunk and they would say, 'Watch, we're going to make her take her clothes off.' They'd play this strip music, *bump-bada-bump*, and sure enough, pretty soon she'd be taking her clothes off."

The power to make women strip was young Santana's introduction to adult attitudes toward the female sex. As days and nights in the Convoy began to blur one into another, he would soon learn other things.

Although Santana has always been uncomfortable talking about his childhood sexuality, he did recently admit that he lost his virginity before the age of fourteen.

". . . I thought it was normal," he explained hesitantly. "My mom or my father, they were very naïve, and so I was thrown into the streets in a certain way. . . . My first encounter with sexuality was not a pleasant one or romantic or tender or wonderful. It was more like a shock kind of thing: gross, disgusting shock."

While Josefina was happy that her son was finding his way with music, she was concerned that Tijuana was a dead end for her family and she did not want her children to continue the cycle of struggle and poverty for another generation. So she took the bull by the horns and, in 1961, filed for immigration to the United States and, in particular, San Francisco, where José was making a good living. José returned to Mexico to be with his family as they immigrated to the United States.

Years later, he would remember that his young son was not happy with having to leave Mexico. "When the family was ready to emigrate, Carlos did not want to come. He said he liked Mexico too much to leave it. We postponed our trip a few days as we tried to persuade our son to come with us. Then, all of a sudden, he hid from us."

Eventually they found their son and, when the Santana family crossed the border into the United States for the first time, Carlos was there (although emotionally and musically, his heart was still back at the Convoy).

The Santana family arrived in San Francisco's Mission District and settled into a modest apartment. Everybody seemed to settle quickly into their new lives . . . except Carlos. His experiences in Tijuana had put too much of the wild side and too much of the adult in him to easily conform to a normal teenage life.

"Because I was always hanging out with adults and seeing all this happening in Tijuana, going back to being a kid in junior high in San Francisco was just a culture shock," he reminisced. "Because when you listened to what the kids talked about in school, it was dumb compared to what the older people talked about."

He settled uneasily into James Lick Junior High School but, not speaking any English, he was immediately branded as an outsider and so was pretty much a loner. It was during these first weeks and months in America that Carlos formed his first band with a couple of musicians named Dan Haro and Gus Rodriguez.

"These guys, where my brother was working making

tortillas, had instruments. My brother's boss was pretty well off and his son had his own drums. But it didn't work out because all those guys wanted to do was play pop music, and all I wanted to do was learn."

Carlos continued to be homesick for Tijuana. And with José once again out on the road, it fell to Josefina to turn her son's head around. She would constantly tell her son how lucky they were to be in America, and of the opportunities that awaited him. But Carlos was having none of it, and it showed in fits of anger and open defiance. He would refuse to eat for long periods, and getting him to go to school was often a losing battle. The hormones were running wild in Carlos Santana, and for his mother, there was hell to pay.

Finally Josefina threw up her hands.

"She just got so disgusted with me, she finally said, 'Okay, I'll give you twenty dollars. That's all I've got. You can go back to Tijuana. But you'll have to go by yourself.' "

So it was with a mixture of fear and excitement that Carlos waved good-bye to his mother as the bus left San Francisco for Tijuana. He arrived back in Tijuana on Halloween eve. People dressed as skeletons and werewolves were racing by Carlos in their Halloween revelry. It was an eerie scene that only added to the young boy's sudden fear and loneliness.

All the bravado had drained out of Carlos. In its

place stood a frightened little boy who had suddenly realized that his family was hundreds of miles away and that he was now all alone. In his vulnerable state, Carlos made a beeline for the nearest church and offered up a streetwise prayer.

"I went to the temple of the Virgin of Guadalupe and said, 'Look, I was here a year ago with my brother, we walked on our knees from the front door all the way to your altar but I didn't ask for a favor. So I figure you owe me one. So I ask that you give me my job back while I'm here and that you take care of my family.' "

Carlos left the church and returned to the Convoy club in hopes of getting back his job in the house band. As luck would have it, Carlos's replacement had recently burned out on the grueling schedule and his old spot was available. But Carlos remembers now that the club owner was concerned about Carlos being underage, and with his family being in another country. Carlos produced a letter from his mother saying that it was all cool and so Carlos was back in the band.

During the next year Carlos continued pumping out music behind the strippers at night and hanging at the beach, reading hot-rod and *Mad* magazines, during the day. Carlos stayed for a time with the drummer of the house band in a run-down hotel until they were evicted. Then he moved in with a friend of his mother's. He was tempted by the prevalence of drugs but never gave in. And, as before, his second stint in Tijuana was dedicated to expanding his musical horizons by listening to musicians who continued to cross the border into Mexico.

"I was really learning again," offered Santana. "The house band was learning things like 'Stormy Monday' and 'You Can Make It If You Try.' I was picking up all kinds of musical repertoire. I was really confident about what I knew about music."

What Carlos did not know was that his mother and father had begun to miss their son and had, with the aid of his older brother Tony, decided to go back to Tijuana and bring him home.

"We made the trip back to Mexico," chuckled José. "We went to the place where he lived and just grabbed him. We did not force him to come with us. We convinced him by crying."

Carlos, who painted a slightly different picture of the abduction, knew the jig was up when Tony showed up unannounced at his home. The guitarist was able to laugh years later as he described how his family just showed up and kidnapped him.

"Tony just showed up, grabbed me, and said, 'Your mama's here.' I tried to sneak back to the club but my mother and Tony were already there. They just put me in the car and we crossed back across the border into the United States. Boy, was I pissed!"

And José remembered that his son remained pissed on that long drive back home. He was silent, angry, and refused to talk to anybody. The scowl on Carlos's face was deep. If he could, he would have jumped out of the car and run away. But then his parents would start to cry again . . . and he did not think he could handle that.

Carlos remained angry and defiant as the Santana family arrived back in San Francisco; Carlos would barely speak and when he did he was radiating anger and frustration like rays from the sun. His father recalled that "all he did was cry, cry, and cry. Then he locked himself up in his room for a week. During this week he refused to eat."

Tensions escalated between Carlos and his mother when he discovered that three hundred dollars he had put aside for the sole purpose of buying a guitar had, unbeknownst to him, been spent on rent.

The young Santana winced as he recalled the day his mother had enough of his tantrums and pouting.

"Finally my mom said, 'I can't stand your silence and your anger. Here's twenty dollars again, but this time I won't go get you back.' I took the twenty dollars and walked out the door. I got as far as Mission Street and my stomach said, 'You don't want to go back over there to Tijuana, man.' "

Carlos Santana turned on his heels and went home.

3

San Francisco Nights

One month later, President John F. Kennedy was assassinated, on November 22, 1963. Not too long after that, the first hints that our involvement in Vietnam might not be so noble began to appear on the back pages of the mainstream press, and in blaring headlines of the first wave of underground papers like the *Berkeley Barb* and the *San Francisco Oracle*.

And just around the corner from the Mission District home of Carlos Santana, a bunch of freaks called "hippies" were beginning to raise a ruckus at the intersection of Haight and Ashbury.

Carlos settled into an uneasy new life in the City by the Bay. His parents once again enrolled him in the nearby James Lick Junior High School. Carlos, whose still-marginal English continued to set him apart, had few friends, and those he did have tended to be of a like mind.

"I didn't hang out with my race or what you would call my race. I always tended to hang out with people who were more soulful. I would always choose people who would have something to say about B.B. King or Jimmy Reed, or some cats who would start singing in the streets."

His father, José, painted a much rosier picture of his son's school days. José claimed that Carlos had in fact picked up English fairly quickly, and also, that he had made a number of friends at school and in their neighborhood. That Carlos was known to embellish the truth was a given in the Santana household and so it is safe to say that the truth lays somewhere between the two extremes.

What was known was that getting Carlos up on a school day was a chore. He would oversleep. He would tell his mother he was sick. He took forever to eat his breakfast. But Carlos knew that, when all was said and done, he would go to school. Because his parents knew that education was his key to a better life. Unfortunately, Carlos did not think so.

The youngster had not forgotten the damage done to his spirit in the Tijuana Catholic schools. And to a degree it carried over to his attitude at James Lick. Carlos was quiet and often distracted in class. Consequently, his relatively mediocre grades did not come as a surprise. José and Josefina were always urging him to do better in school but they, too, realized that their son had no spirit for formal education.

Surprisingly, Carlos refused to take any music classes, feeling that he was already beyond what anybody could teach him. Instead, he would get his fix by playing the dreaded violin in his father's mariachi band in Bay Area clubs on weekends, and daydreamed a lot about the blues and where he fit into the musical universe.

Santana did reconnect with Haro, Rodriguez, and the other musicians he had met during his first abbreviated trip to San Francisco. Happily Carlos found they had grown up musically and they were ready to do things his way. They laid new temptations in the youngster's path. They offered to buy him a new guitar and amplifier in exchange for teaching them a more mature musical repertoire. Carlos became the band's unofficial leader, his relative youth more than balanced out by his musical maturity.

They began doing small parties and the occasional wedding, livening up the expected Top 40 pop covers with a lot of James Brown songs and the occasional shot of down-and-dirty blues. The band took a big step forward when they entered a prestigious Battle of the Bands contest as the backup band for a local soul singer named Joyce Dunn, who would later gain some notoriety as part of Sly and the Family Stone.

"It was amazing, surreal," remembered Carlos of his first high-profile gig. "They had a whole high-school gym with like a thousand bands in it. The first five hundred or so got eliminated because they sounded like the Rolling Stones and the judges were looking for something more original. Our feeling was that we could get into this and so we did things like the blues song 'Steal Away' and 'Heat Wave' and we ended up going into the final round as one of the top three bands.

"But the worst thing happened. We got excited and nervous and so we got drunk. We were loaded when we went into the finals and missed all kinds of changes and we were eliminated. But just the fact that we could reach those heights was really something and it gave me confidence that I really had something."

By the time Carlos entered Mission High School in 1963, his mind was already set on a musical career and everything else took a backseat. He frequently cut class, and had taken an after-school job washing dishes and flipping burgers at a dive of a restaurant called the Tick Tock. Ever the loyal son, he would take his meager paycheck home every week and hand it over to his mother.

Given his halfhearted approach to formal education and his desire to be a musician, it was surprising that Carlos did not just drop out of school. He made no secret about getting nothing out of the experience. But he knew that his parents, and especially his mother, would be disappointed. He did not want to hurt them and so he continued to suffer in silence.

Carlos continued to make occasional trips back to Tijuana where he aspired to soak up the blues, and began building a song list that included Jimmy Reed, Howlin' Wolf, and B.B. King. Of more recent vintage, Santana also found a lot to admire in the Paul Butterfield Blues Band—at the time, the leader of the emerging wave of white blues bands—and in particular, its enigmatic guitarist Michael Bloomfield. Cream and Jimi Hendrix were also high on the youngster's dream team.

He began to squirrel away a few dollars each week, which he eventually would spend in a nearby record shop. Then he would go home, put the albums on the family record player, and listen. Carlos's parents were not happy with these awful sounds, and often told him to turn it off. Carlos would obligingly turn the sound down—but never off.

Carlos did more than admire these groups from afar, like the typical teenager. He got into their music, their playing, and, by degrees, learned to become like them. "That's how everybody learns," he once declared. "You cop an album and you wear it out, pretending you're them. You fantasize being onstage with them until you learn to play your solo after they play their solo."

At Mission High, Carlos once again gravitated toward friends who were into music. Among them was this kid across town at Poly High who always seemed to be banging on the congas—Michael Carabello. Carabello, like Santana, was a free spirit who was totally dedicated to music and not much else. They would occasionally get together and jam, but neither expressed a desire to do anything more formal.

Carlos, despite his obvious talents, was also not interested in getting a formal musical education. He steadfastly refused to enroll in any of the high-school music classes and, although he had heard of palaces of higher musical education such as the Julliard School in New York City, or the Berklee College of Music in Boston, he had no interest in attending, despite the fact that it could have helped him in what would remain a striking lack of formal composing skills.

In later years he would state that he did not miss

furthering his musical education. "I don't understand classical music or jazz the way an academic would," he once said. "I don't have a Ph.D. and I don't want to have one. Sometimes those things just cause you trouble."

It was late in his high-school education that Carlos also made the acquaintance of one Stan Marcum. A recent graduate of barber college, Marcum saw himself as a self-styled hipster who had more on his mind than cutting hair. It was through Marcum that Carlos was introduced to the way-out realms of jazz populated by John Coltrane and Miles Davis.

It was also through Marcum that Carlos experimented for the first time with LSD and found it to his liking. But, if Marcum did nothing else, he will always be remembered for taking Carlos out into the streets and showing him the new musical and cultural experience that was emerging literally around the corner from his home in the Mission District.

Carlos would often remember the sense of freedom he encountered while observing the early days of the hippie movement. He admired the attitude, the bright colors, the weird clothes and long hair, and, most important of all, the music. Through informal jams in nearby Golden Gate Park and other spots scattered around the city, Carlos had the chance to see and hear the likes of the Jefferson Airplane and the Grateful Dead and the strange new music they were playing. He did not understand it. But he liked what he heard.

Carlos recalled his musical world changed forever when "I started hanging around with a different crowd that hung out at Haight-Ashbury. I found myself wanting to be a part of this new wave."

Carlos's erratic formal education continued into his junior year at Mission High School. He would do poorly in all of his academic subjects. Art was a different matter. He would get A's in drawing and B's in his design classes. He was encouraged by his art teacher, Mr. Knudson, to take his talent to art school and a career. Carlos wavered but remained steadfast with music. Surprisingly he could muster no better than a B in his Spanish class. By his senior year, school was all but forgotten.

"I was supposed to be going to Mission High but I would only show up in the morning for homeroom. They would take attendance and then I would split. Mainly what I did was pretty much daydream about playing with a lot of people."

By the mid-1960s the Fillmore West had become a mecca for the quickly spreading wave of emerging psychedelic rock. Local bands like the Jefferson Airplane and the Grateful Dead and emerging supergroups like Cream, the Jimi Hendrix Experience, and the Paul

Butterfield Blues Band were making names for themselves, based largely on legendary performances on
the Fillmore stage. That was the place that Carlos Santana would often find himself, standing stagefront,
studying the masters up close and personal, much as
he had done with Xavier Batiz in Tijuana. Only this
time, the bands would not turn their backs on the
youngster, and would often cast a smile in his direction. Sometimes he would pay to get in. When he did
not have the price of admission he would resort to
drastic and illegal measures.

Bill Graham, an alternately fiery and compassionate
entrepreneur, had caught lightning in a bottle when
he decided to turn big-time concert promoter and
turn the little-used Fillmore hall into rock-and-roll
heaven. Graham, often disliked but never disre-
spected, worked hard at building the Fillmore into
one of the top rock-and-roll venues in the country. He
was a tough-minded businessman who did not get to
the top by being charitable. One night, after dotting
the *i*'s and crossing the *t*'s on a Cream–Paul Butterfield Blues Band concert as a driving rain splattered
the streets around the Fillmore, he fell into a deep
sleep in his second-floor office.

"I heard some noise outside my windows," remembered Graham in later years. "Somebody was trying
the doors. I looked out and there were these two guys

trying to get in. One was Carlos Santana and the other was Michael Carabello. I said, 'Hello?' They said, 'Oh, jeez. You know. Like we wanna see the great Eric Clapton, man. But we don't have the bread.' They seemed so sincere that I let them in."

What Graham did not know was the reason Carlos never seemed to have any money was that, every week, he would turn his paycheck from the Tick Tock over to his mother and then, if a hot act was in town, race down to the Fillmore and bum money to get into the show. If that did not work, Carlos was not above sneaking in. While the promoter would usually cut a little slack in letting Carlos into the shows, he was not above giving him a hard time.

Carlos remembered one hilarious encounter with Graham when Miles Davis was in town, in which the promoter caught him, halfway through a bathroom window. Graham began yelling, "What's the matter with you? Where's your money? Are you too lazy to work?" Carlos took the verbal abuse, after which Graham let Carlos into the show.

Carlos Santana graduated from Mission High School in June 1965. "Between washing dishes at the Tick Tock and cutting classes, I barely got out. I didn't want to know about algebra or George Washington or whatever. I could hardly wait to get out of school. They [the school administration] were very gracious to give me my diploma, because all I knew in my heart was that I didn't belong in Vietnam and I didn't belong in school."

What he did know was that he was ready to make his way as a musician. And he would not think twice about telling anybody who would listen about his plans.

"I validated my existence before I got out of high school," he stated philosophically. "People would ask, 'What are you going to do when you leave school?' I'd say, 'I'm going to play with Michael Bloomfield and B.B. King.' They thought I was crazy. They'd say, 'Man, you're tripping!' And I'd say, 'No, you're tripping because you don't know what you want to do. I know what I want to do and I know who I'm going to do it with. I'm going to play with those people.' "

Not only was Carlos determined to play with those people, but he was finding that his whole approach to music was being turned, by degrees, in a more serious direction.

"When I came to America and saw B.B. King for the first time, I knew I could captivate people with no bull-shit, no gimmicks, just playing. When I first heard John Coltrane, that changed everything around. Then I heard Gabor Szabo and that took me out of there. I was on my way to picking up my own individuality and where I would fit into all of this."

But going down the music road was not going to be

easy. While José Santana was convinced his son would find his way, his mother Josefina was increasingly unhappy with what she perceived as the unhealthy lifestyle and crowd her son was falling in with. They would argue long and loud; Josefina insisting that her son would end up a bum and Carlos insisting that music was his thing and that this was how he was going to find his way.

"It was becoming really strained, the relationship between my mother and myself," Carlos recalled painfully. "Basically she's a very domineering woman who is strong in her convictions. I'm just like her. There wasn't room for two people like that in the same house. So I went home one day and I just said, 'I have to leave the house.' "

José recalled that, after one particularly ugly fight, "he told us he was going to stop living with us and get a room by himself. I asked him why and he said, 'Because I want to see if, one day, I can do something.' He didn't take anything with him, not even his clothes."

Carlos moved into a small apartment in the center of San Francisco's burgeoning hippie district. He continued to work at the Tick Tock and his father would often find a place for him in his weekend gigs as a violin player or guitarist. However, Carlos was continuing to spend more and more of his time in the street, busking in the streets for dimes and quarters and forming informal alliances with musicians in the streets and parks of San Francisco and Palo Alto. He was also taking a lot of drugs and drinking a lot of wine. But, for Carlos, this was all part and parcel of immersing himself in the free-spirited culture that was growing up around him. This, he reasoned, was how he was going to find his way.

On his own, Carlos became determined to have things his way, and was a little bit self-centered in his outlook. The core group of musicians, including drummer Danny and bass player Gus, from his first informal San Francisco band that had formed around Carlos quickly fell by the wayside.

A lot of the musicians he would hang around with still had domestic obligations. Carlos had no patience with the notion of families and day jobs. He would regularly admonish them for their middle-class ways, exhorting them to leave all that foolishness behind if they wanted to hang out with him and be real musicians. The youngster with the now wild, bushy hair saw himself as a true artist, and true artists did not compromise their talent or their destiny.

But Carlos's allegedly strong artistic stance was indeed being compromised by the fact that he still had the relative security of his low-paying job at the Tick Tock. And while he took pride in doing a good job at his menial tasks, he was feeling rather hypocritical. He would often lie to his street friends about the true source of his income, claiming it was money he made panhandling or that was given to him by his parents.

He did not know if his friends were swallowing those lies, but they were adding to his internal struggles. He wanted to break free into the creative life; he felt the hours spent washing dishes and cooking burgers were time lost forever. But something in his psyche was keeping him at the Tick Tock and, he must have felt, in a safer, more predictable environment. Carlos knew in his gut that he needed a push out the door, and it came one day when a pair of limos pulled up in front of the Tick Tock Restaurant and the Grateful Dead piled out.

"I had my apron on and those guys came over to the counter and asked for french fries and burgers. I never talked to the Dead that day. I just looked at them. But something in me just said, 'Man, you can do that thing, what they do.' I walked up to the owner of the Tick Tock and said, 'Man, I quit.' I took my time card, put it in the time clock and said, 'I'm outta here,' and just left."

With no steady income other than the odd gig with his father, Carlos jumped at the offer to move in with Stan Marcum. Carlos and Marcum, one night during a music-and-drugs reverie, made an informal pact: Santana would form a band and Marcum would manage them.

It was a promise born of exuberance and drugs. It was a promise both young men took seriously, because both men felt Carlos Santana had a future.

Under Marcum's tutelage, Carlos continued to explore the sixties music scene in all its facets. Marcum, his ear constantly tuned to the progressive side of things, would often bend his roommates' ears with out-there stuff by jazz artists and obscure European styles of music. But Carlos maintained a steadfast loyalty to the blues.

Santana, Marcum, and a loose array of musician friends continued to haunt the Fillmore West, paying when they could and, recalled Fillmore worker Paul Baratta, relying on goodwill when they had no money. "I knew the kind of money that Carlos and his first manager, Stan Marcum, weren't making. We had a Jefferson Airplane–Jimi Hendrix show one night and I saw them standing by the ticket booth, and came down. I had seen them at shows the last four nights, plopping down their money. Stan said, 'Any chance we can get to see Hendrix? We already paid our way in a few times. We just don't have any more money.' I couldn't say no. From that point on I developed a relationship with them. They paid when they could and, when they couldn't, I would let them in."

At the time, Bill Graham was offering low-priced Sunday matinees at the Fillmore. For a buck, audiences would get two name acts and an unpaid unknown that was auditioning for the third opening-act slot. It was a lighthearted, fun experience geared toward families. There would be balloons festooned all around the hall and Graham would occasionally provide free popcorn.

In 1966, Santana and Marcum attended one of those shows, jazzed at the prospect of seeing two of their favorite acts, the Paul Butterfield Blues Band and Charles Lloyd, perform. As usual Carlos was up front, his chin pressed against the stage as he watched Charles Lloyd perform. He was not prepared for what happened next.

The story is one of those delightful urban myths that has been passed down through the decades. Paul Butterfield had allegedly taken a tab of LSD and ended up on a rather unpleasant trip. As the story goes, Butterfield showed up at the Fillmore late, bare-foot, and had a look on his face like he had just stared into the face of God. It was not a pleasant situation to set before the already stressed-out Bill Graham.

Graham was furious. He had a liberal attitude toward drug-taking but it was his professional credo

that musicians never be too stoned or too high to perform. One look at Butterfield and the promoter knew
his headlining act was not going on.

Graham looked around, saw some familiar faces
in the audience, and quickly pulled together an
impromptu jam that included members of the Grateful Dead and the Jefferson Airplane and Butterfield
Band member Michael Bloomfield, to cover for the
stoned Butterfield. Conspicuous on the stage was a
guitar standing unattended. Marcum saw a chance to
flex his managerial muscle, and boldly walked up to
Bill Graham and told the promoter, "Hey, you know, I
know this Mexican kid from Tijuana. He loves playing
blues and he loves B.B. King. Will you let him play?"

Graham sized up the offer and responded, "I'm not
in charge, Bloomfield is, go ask him." Marcum
repeated his suggestion to Bloomfield who sized up
Carlos for a moment and said, "Sure, man. Go ahead."

Carlos was in a state of shock as he climbed onto the
Fillmore stage, and picked up the guitar and nervously
tuned it.

"So I got the guitar and just started playing
(rhythm) and pretty much stood there waiting and
waiting until finally Bloomfield turned around, saw
me standing there, and said, 'Oh yeah, you're still
here, go ahead and take a solo.' And I jumped on it."

Carlos stepped forward and unleashed a deep soulful series of blues guitar licks. The musicians onstage did a double take, the consensus being, *Where did this kid come from?* The audience was likewise enthralled at the degree of emotion that was flying out of this youngster's ax.

Bill Graham also noticed. He came up to Carlos after the jam and complimented him on his playing. "He said, 'You got a band?' And I said, 'Yeah,' which was sort of true in a way. He took my phone number and we sort of hooked up."

Carlos immediately set about pulling together a band. Danny Haro and Gus Rodriguez, who were still technically in the group, continued on drums and bass. A guitarist named Tom Frazier, who was in the audience on the night of Carlos's impromptu jam, hooked up with him, and in turn introduced him to a Palo Alto keyboard player with a distinctive voice and some songwriting skills named Gregg Rolie. In short order, Danny and Gus once again fell victim to their domestic obligations and were replaced by a couple of local street cats, bassist David Brown and drummer Rod Harper.

This first group of musicians was young and inexperienced in the extreme. Most had gone through the high-school-band phase and had continued to work on the fringes as professional musicians. But, in essence, they were all raw kids, full of bravado and a modicum of skill. In informal meetings, they got high and pledged to each other that they could make this work and that they would soon be stars.

The band was christened the Santana Blues Band in homage to Carlos's heroes the Paul Butterfield Blues Band. The early rehearsals were ragged at best, but everybody seemed to know how to play their instruments; and there was some primitive cohesion in the unit. That everybody seemed to get along fairly well was considered a bonus. It was not much to go on. But, they felt, it was enough to get them out there.

Armed with a short list of blues and soul songs, the Santana Blues Band began playing gigs and informal jams in exotic places like Aquatic Park and Hippie Hill and clubs like the Matrix in San Francisco and the Ark in Sausalito. Those early shows were erratic, owing to the short time the band had been together. Set lists were short and often involved long, tedious, and not-always-in-tune jams. However, the chemistry and raw energy was evident early on, especially in the interplay between Santana and Rolie. Both could sense that, once they cleaned the bugs out, this band could be heading somewhere.

"We started out feeling that we could play blues in a way that was like Paul Butterfield, Cream, and Hendrix," Carlos reflected. "But then we started hanging out in the parks and seeing these conga players and flute players hanging out and playing. And I said, 'Man, this is great!' "

The band began experimenting, mixing jazz and blues with African and Cuban rhythms. Longtime friend, percussionist Michael Carabello, began sitting in with the band on congas. Carlos noticed an immediate change in the way audiences were responding to their new sound.

"We noticed that the hippies and the women started dancing differently than how they danced to the Grateful Dead. It wasn't like they were catching butterflies anymore. All of a sudden they were moving their bodies in a sensual, belly-dancing kind of way and the girls' nipples were getting hard. We looked at what was going on and we said, 'Oooh, this works.' "

Rolie agreed that, for their time, the Santana Blues Band was definitely out there. "We were told we were crazy playing the music we played. But it was original and, to this day, nothing sounds like it."

But while it worked, it was not paying the bills. Shows in the parks paid nothing, and unknown acts in area clubs pulled down little more than gas money.

The band members, playing the whole hippie-musician persona for all it was worth, did not work, and relied on Stan Marcum to pay their bills. "Stan sold his clothes for us," explained Carabello of the band's free ride. "He went out and cut hair while we all stayed home, got high and played music."

While it appeared that the band was doing more hanging out than actual playing, Carlos would often recall that living in a crash pad of a hotel with the other members of the band was like being at a university.

"I would go to some cat's room and he'd be listening to Sly or Jimi Hendrix, another guy to the Stones or the Beatles. Another guy would be listening to Tito Puente and Mongo Santamaria. Another guy would be listening to Miles and Coltrane."

Easily, one of the band's most memorable appearances was on January 14, 1967, when the Santana Blues Band joined a literal sea of musicians, poets, and hippie philosophers in the Human Be-In, a gathering of the hippie tribes in San Francisco's Golden Gate Park. It was the largest group of people the band had played to at that point, and Carlos was ecstatic as he played his heart out and later wandered among the thousands of people, getting high and savoring the whole hippie scene.

The Santana Blues Band was hitting its stride early in 1967 and was getting ready for an assault on bigger venues when Carlos took a random test for tuberculosis. The test came back positive.

Carlos speculated that he contracted the disease drinking the water during his frequent trips to Tijuana. But all the speculation in the world could not remove the fact that Carlos was sick. He checked himself into Mission General Hospital. He would end up staying for three months.

It was not a pleasant stay. Carlos was in a ward reserved for TB patients, and as it turned out, he was the healthiest one in the room. When other patients in the ward began dying, Carlos became extremely paranoid. When the doctors came by on their daily rounds and shot him full of stryptomicon, he was in pain.

Of equal concern to Carlos, as he lay in his bed receiving visitors and the occasional tab of LSD to brighten his spirits, was the fact that the Santana Blues Band was withering on the vine in his absence. The band continued to practice but, with no gigs on the horizon and Carlos not around to keep a sense of order, things got a little sloppy and eventually led to one member of the band being shown the door.

"I was just playing because I enjoyed playing," remembered Michael Carabello, "but I wasn't really serious. When Carlos went to the hospital, we were all waiting for him to get out of the hospital and I stopped going to practice so I got kicked out of the band."

In the meantime Carlos decided that sick or not, he had to escape what he considered a "jail sentence." He called a couple of his friends and asked them to bring him some clothes. He laughed, years later, as he remembered his great escape.

"We visited for a while and I said, 'See you later, guys.' I walked them to the elevator and just walked in with them. I changed clothes and just walked out with them."

Carlos called the hospital the next day and confessed his escape. The doctors were not thrilled but informed him that he was not contagious and that if he continued to take medication, he could resume his life.

That night Carlos celebrated his return to the real world by getting high with a group of friends and playing his guitar. The ax felt good in his hands.

A few days after leaving the hospital, Carlos rang up Bill Graham. The Santana Blues Band was back in business.

4

By the Time They
Got to Woodstock

The Santana Blues Band did not know they were a hot commodity when they formally auditioned for Bill Graham in 1968. Graham knew.

The promoter had long been a champion of Latin music. There was always something by Willie Bobo and Eddie Palmieri on the top of his record stack, and there was usually something by Tito Puente on the turntable. Consequently, he was instantly attracted to the congas and the driving rhythm section riding over Carlos's soaring guitar and Gregg Rolie's soulful vocals.

Bill Graham could feel the music in his bones as he watched the Santana Blues Band play on the empty Fillmore stage. And he knew others would, too.

"Bill was the first person who looked at the music for what it was," reflected Carlos of the first serious conversation the band had with the promoter. "Bill said, 'You guys got something different, something that makes the pelvis move in a different way. Your music is two things that should never be separated: spiritual and sensual. So stop fighting it.' "

Still, Carlos had some lingering problems with the fact that the band's music was appealing to baser instincts. Those fears centered largely on his religious background. "With my Catholic upbringing, I would get that guilt thing. I was horny all the time and I felt guilty because I was horny. That was kind of like my Catholic trip."

Needless to say, Santana overcame any sense of guilt that same year when they made their debut at the Fillmore West, opening for his idols, the Paul Butterfield Blues Band. The Santana Blues Band was a bundle of nervous energy moments before they hit the stage. For Carlos, playing at the Fillmore was like a coming-out party.

"It was really, really crazy," he remembered of that night. "We played all of Paul Butterfield's songs before he went on."

Bill Graham, who was notoriously hard to please, was enthralled with what the band was laying down. Yes, the band sounded a bit ragged around the edges, and his eyes would glaze over when the songs evolved into what he considered interminable jams. But as he scanned the audience and watched the women move, he could also tell that his feelings about the power in the band had been right on the mark.

"What impressed me [about the band] is that it was an attempt at fusing rock and Afro and Latino and getting a rhythmic sensuous sound into rock, which I've always felt it lacked."

What also endeared the Santana Blues Band to Graham was their willingness to play anytime. They were also not above playing on short notice, which saved the promoter's ass on more than one occasion.

"Whenever somebody wouldn't show up, Bill would say, 'Okay. Come on in and play.' " reflected Carlos. "And it happened quite a lot. Somebody would cancel or Bill would get into a fight with somebody. Every time somebody would miss it, we would be there in a second. I mean, we were hanging around anyway. We didn't have no place else to go."

The result was that, when local faves Loading Zone canceled on Graham at the last minute, the group had the opportunity to open for the Who the weekend of the legendary Monterey Pop Festival. It was a turning point for the band, and for Carlos. For the first time, they were sharing the stage with a legitimate superstar act. Carlos soaked in the vibe, watching, enthralled, as Who guitarist Pete Townshed went through his acrobatics; and Carlos mentally filed it all away for future reference.

The Santana Blues Band also opened for the likes of Chicago, the Johnny Winter Group, and Steppenwolf. "We'd open for those bands," said Carlos, "and we'd end up taking their crowd. That gave us a lot of confidence that what we had was really working."

Carlos's coming-out at the Fillmore also proved to be an opportunity to reunite with his family. Since the day Carlos had walked out the door, Carlos had been completely estranged from his family. Carlos had gone off into his own little world of music and his life, and as a result had stopped communicating with his family. Carlos was able to deal with the separation; he saw it as part of his rite of passage into manhood to be totally on his own. He did not, for a moment, think that his parents might be worried.

José and Josefina Santana were indeed concerned. They had not heard from their son in almost two years, and what they did hear from friends and acquaintances who had spotted Carlos hanging around Haight-Ashbury, was not good. Secondhand reports of Carlos just hanging out, playing guitar, and panhandling for money went to the heart of his parents' dashed hopes for their son. It hurt not knowing the truth and expecting the worst. José always tried to put a positive spin on those reports, insisting that their son was doing his musician thing and that he would soon settle into some kind of regular work. Josefina just wanted to know that her son was well.

One day, one of José's sons came to him with the news that he had heard a song on the radio promoting an upcoming show at the Fillmore, and that the announcer kept saying, "Santana, Santana," over the music. Encouraged, José and Josefina began looking for their son, to no avail.

Finally, one day, a week before the band was set to play a Fillmore West show, Carlos made the decision to reconnect with his family. For Carlos, the isolation from his family had been about pride. He had no accomplishments to hold up to them and did not want to appear a failure in their eyes. But with the growing reputation of the Santana Blues Band in the Bay Area, he felt ready to stand up to his family, as an accomplished musician and a man.

"He finally called us one day," reported his father of the conversation Carlos had with his mother. "He said, 'Mama, they're going to let me play at this place on

Market Street called the Fillmore.' My wife told him, 'Carlos I don't know why you like that hippie music.' His reply was, 'Yes, I like it and I am going to continue playing it.' His mother told him, 'You're crazy!' "

But Carlos insisted he had all these big plans and he was going to make a record someday so that he could make a lot of money and help his parents out. His parents seemed unimpressed. It was at that point in the conversation he invited his parents to the Fillmore to see him perform. They agreed to come and listen to their son.

For his parents, the sights and sounds at the Fillmore were a shock. "There was a mob of people there," recalled his father. "I had never gone to one of those places. We saw a bunch of lights and a lot of strange things in that place. During an intermission we talked to our son for the first time in two years. We asked him to come to our house as soon as he could. He came the next week."

The Santana band was fiery yet unpolished, and it was that uncompromising energy and raw style that had spread the Santana Blues Band's reputation all over the Bay Area. Besides the Fillmore, the group soon found themselves performing to packed houses at San Francisco's Straight Theater, and the Carousel.

Audiences for those early shows found a lot about

the band that excited them. First and foremost, there was Carlos, whose passion for the music and his instrument was obvious in a seemingly never-ending barrage of crying, screaming solos. In Gregg Rolie, Carlos had the perfect teammate—a master of the thick, undulating keyboard runs, and the possessor of strident, haunting vocals. Add to that the collective power of one of the roughest, believable rhythm sections imaginable and it was a sure bet that the next time these clubgoers saw the Santana Blues Band, they'd be paying premium concert-hall prices.

But there were changes afoot. Although Carlos was working hard to make the band a team situation, he was slowly but surely emerging as the unspoken leader. So nobody complained when it was decided, for commercial considerations and to appease the local musicians' union, who were complaining about how the band had to have an official leader, to shorten the band's name to Santana.

"The reason we chose my name was because it sounded the best," said Carlos who, years later, still remained uncomfortable with that decision. "Santana was something that could be a galaxy. It could be a planet or it could be the winds. It had a universal resonance to it."

However, the fact remained that Santana, while

musically sound, was far from poised in other areas. They were spending their time, when not performing or rehearsing, doing a lot of drugs and experiencing their first round of willing groupies. Essentially an immature bunch of children, the band was often less than professional as well, and this drove Bill Graham to distraction, their late arrival for the Who show being a case in point.

"We were late for the show and Bill was screaming at me and he asked me what kind of a fucking band we had," admitted Carlos. "The problem was that these other cats were late, just blowing it, putting cologne on themselves and all this other shit. It wasn't the music that was really happening, this was all just a trip for them."

This lack of professionalism weighed particularly heavy on Carlos, who had always taken the music seriously, and so, only months after Santana began playing out, Carlos, with the blessing of Rolie and others, was faced with telling the least two of the more irresponsible members of the band, Frazier and Harper, they were out. Local drummer Bob "Doc" Livingston, an adequate drummer with a penchant for booze, was added on skins and it was just naturally decided that a second guitarist was not necessary.

Carlos, figuratively and literally, had stepped to the front.

The stripped-down Santana lineup continued to grow musically. Carlos's playing style was beginning to move away from a basic blues stance and into a more progressive style of playing. He was weaning himself out of the traditional styles of B.B., Albert, and Freddie King, and into a more progressive mixture of European sounds. Carlos was determined to find his own voice.

David Brown recalled that, as Carlos continued to explore different musical styles, the rest of Santana followed suit.

"We didn't like the music too repetitious, the way Butterfield and other blues bands were playing," offered the bassist. "So we got into improvisation and we'd find the drums in there more of the time. Eventually we just sat back and decided to let them do their thing."

The result was that Santana began moving farther away from the blues and into a more free-form/ improvisational series of extended jams, concocting a heavy Latin musical hybrid that soon began incorporating roaring new material into their set. In the spirit of democracy, the early Santana songs would be credited to the group, but the reality was that Santana and Rolie were making the important decisions regarding lyrics and melody. The lineup changes and the new musical direction cemented the band's reputation as legitimate members of the burgeoning psychedelic scene in San Francisco.

Rolie laughed at the notion that what they were playing was well thought-out rather than something totally unconscious. "At the time, we were just playing. We didn't think about it."

The relationship between Santana and Bill Graham continued to flourish; there was a definite father-son vibe between the two. While Stan Marcum continued to operate as the band's manager, doing little more than collecting the band's money and booking the smattering of non-Fillmore shows, he willingly turned over the lion's share of the bookings to the Fillmore honcho and his Shady Management company.

With Graham's clout and the coming of the big out-door festivals that began popping up in the late 1960s, Santana began reaching out to bigger crowds, outside the confines of San Francisco. In September 1968, they joined the likes of the Grateful Dead, Muddy Waters, the Youngbloods, and Country Joe and the Fish at the Sky River Rock Festival and the Lighter Than Air Fair. Carlos was wide-eyed at the response the band received at this, their biggest concert to date. He was thinking it could not get any bigger than this.

Graham was already thinking about the next step.

By 1968, record companies had jumped on board

the emerging psychedelic music scene and just about every band with a San Francisco zip code was signing on the dotted line with a major label. Graham was convinced that Santana would be snapped up in no time, and so he used his contacts and influence in the record industry to alert selected labels to the fact that Santana was available.

Santana's style of music, even by current rock standards, was pretty far removed from mainstream pop and the current infatuation with psychedelia, and Graham sensed the band was going to be a hard sell. And so he was not surprised when labels did not beat a path to their door. But one day Carlos received an excited telephone call from Graham.

"Bill Graham called us and said, 'Hey, the head of Atlantic music, Ahmet Ertegun, is in town looking to hear us.' I loved Aretha Franklin, but I didn't want to be with Atlantic. I had heard that a lot of musicians were not satisfied with Atlantic's airplay and distribution track record so I told Bill, 'I don't want to be on Atlantic.' But Bill said, 'Just go and don't screw it up.' So I went to the audition but I played terribly, just awful."

The result was that Ertegun came, saw, and went away unimpressed. The Atlantic president reportedly dismissed Santana when he said, "They can't play. Furthermore, they won't sell."

Carlos, who years later would admit that he held back and blew the Atlantic audition on purpose, had his mind set on another home for the Santana band.

"I wanted to be with Columbia because Bob Dylan, Miles Davis, and people like that were over there. Actually what got me to wanting to be on Columbia was that, each year, they put out these posters for Christmas with all their artists on it. I wanted to be on this poster."

Columbia Records was only slightly more interested than Atlantic, but they were willing to roll the dice after seeing the band perform live with the Grateful Dead at a Santa Barbara concert. Carlos would grin in later years when he recalled how the band bowled over the Columbia brass.

"It freaked them out what we would do to the audience. One of the Columbia people told us, 'Your music is so vibrant that you can start with any song and end with any song and your music still comes off orgasmic.' "

In 1968 Columbia signed Santana, for very little money. The music trades trumpeted the signing as a real coup for the label. The band was jazzed at signing with Columbia. Bill Graham was concerned.

"Bill Graham took us aside shortly after we signed with Columbia," sighed Carlos, "and said 'If you're gonna make a record, you guys don't really have any songs, just jams, like seventeen-minute things.' We looked at him and said, 'Yeah, isn't that cool?' He said, 'No, it's not. You have to have some songs.' So he brought us into his office and hooked us up with some things."

Graham's education of the Santana band included words like *verses* and *choruses*, basic elements of a song, which the group of musicians knew nothing about. It was basically Music 101 as the band slowly listened and learned what went into a good commercial song.

The band quickly assimilated such Latin and soul favorites as "Black Magic Woman," "Evil Ways," and "Oye Como Va," and spit them out as stripped-down, pumped-up bluesy rock odes.

Santana ended 1968 with a series of four headlining shows, December 19–22, at the Fillmore West, making them the first band ever to headline the venue without having made a record. But the first steps toward changing that were already in the works. A talented Columbia Records producer, David Rubinson, was recording the performances and making mental notes about how he would effectively translate the Santana concert vibe to a studio setting.

Rubinson was already a minor celebrity in the Columbia Records camp, thanks to the minor miracle of taking another San Francisco group, Moby Grape's, notoriously raw and occasionally sloppy live sound and turning it into a first-rate debut studio album. The consensus was that Santana—whom many insiders considered less disciplined musically than Moby Grape—and Rubinson were made for each other. There was a smile on the producer's face as he watched Santana rock out. This was going to be fun.

It was during this period that conga player Marcus Malone was discovered in a North Beach hangout by manager Marcum, and added to the band in an effort to beef up the band's already potent percussion section. Adding another member to the band at this point did not prove to be a problem. The group was living the hippie ethic and so felt that anybody who could come in and help the band was welcome.

Santana finished the year with an explosive New Year's Eve show at the famed Winterland Ballroom that featured inspired playing and a moment of total strangeness when drummer Livingston, who had almost immediately become a liability because of his drinking, fell off his drum kit in a drunken stupor in the middle of a song.

The strangeness continued shortly after the New Year when conga player Malone was charged with first-degree murder in the stabbing death of his girlfriend's husband. Malone was out on bail the day the Santana band went down to Los Angeles to record their first album, with Rubinson producing.

The sessions for Santana's first album were a nightmare. For ten days, Rubinson struggled to pull Santana together as a musical unit. He quickly found that it would be a losing battle.

The band was suddenly sloppy and uninspired. The magic Rubinson had felt when recording the Fillmore shows was nowhere to be found. A big part of the problem centered on the fact that Malone, still an emotional wreck in the wake of the murder charge, was constantly showing up late or missing sessions altogether. Bob Livingston continued his drunken ways, and the reality was that, while he was a passable drummer in a live setting, he did not have the chops necessary to drive the band in the studio.

However, there were more than individual band members' vices haunting the recording session. Santana were so entrenched in the dynamics of playing before a live audience, that the empty confines of the studio succeeded only in blunting the emotion and passion that Rubinson had seen on the Fillmore stage. Rubinson was admittedly also at fault. For whatever reason, he did not seem to have the rigid sense of control nor the tolerance he had exhibited on previous assignments.

There were disagreements over the quality of the

arrangements. The heavy, percussive sound was sounding a bit tinny. Carlos's solos were sounding strangely uninspired. The band, collectively, was out of tune more often than not. The members of Santana were walking around the studio like a pack of zombies.

The band gave up after ten days and returned to San Francisco, where Malone was promptly fired and replaced by band irregular Michael Carabello who, in turn, brought in percussionist Chepito Areas to help shore up the sound. Livingston was also shown the door and was immediately replaced by local drummer Michael Shrieve.

The latest Santana lineup struggled to finish the album, which was called *Freeway Jam*, in San Francisco, but the end product, which remains unreleased to this day, was a flat, lifeless affair. Carlos, in later years, would dismiss those Los Angeles sessions, and the record that resulted, as "a bad vibe." Rubinson and the band amicably parted company shortly after the completion of that aborted effort.

Carlos's disappointment was salved when he was asked to pinch-hit for his idol Michael Bloomfield, who had collapsed from exhaustion, for the last night of a series of live shows at the Fillmore that would result in the album *The Live Adventures of Al Kooper and Michael Bloomfield*. Bloomfield recalled that he literally got up out of his hospital bed to call Carlos who, he conceded, was an unknown quantity outside of San Francisco.

But Carlos knew full well that a little bird named Bill Graham had planted the bug in Bloomfield's ear; not that Graham was being totally altruistic in suggesting the young guitarist for this important gig. With Bloomfield out of commission, Al Kooper was in charge and, truth be known, he was running the live sessions in a rather uninspired manner. Graham knew that Carlos had the youth and excitement to instantly elevate the proceedings to a higher level.

Carlos was admittedly nervous at the prospect of stepping in for his hero and, when called upon to supply the solo to an obscure blues ditty called "Sonny Boy Williamson," he responded with a serviceable but ultimately unspectacular solo.

"I just went in there, Al Kooper counted off, and we played," he remembered. "And that's really what it was. It wasn't about anything we talked about and it was not really something that knocked me out one way or the other."

Santana continued to search for the ideal situation for recording their debut album and eventually found the answer in producer Brent Dangerfield, a soundman who had worked with the band during their shows at the Straight Theater, and who had never produced anything before being tapped to pilot Santana's maiden voyage. There was no logic in the choice of Dangerfield. However, the Santana band, still smarting from the disappointment in Los Angeles with a professional producer, looked upon this rank amateur guiding their fortunes as both a goof and as a challenge that, at that moment, seemed to fit their collective mind-set. And, as these things so often work out, the sessions that produced the self-titled debut album were amazing.

The band had been through the process once before and so the idea of going into the studio was not as scary a proposition. To help with their arrangements, the band had asked pianist Albert Gianquinto to come in. On the day in question, Gianquinto sauntered into the studio, listened intently to the songs, said, "Cut down on the solos," and walked out. And, recalled Rolie, that's exactly what they did.

"We just had to think a little more," he said. "We had to keep it to shorter statements, but with the same intensity, therefore making it more intense."

Carlos had to agree that stripping things to the bone did have the desired effect. "Our intensity (in the studio) was of a different kind," reflected Carlos. "Altogether that first album took about a week to make. Basically, it took two days to record and two days to mix."

Columbia Records was thrilled with *Santana*, and with good reason: The album was a studio album in name only.

The reality was that the band had literally recorded their live show. Yes, there were the inevitable overdubs but the expected studio smoothness had been replaced by a raw, loud feel which showcased the band as a cohesive unit that had learned what worked and had put it front and center. The band had managed a minor miracle on *Santana*. There were improvised moments all over the record while, at the same time, the band was incredibly tight. Observers at those sessions were quick to report that Carlos's guitar playing was raw and possessed. Gregg Rolie was also cited as a heavy-handed keyboardist whose vocals cut through the tough percussive rhythms like butter. The album was scheduled for a October 1969 release; the folks at Columbia could hardly wait.

In the meantime, Santana continued to play out live, and their growing reputation as a monster band, with their debut album on the horizon, made it easier for Graham to get them on higher-profile bills. The group continued to be a headliner at the Fillmore and toured outside the state, opening for the likes of Janis

Joplin and her band, Big Brother and the Holding Company, and Crosby, Stills, Nash and Young. From a purely demographic point of view, Santana had latched on to the heretofore little-regarded Latin population peppered throughout the Midwest, the South, and the East Coast. The band reasoned that, once their album was finally released, there would be people lining up around the block to buy it.

One of the biggest gigs to date was an August appearance at the Atlantic City Pop Festival in New Jersey, where Santana shared the stage with the Jefferson Airplane, B.B. King, and Creedence Clearwater Revival; but an even bigger platform for their sound was right around the corner. . . .

. . . On the rolling fields of a New York farming community called Woodstock.

The idea of the Woodstock Festival, three days of peace, love, and understanding set to the driving beat of more than thirty superstar acts, seemed good on paper. But Bill Graham was a realist and, to him, the idea of several hundred thousand people and numerous bands at the mercy of promoters with little experience at this big an event worried him.

Graham saw early signs of trouble when the promoters of Woodstock came to him for help when many of the bigger bands they approached were reluctant to become involved. Graham, just as reluctant, agreed to help get the right bands on board . . . in exchange for one big favor.

"I said they could use my name in return for Santana being put on the show on Saturday night," recalled Graham. "I wanted them on during prime time, which was difficult because Santana still had no album out. I didn't want them on at seven in the morning or three in the afternoon. People on the East Coast had heard of them. But they had never seen them."

And for people to see them was almost as important to Graham as people hearing the band, according to Carlos's memory of that conversation with Graham. "Bill said, 'Before you hit one note, you guys are going to show that blacks, Chicanos, Cubans, and Anglos can work together.' "

When Graham informed Carlos and the rest of the band of their upcoming Woodstock appearance, they were excited, and then just a little bit scared.

"We were going on without having an album out and a lot of people didn't know us from Adam," said Carlos, still amazed at the memory. "It was kind of scary going out in front of that much of a crowd. But I felt if Bill believed we could do it, we could do it."

The Santana band was helicoptered into the Woodstock site on August 15, 1969. As Carlos looked down on the hundreds of thousands of mud-caked people openly taking drugs, making love, and grooving to the music, he was amazed.

"The different elements were going like waves. There were the natural elements plus all the drugs people were taking. I saw it as a disaster area but then, at the time, I was in a pretty liquid state."

The band arrived at eleven A.M. They were not scheduled to go on until eight P.M. that night. The promoters told the band "to just cool out and take it easy." Carlos hung out with Jerry Garcia from the Dead and other familiar musicians. He would occasionally watch from backstage as other bands performed.

"One thing led to another," reflected Carlos, "and I decided I wanted to take some mescaline. I figured I had plenty of time to come down before it was time for us to play. But just at the point that I was coming on to it, this guy came over and said, 'Look, if you don't go on right now, you guys are not going to play.'"

Carlos and the band raced onstage. Santana, in the midst of a drug-induced haze, looked out and saw "an ocean of flesh, hair, teeth, and hands." He was scared to death. The drugs were all over him. He said a silent prayer. "I just prayed that the Lord would keep me in tune and in time."

Carlos's prayers were answered.

To this day, the guitarist does not remember much of the band's set, slightly more than one hour long. What the audience remembered was a relentless rush of primal rock and Third World rhythms, racing through what had been dubbed the Woodstock Nation like an out-of-control forest fire. The consensus was that there were occasional timing missteps and, if you listened closely, you could hear an out-of-tune instrument or two on some numbers. As the band prepared to launch into their final song, "Soul Sacrifice," Carlos had returned to planet Earth.

"I wasn't really that on until I sweated some of that stuff out, which was around 'Soul Sacrifice.' The rest of the stuff, my guitar was like a rubberband. The neck was moving around like a duck neck."

"Overall I think we managed," he said in his assessment of Santana's Woodstock performance. "By the time we got to 'Soul Sacrifice,' I had come back from a pretty intense journey. Ultimately, I felt we had plugged in to a whole lot of hearts at Woodstock."

With Bill Graham in their corner, Santana came away from Woodstock with a $35,000 payday, reportedly, the highest amount any act was paid during the three-day festival. Within a week, Santana would add to their Woodstock mystique by playing another electrifying set at the Texas International Pop Festival in Dallas—their third major outdoor festival in a month.

But while the rock-music world was falling all over itself in praise of Santana, convincing the traditional Latino community was a whole other matter. East Coast music lovers were a particularly surly lot. To them, Santana were wild Mexicans from the West Coast. If they could not play salsa, people did not want to know them.

However, this backlash was counterbalanced by the number of superstar Latino musicians who came to the band's defense. People like Ray Barretto and Tito Puente were especially encouraging to the band, and it was that kind of high-powered praise that eventually led to even the most cynical critics giving the band a break.

Santana's first album was released in October 1969 and the band's long stretch of live touring paid immediate dividends. The album raced up the *Billboard* charts, and by November, amid a tidal wave of positive critical response and massive radio airplay, topped out at number 4. Santana's first album would ultimately spend two years on the *Billboard* charts, and would earn the band and its namesake leader their first gold and platinum records.

Why the record was such an immediate success has

been open to much speculation; but the fact remains that, at the height of the hippie movement, a lot of weak music was out there under the guise of psyche-delia. In contrast, Santana was all pulse and rhythm. It was nasty, lustful music in a field of peace and love.

Rave reviews rained down on the band. One of the most praiseworthy came from *Rolling Stone* magazine, which proclaimed the album "an explosive fusion of Hispanic-edged rock, Afro-Cuban rhythms, and inter-stellar improvisation."

Picking a commercial single for the band seemed like an easy task: "Evil Ways," with its haunting vocals and tough, percussive rhythms, was the logical choice. And so it was surprising when the more jam-oriented "Jingo" was selected. While a good song, "Jingo" proved to be a hard sell on Top 40 radio and ulti-mately stalled at number 56 on the record chart.

Carlos, now fully reunited with his family, had kept his parents up-to-date, sharing with them the excite-ment of signing with Columbia and how the record was progressing. Needless to say, the Santana family was one of the first to get a copy.

José would jokingly relate in later years how much of a struggle it was to get into his son's music. "When the album came out, since my music is so different from his, I couldn't understand it. To tell you the truth, I did not even know when one of my son's numbers began or finished. I listened to the record many, many times to see if it made sense. Now, after listening to it many more times, I like it."

Shortly after the release of the album, Carlos was given the opportunity of a lifetime when, on a trip to New York, he had the opportunity to meet one of his idols, Jimi Hendrix. It was a wild night.

Carlos was met at his hotel by Hendrix's girlfriend, who told him they were on their way to a party Jimi was holding in the recording studio where he was working on his new album. Naively Carlos asked, "How can there be a party if he's gonna be recording?" Hendrix's girlfriend admonished him to "not be such a square" as they piled into a cab and headed for the studio.

The cab pulled up outside the studio just as Hendrix emerged from another cab; Carlos finally met his idol. "Jimi said, 'I really like your album, man. I know about you and I like your choice of notes.' Coming from him, that really blew me away. What could I say? What I did say was, 'Thanks, man.' "

Carlos entered the studio and watched as Hendrix plugged in his guitar and began playing the umpteenth take of the song "Room Full of Mirrors." Hendrix, who was notoriously shy about anyone seeing him play, had turned to face the amps. Everything was fine for the first few moments but then, Carlos remembered sadly, Hendrix started freaking out and playing some "wild shit" that had nothing to do with the song.

At a signal from the producer and engineer, two roadies entered the studio, forced Hendrix to drop his guitar, and forcibly dragged him into the engineering booth. Carlos was shocked at Hendrix's drug-induced condition. "His eyes were all bloodshot and he was foaming at the mouth. It was like being in a room with someone who was having an epileptic fit. That's how it hit me and it really shook me up."

It seemed like a good idea at the time. The Rolling Stones, in the midst of a U.S. tour that had the band dodging charges of price gouging and halfhearted performances, decided that it would be a good public-relations move to do a big, free outdoor concert somewhere in the States. When they decided on the Altamont speedway in the small, northern California town of Altamont for the performance, they inevitably turned to Bill Graham to help fill out the bill with local talent. The promoter suggested the Grateful Dead, Jefferson Airplane, and Santana. He also offered some advice: Don't do it.

Graham, still smarting from the negative fallout from Woodstock, was leery of another free show, big crowds, the Stones' unpredictability, and, most importantly, the band's decision to hire a local chapter of the Hell's Angels motorcycle gang to handle security. But Graham held his breath and hoped for the best.

What he got was the worst.

Santana was barely into the first number of their set when Carlos was shocked to look out into the crowd and see a fan being beaten senseless by a couple of the hired thugs. Sporadic outbursts continued throughout the band's set. During their final song, a fan raced across the stage in front of the band with a couple of Hell's Angels in hot pursuit; they caught him just to the left of center stage and beat him to a pulp as Carlos and the band, wide-eyed, looked on in astonishment. Carlos was shaking his head as the group walked offstage. He was suddenly back in the low-class bars of Tijuana, playing to yet another violent crowd.

Things got progressively worse as the day went on. A couple of members of the Jefferson Airplane tried to interfere when the Angels again began beating on fans, and got slugged for their trouble. The day ended in tragedy and murder at the front of the stage when Meredith Hunter was stabbed to death as the Stones played.

In a space of three months, Carlos Santana had seen the birth of the hippie movement as a viable social vehicle at Woodstock, and its death in the mud and blood of Altamont. The end of 1969 saw the guitarist in a reflective mood. He was in a band. He had a hit record and he was a rising star. But inside, Carlos Santana was not completely happy.

"I still could not speak English very well. My accent was straight from Tijuana. I was angry at the world because I could not articulate."

5

Blues All the Time

Bill Graham had warned Carlos Santana. "He told us, 'Listen, when your first album comes out, you guys are gonna be recognized on the street and your egos are gonna get so big you're gonna need a shoehorn to come into a room. And it's just gonna fuck you all up.' But we said, 'No, no it's not gonna happen.' "

Truth be told, by the time Graham got around to giving his dire warning, Carlos was already beginning to have his first pangs of doubt about the stability of the band. Early on, he used to be amused when the band members were primping in front of a mirror before going onstage and surrounding themselves with groupies. Carlos himself was no saint. He jumped right into the frenzy of buying new clothes and cars when the first bit of big money started trickling in. And he did like the ladies. This, he reasoned, was all part of the rock-star thing and he was more than willing to take the trip. Most of the time.

But even Carlos's sensibilities were occasionally put to the test by the antics of the rest of the band. He knew going in that most of the members of Santana ran with a wild crowd but he did not foresee the band becoming the unofficial Pied Piper for the outer fringes of society. That is, until after one particular concert when, after a quick shower at his hotel, "I went down to the hotel lobby to see what was happening and I found it full of pimps, dealers, and weirdos. It was like walking into a swamp."

Carlos felt in his gut that rock stardom and this band would not mix. Here were a bunch of twenty-two-year-old kids with no sophistication to speak of, suddenly having the biggest record on the planet. You couldn't turn on the radio for weeks after their debut album hit the bricks without hearing a Santana cut. They were hanging out with famous people and basically living the high life.

"It was just unbelievable that it was all happening,"

recalled keyboardist Rolie. "We had gone from obscurity to everybody knowing who we were."

And who they were, in the eyes of the music industry and their peers, was a bunch of radical young toughs. Whereas their psychedelic brethren had built up an almost stereotypical image of peace, love, and being laid-back, the members of Santana projected a dangerous vibe, a non-hippie attitude that put off many, but also attracted an equally rabid following. Nobody ever accused the Santana band of putting up a false image. Because being young, horny, and high was what they were all about; that they could actually play their instruments and put out such an enticing sound, was considered by many to be a bonus.

While he kept quiet about his true feelings, inside, Carlos knew that factions were being formed within the band that would ultimately compromise the musical integrity of Santana. On one side were the serious musicians, the ones who practiced long and hard and whose passion for the music was obvious—Carlos numbered Rolie, drummer Shrieve, and himself in that camp. On the other side were those who were in this trip for all they could get. They were the ones who would have to be watched.

Santana released their second single, a remake of the Willie Bobo hit "Evil Ways," in February 1970. Easily the most commercial song on their debut disc, "Evil Ways" became an instant radio staple that made its way to number 4 on the national charts. But even as the sales of Santana's first album climbed past platinum and flirted with two million copies sold, the band was already beginning to exhibit the excessive lifestyle of "Too much, too soon." Within a space of a few months, the band had gone from typical rock-star shenanigans to hard-core consumption.

Even to the casual observer, it was not a pretty sight. And while he was an active participant in the party, Carlos saw his future when, in March 1970, he attended a series of Jimi Hendrix concerts in Berkeley, California, that were being filmed for a planned concert film.

Carlos once again made small talk with Hendrix but it was the deadened look in the legendary guitarist's eyes that spoke volumes to him. "I could see by his eyes that, by that point, he was deeply married to whatever flow he was into."

What Carlos also found out during those Berkeley concerts was that Hendrix was looking for a change in musical direction after his three albums with the Experience. And that he wasn't looking too far.

"He mentioned to Michael Carabello that he was thinking of joining our band," recalled Carlos. "I said, 'Great! I guess I'll have to become a roadie.' But he did mention the possibility of going with us. At the time our band was starting to become big and I guess Jimi thought, 'Okay, this has some potential.' "

All who heard this story felt that a Hendrix-Santana collaboration would have resulted in some brilliant music. Unfortunately, Hendrix's death on September 18, 1970, made it a moot point.

But despite such examples, the Santana band continued to live the high life.

Number one on the band's collective hit parade of vices was drugs, which should not have been a surprise to anyone. The members of Santana were active drug users and, in certain instances, abusers before there even was a Santana. With their success, the only thing that had changed was that money and, by association, drugs, were now easier to come by.

It was a rare day when most of the Santana band was not high on cocaine. In fact, the drug became such a big part of the band's daily life that, when they went out on tour, a representative of their entourage had the sole job of always making sure he had an ounce or two available in case anybody in the group ran out. Michael Carabello never ran out, and could usually be counted on to have at least an ounce of the drug secreted somewhere in his luggage for emergencies.

A temporary touring member of the band, piano player Albert Gianquinto (who had helped out on their debut album), added to the growing drug problem in the band when he introduced several of the band members to heroin. In no time at all, bassist Dave Brown had picked up the habit.

Even Carlos, who always was held up as one of Santana's more enlightened spirits, was not immune. "I developed a sort of thing for LSD, mescaline, mushrooms, stuff like that. I wanted to try everything, just like a little child."

But despite the fact that Santana would never go onstage without at least half the band higher than a kite, they always, much like their Woodstock experience, seemed to be able to put on a good show and survive their professional duties, relying more on instinct than anything else.

Groupies proved to be another vice that the band, including Carlos, embraced enthusiastically. As the top dogs in rock, the band had women literally waiting for them on every stop of their tour. This was the time of free love, it was before AIDS, and women were feeling liberated in the sexual arena. For them, the Santana band was particularly enticing. There was a sense of fear and danger in being around this band, and some women felt it was a turn-on. And in the spirit of friendship, Carlos Santana would often pass the willing women around to the rest of the band.

An incident typical of the band's approach to the pleasures of the flesh occurred during the Miami Pop Festival, when the band made the acquaintance of a girl they dubbed "the Burger Queen" who would continue to show up at various Santana tour dates and service the band. On one occasion, road manager Herbie Herbert had a camera going when the Burger Queen decided to "pull a train" for the entire band. Captured for posterity that night was the site of a naked Carlos Santana finishing intercourse, climbing off the girl and making way as the next band member climbed on.

Problems of the professional kind were also developing between Santana and Bill Graham. Although there was nothing in writing, Graham, early in his relationship with Santana, had come to believe that he was, for all intents and purposes, the band's manager as well as their booking agent. He would recall years later the events that led up to his feeling that way:

"The band came to me and said, 'We would like you to manage our affairs.' I said, 'Fine, and this is the percentage I want.' I never asked for papers from anyone, never. Because I felt, 'I'm good and you're good. If we get along, why have a marriage license? I'd rather just live together.' "

Unfortunately for Graham, the members of Santana

were nothing if not loyal, and in Stan Marcum they had somebody who had been there from the beginning and whom they felt was doing a good job by them. So not too long after "Evil Ways" hit the charts, Graham walked into his office and was given a message by his secretary. A message from the band saying that they were going to go with Marcum as their full-time manager.

Graham was enraged. He raced down to the band's rehearsal room and began screaming at the top of his lungs at the band members. The band, which had pretty much shied away from the business side of what they were doing, did not know how to respond to his tirade and so they called in their road manager, Herbie Herbert, to explain to Graham that Santana had decided to go with Marcum as manager.

Graham was fuming and screaming obscenities as he left the rehearsal room. He would continue to book Santana's concerts. But he would never forget the sense of betrayal he felt that day.

Santana embarked on a two-month tour of Europe in April 1970 to coincide with the release of their first album overseas. Easily, a tour high point was a command performance at the Royal Albert Hall in London. The band also sold out concerts in Germany and Denmark and turned heads with a fiery performance at the famed Montreaux Jazz Festival in Switzerland.

Santana returned to the United States midway through 1970 and began an extended series of big summer shows. This would be an enjoyable tour for Carlos thanks to Bill Graham.

The promoter, who prided himself on being on the cutting edge, had long been a fan of jazz great Miles Davis. And when Davis's most recent album, *Bitch's Brew*, showed signs of making inroads into the rock audience, Graham decided that Davis and Santana would be a good fit, and booked Davis as an opening act for the band on a number of shows.

Davis had been an inspiration for Carlos for years and the idea of playing on the same bill with him was like manna from heaven. As the tour progressed, he found out that the respect went both ways.

"Man! That motherfucker can play his ass off!" reflected Davis of his memories of that tour. "I loved the way he played and he also turned out to be a very nice person. Yeah, I was opening for him but I was comfortable with that because I liked the way he was playing."

Carlos and Miles Davis became good friends on that tour. In later years, the pair would talk and get together with regularity and Carlos was quick to pick the jazz master's brain when it came to all things musical.

The band eventually finished up the tour and began making plans to go back into the studio to begin recording their second album, *Abraxas*. The occasion of their second album brought on the usual speculation from the press and industry insiders. Would the band be one-album wonders, or would they continue to grow as musicians? There was also the circulation of the first stories chronicling the band's drug use and what impact it might have on the band in the studio. Santana responded to the doubters by saying they were confident that *Abraxas* would be an even wilder ride.

But they were also sure that certain elements of their recording process needed to be improved. Santana had been thrilled with the quality of the first album but, with some time to reflect, they now felt the sound quality could have been better on *Santana*, and so the first goal was to make a record that sounded better. Bringing in veteran engineer Fred Castro solved that problem. The rest, they reasoned, would be pure aesthetics: finding the right chorus, the right song, the right note.

Since the recording of *Santana*, Carlos had slowly

but surely emerged as the official group leader. Santana still made group decisions in most situations. But the rest of the band usually deferred to Carlos on any important issue and, with his seemingly encyclopedic knowledge of music, it was a safe bet that when they went into the studio, his word would be law.

But would the occasion of another recording session cause professional and personal conflicts? After all, Gregg Rolie had proven himself an equally strong talent and a vocal advocate of the band's raw style of playing. And, after Carlos, he seemed to have the ear of the rest of the band when it came to musical decisions.

For his part, Carlos seemed to be favoring a more subtle, less primal approach in his playing of late and had given some clues in interviews that he would be pressing for a more intricate, subtle sound on the group's second album.

Some sort of confrontation seemed inevitable. Insiders held their breath.

On the surface, the *Abraxas* sessions appeared to be heading in the right direction. The band members had been listening to a lot of the Beatles' *Abbey Road*, and *Sgt. Pepper's Lonely Hearts Club Band* in the interim, and also favored the Jimi Hendrix albums in which songs would seamlessly bleed into each other.

"That's the concept we wanted to have with *Abraxas*," chronicled Carlos. "We wanted something where you could put the needle in the groove and it's just one breath."

After a long battle, Rolie convinced the band that an interpretation of Peter Green's classic, "Black Magic Woman," would serve to anchor the album as well as give them another, almost certain commercial hit. Soon after, the trilogy that would prove the center-piece of the album came together when the original "Gypsy Woman" and the Tito Puente song "Oye Como Va" were added to the album's set list. In fact, the *Abraxas* sessions were shaping up to be an even tougher fusion of rock and Latin rhythms.

Unfortunately, things turned ugly fast once the ses-sions began. The band camaraderie, which had pretty much survived extensive touring, quickly turned to petty bickering and infighting in the studio. Drugs fueled a lot of the problems during the *Abraxas* ses-sions but, as Carlos recalled, things started getting worse when the much-heralded band democracy began dissolving into separate dictatorships.

"I remember I started to pull rank on the rest of the band," Carlos painfully recalled. "In the past, things had been very democratic. But the band did not want the songs 'Oye Como Va' and 'Samba Pa Ti' on the record. They said it didn't sound like Santana. We went back and forth for a long time before I finally said, 'Either those two songs go on the album or you go find another guitar player.' I had to dig in my heels and it worked."

The sessions quickly degenerated into an ongoing battle that often pitted Carlos against the rest of the band. He would give in on small things in the name of democracy, but it was evident to the other members of Santana that the music was beginning to veer slowly toward something not-quite-so-rough and progressively more spacey.

One night, after yet another in a series of grueling and often combative sessions, Gregg Rolie and Michael Shrieve wandered into a small club in Palo Alto, California, called Poppycock. They had barely cleared the doorway when they found themselves immediately blown away by a young teenage guitarist named Neal Schon. The pair were so impressed with the fifteen-year-old that they got up onstage and jammed with him after his set.

The next day Rolie and Shrieve drove Schon to the studio where Santana was recording and set him up in an adjacent studio where, in between breaks, the band members would wander in and be mesmerized by the youngster's mastery of blues, rock, and all musical points in between. Schon, they reasoned, was cut—creatively—from the same cloth as Carlos: quiet, somewhat innocent and personable, but a monster when he strapped on his ax. A couple of jams later and the rest of the band was already beginning to put pressure on Carlos to add Schon to the band on a permanent basis.

Schon, while excited at the offer and a fan of the band, really was not thinking too much about the impact of joining a superstar group. More the technician and theorist than rock star, the youngster looked upon the prospect of joining Santana as just another opportunity to learn.

Carlos was not thrilled. His growing ego and sense of himself as the true leader of the band would not allow him to add a second, and quite good, guitarist. But if Carlos was not interested, somebody else was.

Guitar legend Eric Clapton and his band Derek and the Dominos were in town and had come over to check out Santana. An epic jam session between the two groups ensued. Unfortunately, Carlos had chosen to take some LSD just prior to coming into the studio. Consequently, he was shocked to find Clapton and his band plugged in and jamming when he walked through the door.

"I came in and Eric and Neal Schon were jamming," the guitarist reflected sadly. "I felt really bad because I wanted to play. But I had just taken the LSD and I was just too out of it."

Carlos's inability to play allowed Clapton to get an earful of Schon—he was impressed. Clapton, during a concert the next night in Berkeley, called Schon onstage to join the group for a couple of songs. Right after the concert, Clapton offered the youngster a job in his band.

Schon called his friends in Santana the next day and relayed Clapton's offer. They in turn raged at Carlos that they would be losing a very good musician if they didn't move fast. Carlos still was not sure about competing with this kid. But he was sure that he did not want Eric Clapton to get him.

Neal Schon became the band's second guitarist the next day.

The *Abraxas* sessions ultimately turned out to be a good object lesson, in that the normally laid-back Carlos had learned how to stand up for what he believed in and the rest of the band had, grudgingly, learned how to be flexible.

Any bruised feelings members had coming out of the studio were salved when *Abraxas* was released in fall 1970 to rave reviews. *Vibe* magazine, in looking back on the past one hundred years, would name *Abraxas* as one of the one hundred essential albums of the twentieth century.

Gregg Rolie's insistence that "Black Magic Woman" be on *Abraxas* delivered immediate dividends when, in

January 1971, it became the first single off the album and eventually made its way to number 4 on the singles charts.

For Carlos, the occasion of *Abraxas*'s release was an important moment in his life as a musician. It was with that album and hearing the likes of "Samba Pa Ti" raging out of his radio speakers that the young guitarist felt he had finally discovered his own voice.

"I immediately knew," he once said, of that moment. "It made me feel grateful and aware that all the guys that I loved, they had a new baby, and it was my sound. That was the moment."

The album shot straight to the top of the *Billboard* charts and stayed there for six weeks, selling over a million copies in the process.

But Santana would admit, years later, that even at the height of the band's popularity with *Abraxas*, he was not really enjoying the success. "*Abraxas* would be on every radio station and I found myself more and more depressed and I'd find myself crying. The band was deteriorating and my friends, who I grew up with, were total strangers to me. We were sounding like crap."

And the main reason Santana was sounding like crap was that the band was spending too much time catting around and not enough time rehearsing. Carlos was the only one in the band who seemed to care about the music at that point, and he admitted that he was fighting a losing battle.

"Everybody was just basically acting stupid and out of their minds," the guitarist recalled. "I would say, 'Why don't we start getting to the music?' Then people started thinking I was bringing everybody down for trying to get to the next thing."

In an effort to ease his discomfort with the way things were going, Carlos, for the first time, offered up his services on other people's albums. The couple of days he spent in the studio with the Jefferson Airplane on their *Bark* session was a joy. To his way of thinking, the Airplane, who were actually going through some tough times of their own, were still the fun-loving street musicians he liked to be around. In fact, Carlos had such a good time that he immediately jumped to working on the solo album of Airplane member Papa John Creach. Creach, a bluesman, gave Carlos the opportunity to play the kind of simple music that had sparked his imagination as a child.

Santana were so excited at the way *Abraxas* was selling, they immediately made plans to go back into the studio and begin recording the follow-up, tentatively titled *Santana III*. Those early attempts at recording the album proved haphazard at best and usually collapsed into lengthy jams that provided little that was usable. Plus there was always the matter of having to drop everything at a moment's notice and go on tour.

There were two schools of thought behind Santana's long stretches on the road. One was the willingness of the band to perform under any and all circumstances; they would not balk at the addition of shows on an already-packed tour and would, on occasion, give up a day off, when a promoter called with a last-minute gig. The other was greed—greed on the part of promoters, to work the band like a pack of dogs, and of the band members themselves, who collectively had the attitude of striking while the iron was hot.

The group began a short series of dates at the tail end of 1970, working Neal Schon in slowly with a few songs each night. The young guitar player made his official debut on December 31, 1970, at the Crater Festival in Hawaii. Schon proved to be a perfect fit and a solid young rock-star presence in the band. Although nobody would say so to his face, it became evident that Schon's presence in Santana was pushing Carlos to even greater creative heights. In Neal Schon, Carlos Santana saw a threat and, in a way, an inspiration.

For his part, Schon never saw Santana as an easy fit. Essentially trained as a lead guitarist, the youngster's rhythm licks were comparatively weak and he had to struggle on the job just to get to the point of being adequate. And when he did take lead on a song, he always felt the presence of Carlos—someone whom he admired—at his shoulder, adding to his adolescent insecurity.

The stay in Hawaii was typical of the temptations thrown in the band's path. Bowls of cocaine were piled high in the band members' rooms at a plush mansion. Local women were instantly drawn to the swarthy, dangerous look of Santana, and band members were constantly sneaking off to rooms and beach-front cabanas for various bouts of individual and group sex.

Professionally, Santana were on top of the world. These poor kids from the San Francisco streets were now living in fine houses and driving new cars. However, internally, the band was beginning to crack apart at the seams. Cliques and factions, true to Carlos Santana's early fears, were beginning to form within the group.

Santana and Rolie were clashing more and more often over the band's evolving musical direction and the increased drug use. While not a heavy drug user, Carlos continued to use psychedelics regularly, while Rolie, except for a penchant for marijuana, stayed relatively straight. Santana and Carabello rarely agreed on anything. David Brown had become a big drug user and one was never sure from day to day whether he would make a gig. But the overriding factor in the sudden disintegration of Santana was Santana.

Carlos was slowly moving away from the more heathen aspects of stardom and deeper into the music and where it would take him. He was also becoming rather good at the subtle art of manipulation. It was becoming more and more obvious to the rest of Santana that Carlos had a hidden agenda. Mike Shrieve, one of the younger and more naive members of the band, recalled the day that he saw the dark side of Carlos Santana beginning to emerge.

The pair were walking out of a rehearsal hall when Carlos suddenly turned on Shrieve and began rattling off a litany of things he felt the band should be doing. Shrieve defiantly responded by saying, "You can't make them do that. It's not your group." Carlos looked at Shrieve long and hard before saying, "Not yet."

Shrieve was concerned at the outburst but chose to keep it to himself, already fearing the band was on the verge of a mutiny against Carlos and that this would only push them over the edge.

In February 1971, Santana began intensive rehearsals for an upcoming European and African jaunt. When Chepito Areas did not show up one day, a couple of members of the band went to his apartment . . . where they found him lying unconscious in a spreading pool of blood. Areas was rushed to a nearby hospital where he was diagnosed with a brain aneurysm. He lay in a coma, hovering near death. At one point, he was given the last rites.

Michael Carabello related what happened next a couple of years later, barely able to disguise his anger.

"We didn't know what was going to happen, if he was going to die or whatever. We had a meeting because Carlos was getting restless, just sitting around waiting. He wanted a gig. I said, 'I don't think we should gig, because Chepito's just as much a part of the band as anyone else.' "

But Carlos insisted that the band should tour with a replacement. The rest of the band bristled at his seeming insensitivity but eventually agreed to tour with a replacement for Areas.

Famed percussionist Willie Bobo was added at the last minute. The early dates on the African portion of the tour went well, highlighted by a concert in front of one hundred thousand fans in Ghana. Unfortunately the band's run of bad luck continued when, shortly before that show, Bobo fell ill. He struggled on until the band reached London, and then had to be hospitalized. Faced with canceling the remainder of the tour, Carlos once again suggested a midtour replacement: veteran jazz percussionist Coke Escovedo.

"There was an understanding that I was temporary," recalled Escovedo. "I told the band there was no hassle with Chepito coming back."

But Escovedo was quick to size up the situation. He sensed that Carlos was the leader of the band and, after a few days, he realized there was some distance between the guitarist and the other members.

Carlos had grown increasingly reserved and, in a sense, insecure around the more outgoing, raw attitudes of the rest of the band. Escovedo knew that Carlos ultimately pulled the strings and so he quickly ingratiated himself with the young guitarist. He began to room with him on the road, sit with him at meals, and soon became his confidant.

It did not take long for the rest of the band to realize what was going on. And they did not like it. "Coke started kissing his ass and telling him, 'Well, your name is Carlos Santana and you shouldn't be listening to anybody else,' " recalled Carabello. "He was telling him, 'You should be the leader.' It went to Carlos's head."

David Rubinson, who kept in touch with Santana through his work with Bill Graham's booking agency, also saw what was going on. He indicated that a big part of the problem centered on what he considered "political bullshit" and that there was a growing resentment from the rest of the band about what they perceived as "ass-kissing" on the part of Escovedo.

For his part, Escovedo vehemently denied that he was a disruptive force in the band, insisting that his suggestions were always put out for the benefit of the entire band.

"I wanted to teach them all I could and, from that, people thought I was speaking into Carlos's ear. Yes, Carlos and I got along, we got into a groove. But, at no time, was I kissing anybody's ass."

Santana returned to the United States in spring 1971. They were greeted with some good news. Areas had made a miraculous recovery from the brain aneurysm. He was immediately welcomed back into the band, and Escovedo was kept on as well.

The follow-up single to "Black Magic Woman," "Oye Como Va," had worked its way into the Top Twenty. But all the joy from the band's commercial success could not mask the disintegration process within the band. Manager Stan Marcum had become almost invisible, due in large part to his increased drug use. There were also complaints that the band's massive earnings over the past year were not being invested wisely by Marcum and his handpicked financial advisor.

Escovedo hinted at problems on the management side when he said, "We started finding out things that he [Marcum] could have told us. It got to the point where no one knew what was happening."

In his defense, Marcum claimed that the charges against him were part and parcel of a general malaise that had enveloped the band and, he hinted, were driven by Coke Escovedo. He offered, in a slightly cryptic fashion, that a lot of negative forces had entered the life of the band and that they were driving a wedge between him and the band, and Carlos and the band. But Marcum ultimately stopped short of naming any particular person as the problem element in Santana.

The European-African tour had proved quite lucrative for Santana; their Third World sounds were a breath of fresh air at a time when most of the rock exports to the rest of the world were white-bread English-speaking hippies. And so, less than a month after returning to San Francisco, the band boarded a plane for a return to Europe . . . but, this time, carrying a couple of spare parts. Dave Brown's escalating drug problems made him a liability and so bassist Doug Rauch was brought along as a standby, just in case. Likewise, while Chepito Areas was feeling healthy enough to travel and perform, Coke Escovedo remained in the band as well.

The tour was an eye-opener in more ways than one. It highlighted the fact that Santana was a monster of a band—capable, on any given night, of expanding the envelope of passion and emotion with their music. Unfortunately, this tour also highlighted how alienated the members had become with each other when not onstage. And especially toward Carlos.

In the past year Carlos had begun to tone down his personal act. He still did drugs, although he had quietly stopped using the cocaine more than a year previous. He still chased women, but it was not the full-time occupation it remained for the rest of the band. Also, Carlos had discovered the spiritual power of meditation which had led him deeper into his own personal and musical exploration.

Carlos knew that the other members of Santana were calling him "Jesus" and "hypocrite" behind his back. And he was frustrated at the fact that he was not being understood.

"I was really straightforward with the band about how I felt," sighed Carlos. "I wanted to be real. I didn't want to be cool. I started to feel weak and resentful towards the band. I was demanding more because my soul was demanding more."

The band returned to the States in the summer of 1971 and went back to the studio, intent on finishing *Santana III*. Surprisingly, though the band was essentially falling apart around their heads, the members of Santana were still able to function on a creative level in the studio. There were still the constant battles over musical direction. Carlos recalled that, with the exception of Shrieve and himself, the rest of the band was going for a harder, Led Zeppelin–type sound, while he was steering a course in the direction of the progressive sounds of Weather Report and Miles Davis.

"We were still at a point where we could sit down in a studio and just talk about something and start playing it," remembered Carlos. "One of us would say, 'Listen,' and the others would listen. It was very much like a think tank. We'd use our imaginations and start tripping."

Rolie agreed that the *Santana III* sessions were fairly cohesive despite the fact that the band was pulling in different directions in terms of musical taste. But he echoed Carlos's statements when he offered that "we never closed doors on stuff."

Which was why, for the first time, a Santana album was conspicuous by the number of non–band members who appeared on the album. After bitter arguments, the band finally caved in and allowed the Tower of Power horn section to appear on the song "Everybody's Everything." There were also small vocal and instrumental contributions made by Luis Gasca, Linda Trillery, Mario Ochoa, and Gregg Errico. And while he was not identified as a member of the Santana band in the studio, Coke Escovedo did supply vocals and percussion on a number of cuts.

Surprisingly, this approach worked. The finished album was a tough-sounding brother to the first two Santana albums which, at the same time, showed that the band, and especially Carlos, were beginning to move to the beat of a different drummer.

But the growing breach within the band into factions was growing worse by the day and so a series of meetings was called to clear the air. In the first, Coke Escovedo once again took center stage, reciting a litany of accusations against Stan Marcum and strongly suggested Marcum be relieved of his duties as manager. David Rubinson related hearing that the meeting had gotten particularly heated.

"Coke wanted to get rid of Marcum and he got a couple of the guys on his side. I think he could have done whatever he wanted and taken over the band because he was a very strong force. He pushed and pushed and ultimately it came down to a choice and the band chose against him [Escovedo]."

A second meeting, held at Gregg Rolie's house, concerned the issue of excessive drug and alcohol use among band members. Surprisingly, Carlos made a spirited defense for continuing to use LSD and other psychedelic drugs but agreed that cocaine and heroin use had to stop. The meeting ended with the members of Santana agreeing to clean up their act.

But as the weeks and months went by, it became evident that the promise was an empty one. Especially when it came to bassist Dave Brown, whose drug use had finally come to the attention of authorities in and around San Francisco. In a short period of time, Brown had been busted a handful of times and had done light jail sentences. Relations between Carlos and Chepito Areas were also becoming more and more strained. *Santana III* sessions were regularly interrupted by screaming matches between the pair, with choice epathets making regular appearances.

The sessions themselves continued to be ragged outings, with hourslong jams that would often result in only a few bars of usable music. Carlos and Schon also were locking horns on a regular basis, with solos recorded and rerecorded when one or the other's efforts had been weak. Schon had been around Carlos for so long that he was, subconsciously, beginning to sound like him. He looked at the comparison with pride in the studio but began to bristle when he would hear those comments on the street. Adding insult to injury, he was now being corrected by his idol in the studio.

According to the band, Coke Escovedo was as disruptive in the studio as he had been on the previous

Santana tour. He fought with the rest of the band over his suggestion that the famous Tower of Power horn section be used on some of the cuts on the album. The band vehemently fought Escovedo, on the grounds "that it should always be the same six cats." Even one of *Santana III*'s best songs, "No One to Depend On," written by Carabello and Escovedo, ran afoul of Carlos's sense of outrage, at a line in the song about junkies. Carlos insisted the line be changed and eventually got his way.

Santana III was completed by the end of summer 1971. It was a powerful album, full of the fire and intensity that had made the band famous. And the reviews were almost unanimous in their praise.

Rolling Stone chimed in with, "Prior Santana albums have had some amazing things but also some downers. This LP stays there all the way."

Years later, The *Rolling Stone Record Guide* would remember *Santana III* as "the culmination of the band's early style."

But the success of *Santana III* came at a price. The members of Santana were mentally exhausted and emotionally drained. Carlos recalled his post-recording state of mind as not being good.

"All of us were fried. I had platinum albums in my

house, drugs, food, flesh, and all those kinds of things. But I felt such an emptiness. Everything felt dead to me."

It was on that pessimistic note that the band prepared to hit the road once again. But before they commenced touring, the band geared up for a bit of payback.

After a long run, Bill Graham had decided to close down the Fillmore West and its East Coast counterpart on lower Second Avenue in Manhattan. He approached Santana to close the final night. And, as always, there was a difference of opinion. Some of the band did not want to do it. Others were concerned that, since the show was going to be broadcast live, that bootleg copies of the show would circulate and take the bite out of the recently released *Santana III*.

Graham finally agreed to Santana's long list of conditions, and on that slightly overcast September evening, Santana played like a band possessed. Guitars roared in a fiery frenzy while the percussion-driven rhythm section moved like a runaway train. Santana's set segued into an all-star, all-night jam that did not break up until five the next morning.

It was fitting and more than a little ironic that the last performance at the Fillmore West would also turn out to be the last performance by the Woodstock-era Santana lineup.

In the wake of the Fillmore performance, Carlos became more reclusive and secretive. Uncharacteristically, he began skipping rehearsals for the upcoming tour and went out of his way to avoid the other band members. The rest of Santana were at a loss to explain the guitarist's strange behavior. Finally Carlos faced the band with the reason for his unexplained behavior: Michael Carabello.

"He like had this thing about me," said Carabello. "The people I hung around with, what I did, how I ran my life."

Carlos admitted that he did have an ongoing problem with Carabello. "I still don't know, deep inside me, why I felt so strongly about him being out of the band. It was our personality clashes. So I told the band, 'I'm not going out unless he's [Carabello] out.' The band chose to leave for the East Coast without me."

The band arrived in a state of total disarray. They were determined to go on without Carlos and felt that Neal Schon was more than capable of covering all Carlos's licks. The Boston show went off without a hitch but the next night, in Washington, D.C., the crowd noticed the absence of Carlos and began shouting their objections in the direction of Schon. By the end of that show, Schon was totally rattled.

With the all-important New York dates coming up, Carabello, despite vocal support from the rest of the band, saw the handwriting on the wall. Manager Stan Marcum painfully recalled the day in New York when "Carabello said, 'Well, look, if everybody is fucked up because Carlos won't play because I'm here, I'll just leave.'" Marcum, Dave Brown, and Chepito Areas immediately sided with Carabello and walked out with him.

The band would get their headstrong guitarist back, but the price was that Santana was suddenly without its entire percussion section.

Gregg Rolie was furious as he paced the New York hotel lobby. He knew Carlos was due any minute. He had had it up to here with Carlos's bullshit and disruptive influence on the band. Carlos walked through the lobby and Rolie was immediately in his face. In no uncertain terms, he told Santana what he thought of him. He also told him that he would finish the tour and then he was quitting the band.

"I'll play," he reportedly told Santana during that hotel-lobby confrontation. "But don't look at me. Don't talk to me."

The first couple of shows with Santana back in the band were nothing if not bizarre. With no percussion section, a roadie was positioned behind a set of conga drums and waved his hands over the drums during the first show. But that ploy did not fool a young conga player in the audience named Mingo Lewis. After the first show, he approached road manager Herbie Herbert, said he knew the band's entire set. Herbert gave the alleged musician four dollars' cab fare to go back to his apartment and fetch his congas. He returned, auditioned, and ended up playing the second show of the evening. Lewis would remain with the band for the rest of the tour.

The tour wound down under a cloud, and some mighty strange circumstances. During a concert in Detroit, road manager Herbie Herbert, in an attempt to lighten up the tense atmosphere, put LSD in the band members' drinks. Unfortunately, Gregg Rolie, who had never taken acid before, had a bizarre reaction in which he felt his fingers turning to rubber. The rest of the band got pleasantly stoned.

The final show for Santana was at a soccer stadium in Puerto Rico. The sense that the band was on its last legs resulted in a particularly high-profile orgy. Women were flown in from the United States. Lobsters were brought in on a daily basis. Rolie in particular was having a hard time dealing with the self-destruction of the Santana band. He was drinking a lot and brooding even more. He was ripe for an explosion.

The fuse was lit one day during their short stay in

Puerto Rico when the band was lounging around a pool. Carlos was feeling playful and began splashing his keyboard player. Rolie warned him to stop but Carlos continued to bait him. Finally Rolie leaped at Carlos, grabbed him around the neck, and pushed him underwater. Those witnessing the scene thought it was just playful roughhousing. But Rolie, in his alcohol-induced state, was trying to kill Carlos. The guitarist was struggling for breath as Rolie continued to hold his head underwater. Finally, road manager Herbert sensed that this was serious business, leaped into the pool, and pulled Rolie off Carlos.

This patchwork-quilt Santana limped through the last concert. The show was not their best. The soul of the band was gone. They returned to San Francisco where Santana officially disbanded. A lot of the rage seemed to dissipate at that point. Rolie and Schon, who were already making plans for a new musical project called Journey, made peace with Carlos to the point where they said they'd be willing to work in the studio with him again. But even Rolie's normally high sense of diplomacy could not hide his ultimate bitterness.

"Everybody had a hand in why it went by the wayside," said the candid keyboard player. "But a large part was due to Carlos's desire to be the true leader of a band that was very democratic and we didn't choose to follow."

Santana performing at the Woodstock Music Festival in Bethel, New York, August 15–17, 1969. *Credit: Archive Photos*

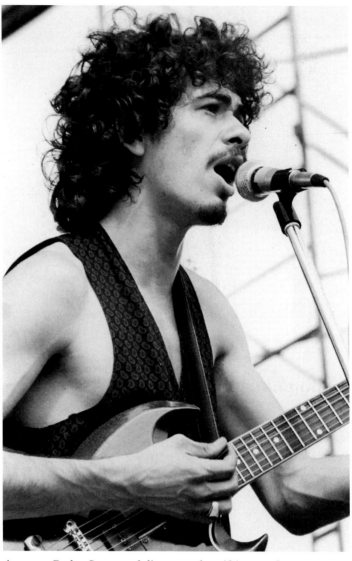

A young Carlos Santana delivers an electrifying performance at the legendary Woodstock concert in 1969. *Credit: Archive Photos*

He was born to perform and mesmerize fans with his innovative Latin blues rock riffs. *Credit: Archive Photos*

The Woodstock concert will forever remain an incredible memory for the fans who witnessed this live performance. *Credit: Archive Photos*

Carlos Santana, lead guitarist and singer of Santana in concert, Ghana.
Credit: Archive Photos

While playing the guitar, Carlos Santana lights a cigarette and creates a moody effect.
Credit: Archive Photos

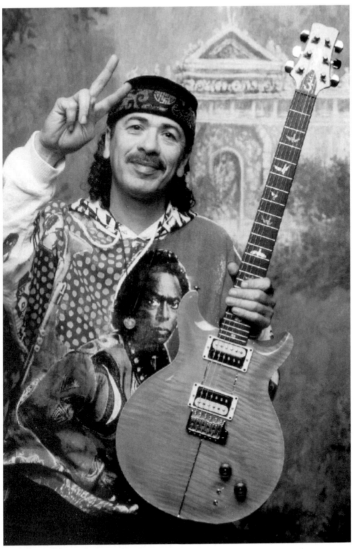

Carlos strikes a pose after he was inducted into the RockWalk along Hollywood Boulevard in 1996. The RockWalk honors the achievements of talented musicians, dedicating an area where their handprints are displayed for the viewing pleasure of fans.

Credit: Reuters/Robert Knight/Archive Photos

The legendary guitarist beams as he looks over his Century Award during the seventh annual *Billboard* Music Awards show in Las Vegas. Santana was honored for his career contributions.
Credit: Reuters/Brad Talbutt/Archive Photos

At a ceremony in Hollywood on August 17, 1998, Carlos Santana was honored with the 2,113th star on the Walk of Fame. Carlos proudly poses with actor Edward James Olmos.
Credit: Reuters/Rose Prouser/Archive Photos

Nominated for ten Grammy awards, he brought down the house performing his hit single, "Smooth" during the 42nd annual Grammy Awards in Los Angeles on February 23, 2000. Carlos Santana walked away with eight Grammies that night and was hailed as the indisputable king of rock guitar. *Credit: Reuters/Staff/ Archive Photos*

Thirty years later, Carlos proves he still has what it takes to give an explosive performance. He performs a number from his phenomenal album, *Supernatural*, while on tour in Mexico City on December 10, 1999. *Credit: Reuters/Daniel Aguilar/Archive Photos*

Over 10,000 people attended the rock legend's second appearance in twenty-five years in Zagreb on October 19, 1999. Needless to say, Carlos did not disappoint! *Credit: Reuters/Hrvoje Polan/Archive Photos*

Despite the fact that he essentially came into the band at the end, Neal Schon also was disappointed at the demise of Santana.

"When Carlos and I first got together, we were really tight and we sounded that way on record," reflected Schon on his departure. "But, after a while, it got to be a constant battle onstage. It was a drag so I decided to split."

Schon's sentiments were pretty much echoed by the rest of the band. When the dust cleared, they saw the rise and fall of the Santana band as the classic rock-and-roll cautionary tale: Too much, too soon. And at this juncture, the band members were ready to rest or try other things.

For, as they would find out in the weeks and months that followed, Carlos was not the only one being lauded for his musicianship. Almost the entire Santana lineup would go on to have long and widely diverse careers in music. Michael Shrieve, who left Santana and spent the ensuing years in a number of experimental music situations, including the progressive percussion group Go, would ultimately look back on his days with Santana as a positive experience. "All in all, it was a good learning experience and a good foundation," he has offered. "I was glad to be where I was."

Carlos remained reflective in the wake of the death of the first incarnation of Santana. He put the blame squarely on drug use and the overindulgence of every vice. And Carlos did not excuse himself from blame. He would cite his ego as a contributing factor in the breakup.

"I think it's what happens in most bands. If you've played out everything you can play with that particular band, you need to let those people go so you can grow musically and spiritually."

6

Quiet Cool

Carlos Santana was not in a rush to get back to work. In the aftermath of the breakup of the original Santana band, the normally assured, upbeat musician was turning inward. He was feeling many emotions. There was guilt for his complicity in the breakup of the band . . . anger at the cost of shattered friendships . . . disappointment at the potential for great music that would now never be realized.

A lot had changed in the past three years with the Santana band. He had gone from being an unknown to being part of one of the most popular bands in the

131

world. He had tasted success and then watched as that taste went sour. Breaking up the Santana band was like leaving a woman he had once loved, and, in a sense, still did.

Nobody would blame him if he took some time off and just did nothing. But while his body was at rest, his mind was in turmoil.

"All of a sudden playing pop music seemed strange," he remembered of the beginning of his spiritual journey. "All the pop guys, like Jimi [Hendrix], Janis [Joplin], and Jim Morrison, were dying left and right. It seemed to me that you either snorted cocaine and shot heroin or you folded your hands and thanked God. But I couldn't see myself in the streets, looking for someone to give me my fix."

He also began to look at his place in the whole so-called San Francisco scene. It had been fun. But ultimately the fun had turned to disappointment. "I never really felt a part of that whole San Francisco thing. I didn't really get along with a lot of the local bands like the Grateful Dead. I never saw myself as a rock star so I guess I just never saw myself as part of that scene." He began to feel estranged.

Carlos was very much in a quandary on the question of freedom versus discipline. Born a Catholic, the musician had—even during his most heathen days with Santana—never completely shaken the hold religion had on him. Now, as he looked at life, for the first time in years, religion was suddenly very much on his mind.

Years later Carlos would concede that his early 1970s religious turn must have sounded pious and pompous, given the years of debauchery he had just come through. But he was not playing games when it came to his spiritual journey. Turning to God was serious business.

"I felt I needed spiritual discipline because everybody around me was being consumed by overindulgence. I hate the idea of discipline but I also love it."

One thing he was certain of—he could not see himself becoming a parody of himself, turning out variations on the first three Santana albums just for the money. This conviction was fed by the comments he heard in the weeks following the breakup. More than one person indicated that he had been the true star of the band, and that a group of faceless sidemen was all he needed to continue the ride. But Carlos would not consider it.

Following the breakup of Santana, Carlos delved deeper into the meditative arts and began listening more and more to the likes of jazz greats Miles Davis and John Coltrane. Spiritually and musically, he saw himself, in the ensuing months, taking the first tentative steps toward a new musical direction.

As he was prone to do before a big tour, Carlos was now making regular visits to his local record store. However, these days, he was more likely to be found browsing in the jazz, classical, and religious sections than in his normal stomping grounds: rock, soul, and blues. He would sit for hours in solitude, listening to music that was putting his head in a different space. A change was definitely coming.

There was the expected, immediate panic at the breakup of the band from forces in the corporate world. Tours had been planned. Records had to be made. Contracts had to be honored. But the record-company executives cynically decided the only one they had to be concerned about was Carlos, and that sidemen were a dime a dozen.

Fortunately there was no urgency for Carlos in keeping his name in the public eye. *Santana III* continued to be a durable album, and subsequent singles, "Everybody's Everything" and "No One to Depend On," had reached high on the national charts. *Rolling Stone* continued to be critically supportive when it offered, "This is music to dance to but it is music that shrieks for more advanced, dexterous and imaginative dancing than some of the freeform body motion that rock dancing has accepted."

Santana, in the meantime, was looking to keep busy

and for something stress-free to take the edge off. He found that in the guise of drummer Buddy Miles.

Miles, who had spent time with fellow San Franciscans the Electric Flag, as well as a stint with Jimi Hendrix in his Band of Gypsies period, and who was currently fronting the Buddy Miles Express, was of like mind and temperament to Carlos. The duo, along with Neal Schon, hooked up and did some informal jamming which turned into a punchy set of their respective greatest hits mixed with a sprinkling of new material that borrowed liberally from funk and soul music.

In summer 1972 the duo agreed to take an offer to do a series of dates that included a live show at Hawaii's Diamond Head volcano. The show was recorded and released as *Live Carlos Santana*. The critics were dismissive of the effort, and the album barely cracked the Top 100, but a medley single, "Evil Ways" / "Them Changes," managed a Top Ten birth. Carlos was happy. Schon, ever the perfectionist, almost immediately disowned the album, citing it as "a total flop."

This mainstream side trip was soon brushed aside as Santana began putting his new musical vision into motion. Initially he turned to drummer Michael

Shrieve, who had remained friendly amid the breakup and whose growing interest in Eastern religions put him on the same wavelength as Carlos. Gregg Rolie and Neal Schon, despite being busy with Journey, agreed to come in and add keyboard and guitar parts to the album. Carlos rounded out his studio band with old Santana touring hands Doug Rauch, Rich Kermode, Tom Koster, and Armando Peraza, and entered the studio to lay down the tracks for the album *Caravanserai*.

The *Caravanserai* sessions were a return to a more relaxed mood for Carlos. It was his album, and while he was open to suggestions, the unspoken agreement was that he was the boss. But he was a boss who was, admittedly, feeling insecure. "I was moving into the unknown. I couldn't read music and I was working with advanced musicians who were well into jazz."

What Carlos found, however, was that these "advanced musicians" were highly respectful of his musical stance and his willingness to push the envelope. In turn, they were patient teachers, answering Carlos's seemingly endless questions and showing him how to bring his musical vision to light.

"Gregg Rolie and Neal Schon already had their eyes to do Journey and so they basically showed up, played their parts and split," recalled Carlos of the sessions.

"So it was Michael Shrieve and I who produced and nurtured that vision together."

And it was a vision that was very much in transition. Carlos seemed reluctant to totally leave behind the raw aspects of the first three albums. But, as the music came together in the studio, it also became apparent that there was room in his music for soft, subtle moments. There was a definite spiritual air to some of the songs. Carlos's guitar was not so much screaming as it was soaring. The vibe was more contemplative than danceable.

"I have a feeling that it is important to transcend every time you wake up," explained Carlos of his new musical moves on *Caravanserai*. "If you listen to *Caravanserai*, you can hear all kinds of things because we were listening to everything at the time."

News of the *Caravanserai* sessions and of Carlos's new direction had made its way to the corporate towers at Columbia, and to its president, Clive Davis. Davis was notorious for leaving his musicians alone to do their thing. However, he was concerned at reports that *Caravanserai* was so totally unlike the first three Santana albums, that nobody who had lived and died by the old sound would be interested in it. Davis had to see for himself, and so—at some point in the mixing of the album—he went down to the studio to listen for himself. He was not thrilled at what he heard and soon there was a tense confrontation between Carlos and himself.

Santana remembered the meeting with some sadness. "He [Clive Davis] was saying that 'there's only one Weather Report and there's only one Miles [Davis] and you guys should just stick to this.' And I said, 'Well, man, thanks for taking the time and coming over, but you said what you have to say and now we're going to do what we have to do.' "

Clive Davis was not a happy man when he left the studio. But there was not much else he could do.

Caravanserai was not an easy album to get into. It was understated in a very jazzy way, and miles removed from the trademark rock-and-roll roar of Santana's first three albums. But Carlos, in the first of many cosmic pronouncements in defense of his creation, exclaimed, "With *Caravanserai* people will discover the inner love that dwells in the center of their hearts."

This was not what a lot of industry people were hoping to hear. There was a bottom line to consider, and *Caravanserai* did not sound like something that was going to swell bank balances at the corporate level.

In particular, Clive Davis was on the horns of a dilemma in regards to Carlos's latest effort. The head of Columbia Records had developed a father-son type

of relationship with Carlos over the life of the first Santana band and he wanted to be supportive in the face
of Carlos's change of musical direction.

Carlos recalled how they finally agreed to disagree.
"At that point I did not care about hits. Mr. Clive Davis
warned me, he would say I was committing career suicide. And I said, 'Thanks for telling me. I actually
know that you're saying this from your heart. But I've
got to do this.' "

Caravanserai was released late in 1972 and, true to
Carlos's new anti-commercial attitude, the record
spawned no hit singles. In fact, even the most progressive jazz stations were hard-pressed to find a single
track that would fit in with their format. But record
buyers flocked to Carlos's new musical direction and
ultimately catapulted *Caravanserai* to number 8 on the
national album charts.

Rolling Stone weighed in with positive notices when it
said, "Carlos need never play another note to rank as
one of the most satisfyingly beautiful players of his
instrument, charming and moving melodic lines as
the music swells and climaxes to swell again."

Carlos Santana toured behind the album and was
encouraged by the fact that he could still fill concert
arenas and gather rave reviews with a concert set that

paid only limited attention to the material from the first three Santana albums.

Professionally, he seemed relaxed and fulfilled. Personally, he was in the dumps. He still savored his adoring female fans but the momentary sexual highs were fleeting and ultimately unfulfilling.

Carlos, in his private moments, would often lament the lack of a personal relationship. "The more successful you are, the more lonely it gets. When you see people coming and approaching you, you know they're approaching you with different intentions than someone who knows you. It becomes a weird loneliness and so you crave to be ordinary."

Santana salved his loneliness in a rush of creative and spiritual pursuits. Once again he agreed to appear on another artist's album, *Stories to Tell*, by jazz musician Flora Purim. This session, with its progressive Latin staging point, allowed Carlos to experience his first taste of music that truly challenged him, given his new spiritual direction. And he liked the feeling.

In 1973, while in New York, Carlos went to a club called Slug's, where pioneering jazz guitarist John McLaughlin was performing. Santana had long been an admirer of the guitarist's spacey, progressive style of playing with the Mahavishnu Orchestra, and Carlos sat riveted as McLaughlin created unorthodox melodies and complex chord progressions. It was safe to say that nothing had prepared Carlos for the aural experience of hearing McLaughlin live.

"It was actually scary to walk in and hear John McLaughlin playing," he reminisced. "I have yet to see anybody create that kind of total assault on the senses."

Santana introduced himself to McLaughlin after the show. The pair hit it off immediately. McLaughlin was a beacon for Santana. Musically he was exploring places and feelings that Carlos could only dream about at that moment. Carlos admitted being intimidated by the guitarist. But he was also excited at the opportunity to learn new things. They began hanging out together and throwing musical ideas at each other with reckless abandon.

The friendship eventually turned to the question of belief. Carlos expressed his interest in Eastern religions and his growing adherence to the meditative aspects of the religion Paramahansa Yogananda. McLaughlin, in turn, mesmerized him with his own spiritual turn in the direction of a religious way of believing headed up by the Indian leader Sri Chinmoy. Pete Townshend of The Who, was also a devoted follower of Sri Chinmoy. Through McLaughlin, Carlos met others into the teachings of Sri Chinmoy—including jazz musician Larry Coryell, who would open Carlos's mind during subsequent visits to Carlos's home.

"He would go to his room and meditate and he had a picture of Sri Chinmoy with him. The first time I saw it, I was really afraid of it because I believed, to a certain extent, that Jesus is my guru. But Larry showed me Sri Chinmoy and where he was coming from and I started to realize that everybody imitates everybody."

It was at this point in Carlos's religious search that he met his soul mate.

"Somebody invited me to go see Tower of Power and the Loading Zone at the Marin Civic Center. I went there and that's where I saw Deborah. I was captivated. I looked in her eyes and I knew it was the end of my bachelor thing."

Deborah King was a bright, assured, attractive woman with soft features who carried herself with an air of grace. It was easy to see why Carlos was smitten. Deborah, standing across the room, was also interested. The first thing she noticed was his soulful eyes. Then she took in his skinny frame and long hair. But there was also something else, an aura of softness and tenderness that was unlike the macho men she had crossed paths with in her life.

Deborah was attracted to Santana but, aware of his celebrity status and his rumored reputation as a womanizer, she was cautious. They talked easily that first night. She was a fan of music. She was spiritual. Carlos was nervous, feeling like a young boy with his first crush. One thing they both sensed was sincerity.

That first conversation ended with Carlos asking her out. Their first date was at a vegetarian restaurant. There was no second date—at least not at first.

"I started going to other shows," recalled Santana, "and I would see her there. We would go home together. Soon we were living together."

The relationship progressed rapidly. Both felt real love for the first time. After a whirlwind romance, Carlos and Deborah married in April 1973. Always one for wearing his heart on his sleeve, Carlos recalled that, the first time she came to his house, "She smelled like something I wanted to wake up next to for the rest of my life."

Theirs was an evolving relationship that, in the beginning, was very much self-oriented. But in short order, their relationship became one of feeling for and reaching out to the needs of the other.

One of the more binding elements of their relationship was a strong religious belief. Both were Catholic by birth but, as they delved further and further into meditation and the teachings of Sri Chinmoy, they found themselves pulling away from traditional beliefs.

"It was all because my wife and I were disenchanted

with the Catholic thing and we were looking for some Eastern spiritual values. Anything that didn't deal with condemning and judging. Catholics were a lot into that. We were more into perceiving and embracing our totality as individuals."

The couple, with the guidance of McLaughlin and others, soon became total devotees to Sri Chinmoy and his teachings. Carlos came away from a personal meeting with the Indian guru with renewed faith and a new spiritual name, Devadip, which means "the eye, the lamp, and the light of God." Carlos was convinced that his newfound religion was the right path. He felt he was being helped a lot in terms of self-trust and self-discipline. He felt it was a necessary step to help him focus his life and his music.

"At the time I got into Sri Chinmoy, everyone was dying, and I felt it was either put the junk in my veins or fold my hands and give myself to the Lord. I never wanted to be a casualty. I didn't want to be a loser. For a long time I was afraid that I wasn't strong enough to shake off the road that was booze and drugs. But with Sri Chinmoy I saw a very simple clarity."

The transformation continued as Carlos became obsessed with learning everything he could about the history and requirements of this religion. Carlos cut his long hair conservatively short and, according to the teachings of Sri Chinmoy, began wearing all-white clothing. He was also spending more and more time with John McLaughlin and found himself pulled deeper into the finer points of the fusion-jazz movement.

McLaughlin, who had traveled a similar path to spiritual enlightenment, embraced Carlos as only a brother would. "We're closer than brothers," he once said. "He has so many divine qualities in his life. He's so lyrical and so pure."

Carlos felt the same way. "My brother John McLaughlin was very gracious in pulling me out of the three-chord songs and into things like John Coltrane's 'A Love Supreme' and 'Naima.' Through meditating I'm beginning to have the confidence in knowing which way to channel my energy."

Musically, Santana was excited about what he perceived as his new musical possibilities but with cautions about going in too esoteric a direction continuing to rain down from the corporate tower—he chose to begin his new musical life in collaboration with McLaughlin on an all-instrumental album called *Love Devotion Surrender.*

The album was a total departure from the raw rock side; subtle melodies and an introspective outlook were moving Carlos more and more into the unexplored world of jazz. Carlos was in a state of grace during those sessions. He would sit for hours, enthralled at the new ways to play that McLaughlin was teaching him. Raw power had given way to light, undulating passages. Heavy rhythms were being replaced by smooth, measured patterns. While nobody would admit it, the feeling was that Carlos's newfound faith was present in every groove.

"It was really intimidating," reflected Carlos of the first time he played with McLaughlin in the studio. "It was like a turtle playing with a hummingbird."

And that uneasiness persisted during the early days of a series of concert dates the guitar duo did in support of the album. "By the third concert on the tour that John and I did together, I realized that, if I got my tone together, my phrasing and whatever musical vocabulary I do have, that I'd be all right."

Flush with the creative energy he had derived from recording *Love Devotion Surrender*, Carlos immediately plunged into his own album. It became evident during the sessions for *Welcome* that, musically, Carlos was on the move.

There were still remnants of Santana's raucous days but, from the song selection to the choice of players, Carlos was going for a much more hybrid sound that incorporated the old Santana with a more jazz-oriented, new strain of music. The musician was very much a serene presence during the recording of *Welcome*, playing leads and subtle melodies with a seeming enlightened sense of touch and feel.

He would often look skyward when laying down his soulful runs. Even the most cynical musicians involved in recording *Welcome* had to admit that Carlos was getting divine inspiration from somewhere. There was quiet confidence, but also twinges of doubt that Santana was capable of taking his music and his life to the next level.

"The most important thing for me is to be able to relax with the other players and listen myself into a state where we can get to a higher understanding of peace, joy, and love."

Carlos's cosmic pronouncements were becoming more frequent. He was exhibiting the traits of the recently converted. And his zealousness had many people concerned.

The press had quickly picked up on his life changes and were, in many cases, making fun of it. "It's always, 'This dumb Mexican discovers God,'" Santana ruefully explained, of the often brutal press he was getting at the time. Consequently, record-company executives held their breath as *Love Devotion Surrender* and then *Welcome* were released, scant months apart, in summer and fall of 1973.

The summer 1973 tour turned out to be a mixed

blessing for Carlos. The music had been well received, but he was uncomfortable with the fact that his all-star touring band—Billy Cobham, Larry Young, and an old Santana band alum, Doug Rauch—did not seem to share his enthusiasm for his new music and his new life. To his way of thinking, the music was coming across as dispirited and disjointed.

Looking to ease his disappointment after what he perceived as another soulless gig in Seattle, Carlos dropped by a local club after the show, where his old Haight-Ashbury buddy Elvin Bishop was playing. Carlos was amazed at the truly free jazz-blues riffs his friend was laying down. He could not only sense that the music was out there, but that the band was actually having fun on the stage.

When Bishop spotted Carlos in the audience and invited him onstage, Carlos did the most spontaneous thing he had done in two years, and joined him. Carlos and Bishop jammed for what seemed like hours. At one point, Carlos even started to dance. By the end of the evening, Carlos had received a wake-up call: He had been reminded that playing music can be fun.

Not surprisingly, *Love Devotion Surrender* appealed to McLaughlin and the whole Mahavishnu Orchestra crowd. But Carlos was thrilled when feedback indicated this his old Santana fans were finding much to like in the music as well. The record *Love Devotion and*

Surrender would top out at number 14 on the national album charts. *Welcome* duplicated the previous Santana record's success, reaching number 25 on the charts despite being the first Santana album that did not spin out at least one commercial single.

Santana, with what seemed like a constantly rotating group of musicians, once again hit the road. The majority of the set contained samplings of *Caravanserai, Love Devotion Surrender,* and *Welcome*. But a smile inevitably came to Carlos's face when he would lapse into "Jingo" or "Oye Como Va" and watch as the still-very-much-rock-and-roll crowd went nuts. For Carlos, there was still a lot of pleasure in looking back . . . even if it was only for a few moments.

The year 1974 began quietly for Carlos Santana. By now deeply into the religion of Sri Chinmoy, Santana/Devadip and Deborah, who had taken on the name Urmila, were totally immersed in the regimen. But for Carlos, it was occasionally annoying. "Cut your hair, no drugs, total vegetarian. Five o'clock in the morning, meditating every day. It was like the West Point approach to spirituality."

When Santana toured these days, his new religion and his devotion to Sri Chinmoy were a part of his performance. He would meditate behind closed doors for fifteen minutes prior to going onstage, and Sri Chinmoy's meditations would often turn up at various points in Santana's concerts as introductions to songs, and, to Carlos's frustration, would often be credited to him in reviews.

Santana's relentless curiosity and excitement surrounding the possibilities of jazz-fusion and world music had not dimmed after the release of *Love Devotion Surrender* and *Welcome.* Far from getting it out of his system, as many cynics had predicted would happen, the experience of working with John McLaughlin had only whet his appetite to explore further.

"Once I got the craving of playing with another guitarist [John McLaughlin] out of the way, I wanted to learn why I was so fascinated with John Coltrane and that sky-church music of his."

His search for continued inspiration and guidance landed at the feet of another Sri Chinmoy disciple, Alice Coltrane, the widow of John. She skillfully played the harp and keyboard and was a noted musician in her own right. The result of their collaboration was an all-instrumental album called *Illuminations,* a progressive foray into the outer reaches of improvisation that moved Carlos Santana even farther away from the commercial world.

In a sense, Carlos was once again the child during the recording of *Illuminations.* He would always be after Alice to tell him stories about her husband John. And Carlos was at all times respectful of the talents of the musicians he was playing with.

With his creative juices flowing, Santana took the rest of the year off and went into the studio once again. The sessions for *Borboletta* were an exciting time for Carlos. Word of his musical worldview had spread throughout the jazz and fusion community and so he was thrilled when jazz greats Stanley Clarke, Airto Moriera, and Flora Purim rang him up with offers to help out on the disc. While it was much more accessible than *Illusions, Borboletta* was still very much a progressive jazz album, although its songs tended to race and jump rather than meander.

Fall of 1974 was shaping up to be a true test of how Santana's musical changes were resonating with the public. There was both excitement and concern when *Santana's Greatest Hits*—essentially a repackaging of the best of the old Santana band's first three albums—was released and immediately raced into the Top Twenty. This was an album that was preaching to the choir, and not a true indicator of how well Santana's new direction was sitting with the fans.

Illuminations came out a month later, and the difference in response was immediate. The album received sporadic notices overseas, and decent reviews State-side, but the lack of commercial appeal was evident when the album failed to chart on the national pop charts. *Borboletta* arrived in time for Christmas, and record-company executives heaved a sigh of relief when the more upbeat disc crashed the Top Twenty despite the lack of a commercial single.

Q magazine praised the album as "a scorcher": "*Borboletta* is more space for Santana to strut his stuff and achieve white heat."

The commercial success of *Borboletta*, and the critical praise heaped on *Illuminations*, was important to Carlos. He was very consciously attempting to put some distance between the Santana of old and the Santana of now. He reasoned that the split would not be complete until a *Borboletta* duplicated the success of an *Abraxas*.

By 1975 Carlos Santana had fallen into a nice but predictable routine. His albums were all selling gold and his tours—with old Santana songs barely hanging on against the onslaught of the spacier new music—continued to sell out. Carlos again turned his attention to an outside project, offering his guitar services, in the name of spiritual jazz, to musician Narada Michael Walden on his album *Garden of Love Light*.

But there was some tension beneath the good times. There was the cold, hard business side of music that Carlos still had to deal with. He dealt with things like money, contracts, and tours in what he thought of as an enlightened manner. However, Carlos was smart enough to realize that he needed a smart and—yes—a tough business hand to guide his career if he was going to advance to what he perceived as the next level.

Once again he turned to Bill Graham.

The feeling-out process was cordial but tentative. The pair had remained in contact over the past years and each considered the other a friend. But, for Graham, there were the hard feelings of the past to deal with and, hopefully, put behind him before he would agree to become Santana's manager. Carlos could do nothing more than apologize. That was enough for Graham, who officially became Santana's manager in June 1975.

Carlos knew that in Bill Graham he had a manager who would not pull any punches, and it was not long before Graham delivered his first right hook. In no uncertain terms, he told Santana that his progressive jazz albums, while selling well, were not producing the numbers that the earlier Latin-rock albums had. He added that, while his progressive spiritual music was fine for solo recordings, he should seriously think about downplaying those elements and returning the Santana band albums and tours to their rockier roots: the hot, sweaty stuff that everybody seemed to like so much better than the religious stuff.

Carlos did not like what Graham was saying. But he had to agree that his new manager made sense. "I have to be realistic," said Carlos in response to Graham's strong suggestions. "People like myself don't go out much. But kids go out and they have this tremendous energy. They are the people I like to play to."

Graham's words took on even more meaning when a long, import-only, three-record live set called *Lotus* (which had been available only in Japan) appeared in the U.S. but failed to chart. The album was considered very good but was also very expensive, and there was a limit to what U.S. record buyers would shell out, even for a Santana set. Many in the industry reasoned that the bottom line was that Carlos's new material was not worth the high price but that a similar package of the old Santana music probably would have done quite well.

Carlos took the failure of *Lotus* a lot harder than anybody expected him to. He made some attempts to defend the album, pointing to the price, and the fact that the album had been available for a long time as an import, as the reasons for the less-than-stellar performance. Once again Graham's admonishment to rock things up was ringing in Carlos's ears; the guitarist hated to admit it, but "I realized I had gotten too far away from my own roots. I was lost."

Graham kept at Carlos to lighten up musically. Rare was the meeting where the manager did not show up with a stack of Tito Puente or other danceable Latin records from his private collection. Carlos would sit and listen and, already a fan of this kind of music, found little he could argue with. He knew he could do this stuff. It was just a matter of fitting it into his new way of thinking and playing.

Graham also suggested that Carlos go with an outside producer on his next album. Carlos took the suggestion seriously but his heart skipped a beat when Graham suggested David Rubinson for the job.

He did not have to jog his memory to recall the disastrous Los Angeles sessions with Rubinson. But Graham insisted that time passes, people change, and that the producer was a different person now than he was then. Never one to carry a grudge, Carlos finally agreed to sit down with the producer and just talk. During this conversation, Rubinson conceded that he could have been more tolerant of the band during those early sessions, and assured the musician that he had grown in his ability to communicate with musicians. Carlos, in the spirit of his newfound faith, sensed that Rubinson was sincere, and agreed to work with him again.

Rubinson echoed Graham's suggestion that, in the guise of Santana, his fans were looking for a more basic, danceable sound than he was offering as Devadip. However, Rubinson was equally insistent that the musician would not have to sacrifice his more spiritual direction in order to make that happen.

One of the producer's first suggestions was that Carlos temporarily put aside his highbrow listening habits and tune in to the world of Top 40 for an education on what was selling and being heard in the commercial world. It was not easy task for Carlos's sensitive ears. Many times he was tempted to turn the radio knob in the face of what he deemed was "garbage" coming out of the speakers. But Rubinson insisted that his charge need only absorb the music and not be critical. Carlos followed his advice and soon, often grudgingly, was finding things he liked.

In this reintroduction to pop, Carlos would mentally erase the words and concentrate on the music and, in particular, on the melodies. This approach made reeducating himself a lot easier, and in fact he did come away with bits and pieces of music and stylings he felt would help him in the studio.

Carlos returned to the studio in 1976, and to his Latin roots, for the recording of *Amigos*. For Carlos, it was fun playing more rock-oriented tunes for the first time in several years, and the musicians he had assembled for this obviously commercial effort carried a less spiritual, more fun-loving attitude that part of his psyche still craved.

"I was trying to find my place in the sound at that time," he recalled of the *Amigos* experience. "What I did was open up all the windows and doors. I let a lot of people infiltrate with their ideas. It was a period of being very naive and the handing over of a lot of things to other people."

But there were struggles as well. Ever the perfectionist, Carlos would often roll his eyes and look skyward for guidance when the music for a particular song seemed almost too simple to be bothered with. Producer Rubinson sensed that this was not Carlos's cup of tea, and constantly encouraged him, telling him the music he was making was good and nothing to be ashamed of. Still, recording *Amigos* was an emotional challenge because the guitarist had to admit that the music of *Amigos* was not as meaningful to him.

He saw himself as a musical Jekyll and Hyde. As the

mild-mannered Devadip, he was the creator of moods and of extended long-form musical expressions. When he was Carlos Santana, his soul craved dance music and songs.

"Santana is my nose, Devadip is my heart," he explained in cosmic tones. "My nose is still important because it's part of me. But what's important is my heart."

Amigos turned out to be a turnaround. The record did respectable, if not quite superstar-caliber, business, and the reviewers wisely picked up on the fact that, musically, Carlos still knew how to play the stuff that had made him popular in the first place.

What also turned out to be important for Carlos throughout 1976 was charitable good works. As early as the late 1960s Carlos always had been available to perform free for what he considered a good purpose. It was not uncommon for people to knock on his door or call him up at three in the morning to ask him to play for a myriad of causes. Given his new religious turn, Santana was now even more willing to help out if the cause seemed right.

In 1973, he had joined the Rolling Stones in Los Angeles for a concert to benefit Nicaraguan earthquake victims. Carlos became interested the plight of boxer Rubin "Hurricane" Carter, who was reportedly doing time for a crime he did not commit, and so when Bob Dylan and his Rolling Thunder Revue agreed to do a benefit concert for Carter in the Houston Texas Astrodome, Santana was there. Carlos saw it as part of his karma to do good works with his music, but also, from a purely selfish point of view, the opportunity to play with the likes of Dylan and Stephen Stills was too good to pass up. For Carlos, it was a glorious night in which good intentions and good music carried the day.

Touring heavily, especially on what he considered the rock-and-roll circuit, continued through 1976. There was no great financial incentive to be on the road. Once all the financial mismanagement from the old Santana days had been straightened out, Carlos had surrounded himself with sound advisors and had invested his money wisely. No, the guitarist was touring simply because he loved playing live.

He appeared as a headliner for most of that year's U.S. dates and joined some buddies from his Haight-Ashbury days, the Grateful Dead and the New Riders of the Purple Sage, for shows in London. The shows were standing-room-only. The reviews were uniformly positive. Once again Carlos Santana was in an area he felt he could control.

The late 1970s were conspicuous in their consistency. Santana released two albums in 1977, *Festival* and the live album *Moonflower*. *Festival*, following in the footsteps of *Amigos*, was again a more commercial, pop-oriented effort. This time around, Carlos seemed more comfortable with the notion of creating radio-friendly music. He smiled more and seemed intent on blurring the lines between spiritual leanings and commercial reality.

Festival reached a respectable number 27 on the album charts and, more importantly, spun off Carlos's first chart single since 1973, a cover of the old Zombies hit "She's Not There." *Moonflower*, a double live collection of some of Carlos's best concert moments over the past few years, crashed the Top Ten.

The reviewer for *Q* magazine gave *Moonflower* four out of five stars, saying, "The hits sound as joyful as ever and the carnival spirit fuses both live and studio cuts into one seamless whole."

Throughout 1977 and into 1978, Santana continued to tour and, thanks to the success of *Amigos* and *Festival*, began playing bigger venues on both sides of the Atlantic. He continued his charitable good works when he joined Joan Baez and a host of other politically-minded performers in a free concert for prisoners' rights at California's notorious Soledad Prison. At the other end of the spectrum, he cashed in as part of the monster hard-rock show California Jam II held in Orange County, CA, in a field in front of an estimated 250,000 people.

And when there was time, he guested on the albums by the rock group Giants, jazz great Gato Barbieri, and his spiritual and musical brother John McLaughlin, on the album *Electric Guitarist*.

But while each Santana record almost automatically went gold, there were signs, by the tail end of the 1970s, that Carlos Santana was slowly but surely falling out of favor with his audience. This was evidenced by the fact that the more commercially-oriented *Inner Secrets* struggled to peak at number 27 on the charts, while the first single off the album, a cover of the Buddy Holly classic "Well All Right," stalled at number 69. A second single off *Inner Secrets*, a cover of the old Classics IV hit "Stormy," made it only to number 32 before beginning a quick descent early in 1979.

Both Santana's record company and Bill Graham were concerned. They did not doubt that Carlos was putting out first-rate material. What they agreed on was that the audience for Santana records was dropping out fast. And the only reason they could put their finger on was the fact that musical styles were changing at a rapid pace. Carlos had done well to survive the last gasp of the psychedelic scene, and his myriad musical influences had helped him craft music that had proved a strong counterpoint to the vapid disco scene of the 1970s. But the return of hard rock and heavy metal, coupled with the rise of the punk-rock movement, was pointing toward a coming decade when truly cerebral music would seem to be taking a backseat. Music-industry insiders expressed concern that what was happening to Carlos Santana, was happening to all the so-called graybeards; their audience had peaked, and while they might hang on with a core group of fans, the chances of capturing enough of the current crop of teens to return to the top of the charts was highly unlikely.

Early in 1979, Santana once again donned the mantle of Devadip, with the album *Oneness / Silver Dreams–Golden Reality*. The album—half new studio material and half live material from a concert in Japan—was a welcome return to Carlos's spiritual comfort zone. He felt that his time with the old Santana sound had primed the pump for the acceptance of his preferred form of music.

Unfortunately, *Oneness / Silver Dreams–Golden Reality* made a little noise in Europe but did not chart in America. In the meantime, a third desperate attempt at spinning a single out of the doomed *Inner Secrets* album—yet another cover, of a marginal hit by the Four Tops, "One Chain (Don't Make No Prison)"— could do no better than number 59. During this period Carlos also made the time to once again offer his musical support to the spiritually-minded Narada Michael Walden on his album *Awakening*.

On the surface, Carlos was unfazed by the seeming dip in his musical fortunes. He considered it merely a temporary drop-off that would soon begin to climb. But at home, Deborah was noticing something about her husband she had not noticed before. Carlos was suddenly more quiet and sullen than usual.

She also noticed something much worse. Carlos Santana was getting angry.

7

Lost in the '80s

The anger was coming from a lot of places. First and foremost was the never-ending struggle between the musical identities of Santana and Devadip, and the pressure he felt for both elements of his personality to do well.

"For a long time, I felt I was at war," he reflected, on the duality of his musical being. "The Santana thing was on one side and the Devadip thing was on the other. I was feeling that if the Santana albums didn't do well, then I would not be able to do Devadip albums and get to play with real cool people."

Truth be told, the opportunity to play with "cool people" had never been a problem. The guitarist's growing notoriety in jazz and world-music circles made him a natural choice for artists wanting to add a bit of "hot" to their albums. In 1980, while struggling with his musical identity, Carlos found time to deliver the goods on solo albums by yet another Haight-Ashbury alum (and former Steve Miller Band member), Boz Scaggs, and out-there jazz-fusion giant Herbie Hancock.

The duality of those outside projects was not lost on him. With Scaggs, Carlos found the opportunity to get back into a structured funky blues area that he still found enriching. On Hancock's album, all bets were off as the free-flowing, progressive nature of the music allowed him to fly in a more free-form setting.

Another problem Carlos struggled with was his growing discomfort with the teachings of Sri Chinmoy. Like a kid with a new toy, Carlos had jumped headfirst into the guru's teachings, but over the years, he had begun to shy away from certain elements of the teachings.

"My time with Sri Chinmoy gave me some discipline and an awareness of Eastern philosophy," he offered in defense of his involvement. "But, after a while, I began to look at it like my old tennis shoes from Mission High School that didn't fit me anymore."

Adding to Santana's inner conflicts was Deborah's announcement that she was pregnant with their first child. Santana was thrilled at the prospect of being a father but, like all fathers, the sudden specter of another mouth to feed and the added responsibility began to weigh on him. He felt he had to do whatever it took to provide for his growing family. For Carlos, that translated into *compromise*. The highly spiritual man began to reason that Devadip might have to take a backseat to the more commercially viable Santana.

For Carlos, the struggle would continue on many fronts. He continued to hang on to what he perceived as the better aspects of the Sri Chinmoy's religion. He thought that without his spiritual guide, he might slip back into old, self-destructive habits. He remained adamant that there was a lot in the spiritual path he had chosen that made him a better person and a better servant to God. Finally, he maintained that the world of Sri Chinmoy was a world where he felt at peace. But to those in his inner, circle, the proclamations began to sound a little hollow.

All these conflicts did not stop Carlos from exercising both of his creative sides in 1980. The more old-school Santana album *Marathon* did typical Santana business as it rose to number 25 on the album charts. Unfortunately, two singles from the album, "You Know that I Love You" and "All I Ever Wanted," finished well out of the Top Twenty and received almost no radio play.

In the guise of Devadip, he entered the studio with renowned jazz players such as Herbie Hancock, Ron Carter, and Wayne Shorter, and emerged with an all-instrumental double album called *The Swing of Delight*. The recording experience was a wonderful time for Carlos. Playing his kind of music with many of the people he considered both his peers and friends was a pleasure. He reasoned that if the vibe in the studio was any indication, *The Swing of Delight* most certainly would be a successful album. Unfortunately, the album, while receiving good notices from the jazz and progressive press was, not unexpectedly, totally ignored by everybody else. Consequently, *The Swing of Delight* topped out at number 75, with an anchor.

There was frustration in every corner of the Santana camp. Carlos was making some of the best music of his career, and yet could not produce a Top Ten hit.

Santana's growing dissatisfaction with Sri Chinmoy finally reached critical mass in 1980 when he heard his guru rail about the lesbian relationship of tennis superstar Billie Jean King. "And a part of me was like, 'What the fuck is all this?' This guy's supposed to be spiritual. Why couldn't he mind his own spiritual business and leave her alone?"

Carlos split with guru Sri Chinmoy shortly after that disagreement. But it was not an amicable split. "He [Sri Chinmoy] was very vindictive for a while. He told all my friends to not call me ever again because I was to drown in the dark sea of ignorance for leaving him." Happily, the people who knew Carlos best, ignored the advice of Sri Chinmoy.

The break with Sri Chinmoy ultimately had a positive effect on Santana. Carlos and Deborah traveled, ate meat for the first time in a long time, and indulged—or, as in the case of Sri Chinmoy's stand in favor of vigorous exercise, did not indulge—in things they wanted to do.

Shortly after the birth of the couple's first child, Salvador, Deborah became a born-again Christian. Carlos followed her lead, but while he attended church and turned his thoughts to Jesus, in reality once again he was on a spiritual search. But it was a search without the heavy load, and that search extended itself to Santana's next trip into the studio and the recording of the album *Papa Re*, which, literally translated, means *High Priest*. Rather than being apprehensive, Carlos was exuding an air of almost little boy–like enthusiasm.

"I had just gotten out of the Sri Chinmoy thing," he recalled. "So it was like, 'School is out, let's play. Let's experiment!' I was just learning how to have fun again."

"Fun" meant bringing on manager Bill Graham to executive-produce the album. Although in later years Carlos would laughingly relate, "The band didn't really need a producer, just an engineer who [was] up on the latest sounds." But Graham did more than his share by gathering and sorting through songs, from some decidedly unorthodox sources, for the album. The *Papa Re* song list ultimately included tunes by the likes of Cat Stevens, aka Yusuf Islam, Russ Ballard, and J. J. Cale, as well as a number of Santana originals—all done up in a poppy, uncharacteristically light manner.

But what started as a tension-free session, which took place from November 1980 through January 1981, quickly became a tug-of-war between designated producer Keith Olsen and the band regarding the direction of the album. The tracks being laid down did not sound right to Carlos, and neither he nor Olsen seemed to be in a happy place. Finally, after a month, Carlos called a halt to the sessions, parted company with Olsen, and scrapped everything that had been recorded to that point.

"It didn't sound like us," lamented Carlos. "I just couldn't put it out."

Bill Graham stepped into the breach and, along with engineer Fred Catero, finished the album. The vibe definitely improved with this makeshift production team; so much so that Carlos decided to change the name of the album from the serious-sounding *Papa Re* to the much more fun-sounding *Zebop!*

Zebop! was released early in March 1981, and was immediately hailed as Carlos Santana's return to commercial respectability. You could drop the needle just about anywhere on the album and find a spirited, usually danceable song. The album broke the Top Ten. The first single, "Winning," also broke through to the Top Twenty, and while a follow-up single, "The Sensitive Kind," stalled at number 56, the consensus in the recording industry was that Carlos had come back from the abyss. And, in the spirit of goodwill, he took the first step toward mending an important fence.

Of all the members of the old Santana band, Gregg Rolie was the guy Carlos had missed the most. They had spoken, periodically, over the ensuing years but had not been in the same room since the recording of *Caravanserai*. Carlos had watched as Rolie's and Neal Schon's band Journey had gone on to commercial success. Carlos had felt he wanted to rekindle the relationship with Rolie but there never seemed to be a right time or a situation that would be comfortable. Finally, one day, Carlos simply jumped into his car, drove over to Rolie's house, and knocked on the door.

"When he [Gregg Rolie] came to the door," laughed Carlos, "his jaw dropped to the floor. It was funny. I said, 'Hey, I'm sorry for whatever I did. Why don't we just get things together?' "

The pair sat down and had a serious talk. A lot of sadness, frustration, and anger were laid out on the table and dealt with. Then they took out their instruments and started jamming like the old days. It felt familiar and good. By the time the dust settled, the pair had cut a handful of demos and Rolie had agreed to play on the next Santana album.

Never one to sit still too long, Carlos was barely out of the sessions for *Zebop!* when he was once again guesting on a number of other people's albums. With jazz legends McCoy Tyner and Stanley Clarke, he got deep into the intricacies of both traditional and progressive forms. Guesting on albums by José Feliciano and Leon Patillo had him picking out old school latino and blues chords.

Santana and his latest lineup toured extensively in support of *Zebop!* through the rest of 1981 and well into 1982. Onstage, Carlos was also finding more joy, unveiling newer songs and marveling at the passion he still had for the likes of "Jingo," "Evil Ways," and "Black Magic Woman." And he was encouraged to see that, at least in a live setting, the audience was showing a measure of respect for his new songs.

On the business side, promoters and record-company executives were encouraged that *Zebop!* had given Santana the shot in the arm his career had badly needed. While privately they would often express the wish that Carlos would devote all his time to Santana material and permanently shelve his spiritual alter ego, they were just grateful the legendary guitarist was no longer the musical liability they felt he had become.

Early in 1982, Carlos returned to the studio once again and recorded the album *Shango*—an album that continued to steer him in a more upbeat direction but not at the expense of his ever-widening musical vocabulary. There were some familiar faces in the studio for the *Shango* sessions, as well as a smattering of new musicians who were constantly drawn into the Santana mix. Carlos had no problem with the revolving-door nature of the Santana band, and felt new influences and ideas could only help the music.

Unfortunately, the spike of popularity of *Zebop!* was short-lived. *Shango* would go no higher than number 22 on the album charts; once again, a respectable showing but not what one would consider the sign of a superstar. And when two singles from the album, "Hold On" and "Nowhere to Run," could do no better than numbers 15 and 66, respectively, Santana began to wonder if the blame lay in his musical direction, or in the ability of Columbia to market him.

Admittedly, Columbia Records had undergone a metamorphosis of some magnitude in recent years. Clive Davis, the man who had signed the Santana band in the late 1960s, and whom Carlos considered a guiding spirit, had been fired by the company in 1973. In his place, a new regime, more intent on the bottom line and promoting the then-trendy sounds of heavy metal and punk, had emerged. Early on, Carlos all but dismissed the notion that the record company was not really in his corner. There were the occasional squawks when Carlos deviated from the Santana main road into what Columbia considered his riskier solo projects. But he never felt that he was not wanted. Until recently.

Carlos would often speculate to family and friends that the reason his records were not doing as well as they had done before, was that he was more of a "prestige" item for the label—somebody to be kept on as a sign of cachet, but not to be marketed in a major way. These feelings continued to gnaw at the guitarist; especially when a much-vaunted solo album, *Havana Moon*—which had received all-star support from musicians Willie Nelson, Booker T. Jones, and the Fabulous Thunderbirds—was basically dead on arrival in 1983.

Carlos's resolve at this point was truly being tested and it resulted in some deep soul-searching. Maybe, he reasoned, his lack of continued success in the eighties was not entirely the fault of his record company. Yes, he had not been marketed the way he would have liked. But he had to admit, many of his records had not been the brilliant efforts he had produced in the 1970s. In many cases he had come to rely, often too much, on studio technology rather than raw inspiration. Unfortunately this shared blame did not ease the creative pain he was feeling.

"In the middle of the eighties, I was thinking very much like a victim," he recalled painfully. "I was angry, bitter, disillusioned. For a while I felt lost in a creative way."

But while his record sales continued in free fall, Santana's prowess as an electrifying live performer allowed him to shine on the road. His was one of the finer moments at 1982's massive outdoor U.S. Festival. And some of the most memorable music of 1983 was made when Santana toured Europe with Bob Dylan.

Touring with Dylan was yet another eye-opening experience for Carlos. He found the legendary singer-songwriter to be generous with his time and experience. Never too old to learn new tricks, Carlos found himself learning much about music and the art of survival from a musician who knew a lot about both. This was a time that Carlos would always remember.

But eventually, Carlos had to return to the reality of the studio. And it was a reality he was not looking forward to. The time of the year when Carlos would normally record a new album came and went without any announcement. There was the usual smoke screen floated by Bill Graham that Carlos was looking for just the right producers and just the right songs. But the reality was that Carlos, feeling a bit leery after the recent string of commercial failures, was not about to test his ego by rushing out another album only to have it fail. With these insecurities set in stone, Carlos avoided the studio for most of 1984.

Once again he concentrated on touring and turned his attention to contributing music to an electic array of other musicians' albums that included Jim Capaldi, Gregg Rolie, and the First Lady of Soul, Aretha Franklin. The guitarist found comfort in just being a hired hand, and in the quality of the relatively simple blues and rock licks he was asked to supply to those albums. When he was not making music, he was taking some time to be with his family, which had grown with the recent birth of his first daughter, Stella.

Deborah was happy to have her husband around the house a bit more. She had always been an advocate of her husband shouldering his share of the domestic duties and, when he was home, Carlos was more than willing to play the role of househusband.

Unfortunately, when Carlos was home, she could also see that her man continued to be moody and would occasionally lash out in anger at the slightest hint of things not going his way. Part of her dismissed his actions as the result of having too much time on his hands. But in her private moments, she would wonder if there were demons lurking behind her husband's soulful eyes. And that thought scared her to death.

Carlos finally went into the studio late in 1984 with high hopes for his next album, *Beyond Appearances*. He had some solid players behind him and he felt the songs were consistent with what was being played on the radio. Carlos did not feel he was selling out by thinking this way; he had just decided that, for now, he could play the game.

But the sales drought continued when the album was released early in 1985. *Beyond Appearances* stalled at number 50, and a halfhearted attempt at a single, "Say It Again," died at number 46. There was no record-industry postmortem for *Beyond Appearances*. The true fans shook their heads. The true cynics considered it more of Santana's downward spiral into oblivion.

In light of this latest failure, Carlos was peppered with more tough questions about whether or not he felt his career was in decline. Carlos, never one to avoid the tough questions, denied that it was, and said that he was just going through what had become a prolonged slump. But inside, Carlos Santana did not really have an answer. Like the reporters, all he had was a bunch of questions.

The guitarist once again turned his attention to the road and, in particular, to charitable causes. He performed at Live Aid in 1985 and did a benefit concert for Amnesty International in 1986. Carlos also continued to slowly but surely mend fences with many of the former members of Santana. This was not always easy. Many of the original members of the band had gone through rough personal and professional times since the breakup in the 1970s and still blamed Carlos. But the vast majority were willing to bury the past.

In fact, his attempts at reuniting with those members was so successful that it resulted in a spectacular July 1986 concert in San Francisco to celebrate the twentieth anniversary of the inception of the Santana band. A total of seventeen former and current members of the band took the stage for a spectacular concert retrospective. And on that night, the magic was there once again. There were smiles all around as the band roared through the old songs and a smattering of the new. The chops were definitely there—a case could have been made for the old Santana to get back together. But the musicians knew in their hearts that this night was one to embrace, enjoy, and remember. Because it would never happen again.

Carlos was once again the hired gun in his spare

time; this time pointing his guitar in the direction of primitive rhythms and jazz-fusion flights on albums by Babatunde Olatunji and Weather Report.

By 1986, Carlos Santana was in a strange place. While his status as a successful recording artist had been tarnished by an erratic eighties output, his worldwide reputation as a cultural ambassador who had brought world music and diverse musical cultures to the public's attention had elevated him to a level of universal respect. Carlos Santana had become an icon which, in turn, brought the inevitable extracurricular offers.

One of the most enticing came from Hollywood in the form of an offer to be the musical director for the movie chronicling the life of 1950s rock-and-roll singer and guitarist Ritchie Valens—*La Bamba*. Carlos jumped into the job with his trademark enthusiasm and grace. And he was overjoyed at the opportunity to work with Willie Dixon and Los Lobos on a number of songs that would ultimately make up the soundtrack. But he would emerge from the experience vowing never to work in Hollywood again.

"It was my first and only encounter with Hollywood's moviemaking machine," he sighed. "It was really frustrating because of the egos that are involved in making movies. The experience just confirmed why

I don't live in Los Angeles and I don't gravitate toward making movies. The Hollywood machine is very insensitive to people's souls. I just felt like saying, 'Look, just take back this money you're giving me. I'll pay you to just get out of my face.' "

Santana continued to be in a commercial slump in 1987. The latest Santana band album, *Freedom*, topped out at number 95.

The lengthy Freedom World Tour proved to be a lot more rewarding. This was Santana's tenth international tour and he was making it personally and professionally fulfilling by mixing in such out-of-the-way places as Austria, Helsinki, Jerusalem, Paris, East Berlin, and Budapest with his normal tour stops. Moving through the rock-starved countries in the Mideast and behind the Iron Curtain was proving particularly rewarding to Carlos.

"Man! We've played everywhere," said Carlos early one morning as his tour bus crossed the border from the Austrian frontier into Hungary. "In a lot of these countries you have to be officially invited by the government to appear and so we all feel pretty honored."

He realized any tour of the Middle East cannot totally get away from that region's political and religious strife. But he was looking at the tour as being something bigger than flags or countries. "It's about music being above such considerations, and the way it can bring people from very different backgrounds together."

Gregg Rolie finally came out with Carlos, and his current touring group, which included Buddy Miles, ran the gamut of ages and nationalities. It was old-fashioned good fun akin to the halcyon days of the 1960s and Santana happily bathed in the applause and the knowledge that, in some corners of the world, he was still considered a superstar. But once the tour ended and he returned home, Carlos was nothing if not the perfect father.

Despite being in love with his wife and his two children, domestic life was something that had not come easy for Santana. For Carlos, worldwide adulation had been hard to leave on the road and there were moments in the early years of their marriage that Deborah had to fight tooth and nail to put her husband's ego in check and get him to pay attention to her and the children. But eventually she got Carlos to conform to what she called "the house rules."

"When he comes home, I don't want to hear about Carlos Santana," related Deborah Santana. "I want him to hear about the children. I want him to take over some of the responsibility. I'll warn him, 'Remember, when you come home, you are a father. There is recycling to be done. You're going to be driving the car pool because that's my reality' "

But Carlos was never far from an opportunity to play, and in the later part of the 1980s, he continued to stretch his muscles on other people's music. His stint with Dylan had resulted in an appearance on the live disc *Real Life* while, with the studio efforts of Clyde Criner and Terri Lyne Carrington, he was once again doing a jazz thing. In all cases, the guitarist never flexed his ego. There was no need for that because he was learning new music from good people. He had no problem continuing to be the student well into his forties.

Midway through 1987, Santana went into the studio to record his latest solo album, the all-instrumental album *Blues for Salvador*. These were not the best of times for the guitarist. He was feeling more and more alienated from his record company, which he believed had given up any sense of support for his music. Consequently he was pessimistic at the prospect of this album doing much in a commercial sense.

"Around that time I just said, 'No, I don't want to appease producers. I just want to play my own music.' So, in my own mind, that album was the beginning of regaining my persona again."

And it was this positive state of mind that gave Carlos Santana pause to reflect that in a pop-music arena not known for longevity, he was well into his third decade as a thriving, still-viable musician. Growing up emulating real musicians like Miles Davis and B.B. King rather than personalities like Elvis Presley and Fabian was a big reason for his continued survival.

Part and parcel of gearing up for the *Blues for Salvador* sessions was recruiting yet another group of musicians. In this area Carlos Santana had become an expert for, since 1968, the guitarist had formed an amazing thirty-five different lineups for both studio and touring duties. The Santana band was a revolving door through which musicians entered, played, and left. And, if the chemistry was right, they stayed awhile.

There had been a number of reasons for this. The most obvious being that the centerpiece of all of Santana's music was his guitar and, beyond that element, everybody else was interchangeable in the ever-changing Carlos Santana musical landscape. Picking musicians, Carlos has often explained, is something that he learned from his jazz peers.

"I can tell by their eyes or what comes out of their mouth," he once said of his criteria for picking musicians. "I try to pick musicians who, I feel, can see their vision and their mission and lifestyle can enhance and complement what we're trying to say and how we're trying to say it."

Given his positive outlook going into *Blues for Sal-*

vador, it was not surprising that the creative interplay with talented musicians continued to make the recording process an exciting time for him, full of small moments and unexpected pleasures. One of the latter came about one day when Santana and keyboard player Chester Thompson were involved in an impromptu jam while the recording engineer was changing tapes.

"We were in the studio and I was just getting some tones together with Chester, and we came up with this thing we called 'Blues for Salvador,' " reflected the smiling Santana as he savored the moment again. "All we had to record on was a two-track. So we captured it on a two-track and, at first, I didn't think anything of it. But I gave a cassette of the music to my wife and she came home from shopping one day and she said, 'Man, I had to pull the car over when this came on.' She asked me what the name of the tune was. I told her I didn't have a title for it. I said I was just stretching out with C. T. She said, 'No, you don't understand. I couldn't drive when I heard that.' "

At Deborah's insistence, Carlos put the haunting instrumental ballad on the album. And the good vibe continued to grow on him as he contemplated a title for the song and the album.

"At the time I was really involved with a cause with Bill Graham, a benefit for the children of San Salvador. I looked at my son, who is named Salvador, as the song was playing. When I saw that and the reaction on his face I said, 'Yes, this is "Blues for Salvador." ' And I decided to give the whole album that title."

Santana was heartened by the fact that, even though *Blues for Salvador* was yet another commercial failure, reaching no higher than 195 on the album charts, the title track garnered considerable airplay on jazz and New Age stations. It was an oasis for Carlos in what would be a rather uneventful and largely unrewarding year in 1988. On the upside, Carlos exercised his creative chops on an eclectic jazz-rock tour with sax player Wayne Shorter. It was a decision that once again drove Bill Graham to distraction.

"Bill warned me, saying, 'Are you sure you want to do this?' I said, 'Yes,' and it turned out to be one of the highlights of my life. In the past I would not have been ready to climb those kinds of mountains. It would have been like jumping into the deep end of a pool. I could have drowned. But now I just want to climb whatever mountains are out there."

The tour with Wayne Shorter produced a recording at the Montreaux Jazz Festival that Carlos felt would eventually be released as a live album. But Columbia would not commit to releasing the album, which led to the latest round of complaints about how his label went about their business. He accused the company of "only listening to the cash register" and "not knowing one note from another." Carlos angrily felt that the corporate side of Columbia felt that they were the artists.

The growing ill will and distrust between Carlos and Columbia continued when a live album, *Viva Santana*—a collection of studio cuts, outtakes, and live recordings from 1969 to 1987—was proposed. Carlos was given carte blanche to assemble the representative cuts. What Columbia Records was essentially hoping for was a *Santana Greatest Hits Volume II*.

Carlos had other ideas, ignoring some of the band's most recent hits, including "Winning," in favor of earlier songs and live material. "I basically knew I wasn't going to please everybody so I went in to please myself. I wanted to capture moments, like a bouquet."

Unfortunately, Columbia did not believe in Carlos's approach. There was a lot of fighting between the musician and the record company. The upshot was that Carlos won the battle but lost the war. Columbia put only a lukewarm promotion behind the record and the result was that *Viva Santana* reached no higher than number 142 on the national album charts.

Carlos just threw up his hands and shook his head.

The new stuff was not selling. Now even the old stuff was withering on the vine. If Carlos were not a religious man he probably would have sold his soul to the devil a long time ago. But he was and so the drought continued.

It was during these dire days that Carlos would occasionally entertain the thought that maybe it was time to pack it in. He had invested his money wisely and, if he chose, would never again have to work a day in his life. But ultimately the desire to play was too strong to cast aside.

"I haven't reached that point," he said in 1988. "I'm too much involved in discovering notes every day. There's only so many notes but, to me, each one is like an ocean."

The year 1988 was also a time for rest and reflection. Columbia was releasing a massive retrospective package of largely early Santana material and felt it would be nice if a representative lineup of that superstar band could get together for a series of concert dates. This was not as difficult a task as it first appeared. The group members had pretty much mended fences long ago and the time away from the music that had put them on top had made the members of Santana anxious to try it again. It also did not hurt that the 1986 show in San Francisco had been a success. And so in August 1988, Carlos Santana, Gregg

Rolie, Michael Shrieve, Chester Thompson, Alphonso Johnson, Armando Peraza, and Chepito Areas came out with the announcement—appropriately, at the Fillmore West—that the Santana band would once again hit the road.

It was a time of looking back and looking forward. Gregg Rolie felt that once the original lineup had gotten out of their twenties in one piece, the world was their oyster. "We survived, somehow, and now we want to put the pieces back together and see how the music sounds."

He was also candid in assessing what had destroyed the original Santana band lineup. While he conceded that drugs and money were a big part of the problem, Rolie indicated that ego and illusions of grandeur had been real obstacles in the band not hearing the music.

Carlos agreed with Rolie's assessment but preferred to look to the future and not to the past. "We're not going to play the old music. We're going to take the old music to a new place."

As he walked around the Fillmore, looking at pictures of familiar faces and walking through hallways and backstage areas he had not walked in years, Carlos, for the first time in years, reflected on the good and the bad that had come out of his experiences in these hallowed halls.

"I miss those days," he said of the 1960s. "Every time I came here, the Fillmore looked different and the music sounded different. There was a lot of pipe dreams around, a lot of stoned people who settled for chump change. I don't miss that. I miss the fire and the hunger people had, the urgent sense that things had to change."

Santana's legendary status in the world of music was finally recognized in 1989 when "Blues for Salvador" was nominated for and captured the Grammy Award for Best Rock Instrumental Performance. For the moment Carlos Santana was happy as he savored the reward for a song that was highly personal and close to his heart.

The creative high continued into later in the year when Carlos had the opportunity to work with one of his idols, blues great John Lee Hooker, on the title track of Hooker's album *The Healer*.

Carlos turned forty-one in a positive state of mind. He was looking to the future with a lot of ideas to expand his creative universe. The musician was thinking of doing a television show, symphony concerts, and recording with a wide variety of world-music artists. And, at an age when most artists begin to think of resting on their laurels, Carlos looked in the mirror and still saw a revolutionary, a street-fighting man.

"Like anybody, you have peaks and valleys and you step in doggie doo-doo sometimes. But I want my life to be a triumph, not a tragedy."

But it was not long before Santana was back in the troughs of frustration . . . and anger.

Carlos's relations with Columbia Records were at an all-time low and the label executives were in a quandary. They knew Santana was one of the few legitimate jewels in their record-company roster and they were fearful that Santana would take his act elsewhere when his current contract ran out.

They had every right to be afraid.

8

Angry

Carlos Santana entered 1990 in a euphoric state of mind.

Despite nearly a decade of professional disappointments, the musician was able to take heart in the recent success of "Blues for Salvador" and the fact that he had become, for millions of followers, a musician for the ages. A growing number of the current stars of the rock-music scene were coming forth to say that Carlos Santana was their idol and, in many cases, had been a prime influence in their own career. In recent years his audience had gone from being primarily his contemporaries, to a mixture of ages ranging from the old to the very young. On more than one occasion, he would visibly blush onstage when a screaming chorus of "Carlos!" would rain onto the stage from a group of teenage girls.

Always leery of the idea of stardom, Carlos always had had a problem with the idea of being considered a cultural icon. But he admitted to being more than a bit amused at the idea that kids who possibly had been conceived to the sounds of Santana, were now cheering him on.

"I've found that a lot of people my age don't come out to shows anymore, but the kids come out," Carlos chuckled. "And it's kind of funny when the kids come up to me and say, 'Hey, my father was really into you, man, and he turned me on to you.' I just go, 'Oh God!' On the one hand they were complimenting me, and on the other hand they were telling me that I was old."

But the idea that there were young people in the audience gave him hope: If only they would connect with his new music the way their parents did before . . . That kind of icon, Carlos would be very happy to be.

Carlos and Deborah welcomed their third child, a second daughter, named Angelica, into the world in 1990. Carlos continued to be the doting father, and although Deborah would occasionally find her husband moody and depressed, she just assumed it was the recent run of bad luck, musically, and she would assure him that it would eventually turn around. Carlos was grateful for her concern and agreed that he was a little down and that the lack of popular success in recent years had a lot to do with it.

But, in his private thoughts, Carlos was nursing deeper hurts.

Santana went into the studio in 1990 to record his latest album, *Spirits Dancing in the Flesh.* The lineup for this record was stripped to a core, guitar-bass-drums-keyboards; an homage of sorts to the lineup that had catapulted Carlos to stardom in the sixties. But for Carlos, there was more on his mind than hanging out with cool people and making beautiful music.

The musician was well aware that this would be his last album on his current contract with Columbia. He had been having many conversations with his manager, Graham, on this subject—raving emotionally at the lack of support by the company and his growing desire to go elsewhere when his contract was up. Santana made a strong argument for switching labels, an argument Graham could not argue with; the best he could offer was to see what would happen with this album and then think in terms of going elsewhere.

And so it was with a sense of defiance and determination that Carlos forged the music on *Spirits Dancing in the Flesh*. This was going to be a true test of what Columbia thought of him. He would give them the best music he could possibly make. Then it would be up to them to get it to the people. However, Carlos realized that Columbia was only part of the food chain. If the radio programmers did not embrace his music, then there was nothing Columbia could do.

After completing *Spirits Dancing in the Flesh*, Santana hit the road again for a series of concerts in Europe and the United States. Given his ongoing tensions with Columbia, Carlos was surprisingly laid-back in his demeanor, and electric in his playing. To many observers of that tour, Santana was playing like a man possessed, like a man with something to prove. What he was feeling was the freeing of spirit and soul he always felt when he was performing. The record company, the radio stations, and his critics could not touch him onstage. The stage was the place where Carlos Santana could be real.

The rave reviews began filtering back to the States from the tour's European leg, and, in particular, highlighted the three nights the band blew the roof off London's famed Hammersmith Odeon Theatre. Carlos had to believe that this renewed excitement surrounding his live performances would translate into equal enthusiasm on the part of Columbia's marketing and promotion department and the radio stations across the land who had seemingly forgotten his name. In his heart he felt *Spirits Dancing in the Flesh* would take him back to the top.

Santana was wrong.

Spirits Dancing in the Flesh landed in the summer of 1990 with a resounding thud, managing to drag itself no higher than number 85 on the pop-music charts. Watching the record crash was painful. The reviews had been mixed. Even radio stations who were sympathetic to Carlos could not find room for him on their superficial pop-music playlists. Almost as an afterthought, the record company released Santana's cover of the Curtis Mayfield classic "Gypsy Woman," which failed to chart.

The failure of *Spirits Dancing in the Flesh* was the last straw for Carlos. While he continued to tour well into 1990, his heart really was not in the record business anymore. He felt totally betrayed by Columbia and told anyone who would listen that he had done his last album for the label. Adding insult to injury was the fact that once Carlos's threats got back to the label, they did nothing to try and persuade him to stay; and so the two sides sat waiting for the clock to run out on a nearly twenty-five-year relationship.

In the meantime, Carlos continued to put up a defiant front. He pointed to figures that showed he out-sold a lot of pop artists that were currently dominating the airwaves and insisted that he would rather be where he was at that moment than to be an insubstantial creation of some marketing department. He reasoned, if nothing else, he was being true to his music and his soul.

Carlos continued to tour. When not on the road, he would play at being the stereotypical househusband and father. Deborah smiled as she watched her man play and laugh with their children. Carlos was also spending a lot of time alone in deep meditation, searching his heart and soul for an answer to the professional demons that bedeviled him.

On October 25, 1990, at 9:55 P.M., a helicopter slammed into some power lines during a driving storm, and crashed. There were no survivors. Among the dead was Bill Graham.

Santana cried like a baby when he heard the news. Fate had taken one of his closest friends and confidants. In a professional sense, he now felt totally alone. Carlos turned inward in the face of this tragedy.

"When Bill left, it really made me face up to the fact that time is short and I have to get to the heart of whatever it is I'm trying to do. I'm more clear now as to why

I'm doing everything. It's not just to make people happy or make them dance. It's to change things so that we can have a clearer vision of our life and ourselves so there won't be so much disharmony in the world."

By acknowledging his mortality, Carlos immediately put himself, spiritually and mentally, back to square one. He would not waste any more time placing blame and turning mental gymnastics in the name of material gain. He had decided to go where his heart and soul led him and the rest be damned.

Greg DiGiovine was the perfect person to step into Bill Graham's empty shoes. Equally comfortable in a lawyer's office and in the wild world of rock and roll, DiGiovine and Santana seemed on the same wavelength almost from the moment they met. Carlos made it plain that he was not going to be guided by anything other than creative and spiritual interests. Instinctively, Carlos felt he could trust this man to guide his fortunes as his new manager.

Word soon got out that Santana was free of his Columbia contract. And Carlos made it plain that he was not going to sign with any label that would not treat him with the same respect and care as their younger artists. The guitarist was soon fielding offers from a number of major labels who all promised him the moon.

Finally Polygram Records and Davit Sigerson, the head of Polygram's Polydor label, made Carlos an offer he could not refuse: total creative control and the freedom to create his own private specialty label. Santana had long been interested in releasing some of his vast collection of unreleased live tapes by the likes of Jimi Hendrix, Miles Davis, and John Coltrane under the moniker of Guts and Grace Records.

He wanted to release some of his music, by going through the estates of the artists and their families, in an effort to honor their memories and perpetuate the legacy of their music. Musician Wayne Shorter suggested that he name the label Guts and Grace in an homage to the trials and tribulations Santana had endured throughout his life.

Carlos signed with Polydor in 1991. He would now sit back and hope for the best.

Despite having lived years on the rock-and-roll fast track, and being an active proponent of certain hallucinogenic drugs, Carlos had managed to maintain a spotless criminal record. However, in June 1991 Carlos Santana was stopped and searched on his way through a Houston airport. Five ounces of marijuana were found in a film canister. He was immediately arrested and released on bail in a matter of hours. His case was heard in August. Carlos pleaded no contest and, since it was his first offense, his case was reduced to a misdemeanor. The musician was fined $100 and ordered to do a series of antidrug public-service announcements. But the true punishment was in the shame he felt he had brought to his family with the arrest. While he did not give up smoking marijuana, Carlos made a concerted effort to be a little more low-profile in his recreational drug use from that point on.

It was a rejuvenated Carlos Santana who went into the recording studio midway through 1991 to record his first album under the Polydor banner. *Milagro* turned out to be a true reflection of where Carlos's head was at. The death of Bill Graham, as well as the recent deaths of two of his heroes, Miles Davis and Stevie Ray Vaughn, had put him in a deeply introspective state that played out in slow melodic moments and spiritual lyrics. But the album was also conspicuous by its lighthearted, playful moments; an indication that the guitarist had come through an emotional tunnel and was slowly emerging into the light.

Milagro, released early in 1992, received a mixed bag of reviews and did only modest business. But Santana took heart that some of the more respected music publications had backed him up.

A four-star review from *Down Beat* said the album "combine[d] the fiery abandon of *Abraxas* and *Caravanserai* with the catchy pop sensibilities of *Zebop!* Guitar fans will have plenty to drool over as Carlos unleashes with the kind of vengeance we haven't heard from him since the mid-seventies."

Rolling Stone echoed those sentiments when it said, "One of the finest sessions Santana has ever done. This album reaffirms Santana's position as the standard-bearer for fusion music. His attack is razor sharp and his solos rank among the best."

Musician magazine exclaimed quite simply, "Awesome. Santana's guitar-playing remains clear-eyed and invigorating."

Carlos returned to the road where he found that he was still an attractive draw for concert audiences. He savored the limelight and the applause. Those nights in front of thousands of adoring fans who, he perceived, were showing respect for all the right reasons, were some of his most memorable.

Respect would not come this easy again for quite a while.

When he returned from the road he discovered that all was not well at his new label. As often happens in the music business, Polygram, the parent company of Polydor, was going through some internal shakeups and the result was that Davit Sigerson was no longer the head of Polydor. Santana was concerned that with Sigerson gone, all the promises that had been made would go with him. But the executives at Polygram assured him that nothing had changed.

Carlos continued to take Polygram at their word, and returned with the live album *Sacred Fire*. The record, a series of live songs taken from recent South American concerts, was obviously more immediate in tone than *Milagro* and it contained a sense of raw, primal energy that signaled a resurgence of presence and purpose. Santana, in the performing arena, continued to wield a taut, creative hand. He hoped against hope that *Sacred Fire* would finally be the album to put him back on top.

Santana was furious when *Sacred Fire* was released midway through 1993 and did good-but-not-great business. Carlos reasoned that, yes, he was being given creative freedom in the studio. But the promotion and the marketing of his first two Polydor albums had been sorely lacking.

In the wake of *Sacred Fire*'s failure came the not-too-veiled comments to the performer by Polydor label executives that he was, in essence, too old for this game. Carlos maintained all along that "I never thought that I had gone out of style," and that he was playing with the same sensuality and spirituality that he always had. But he had to concede that he would rarely hear any music other than the early Santana music on the radio and that radio programmers were not lining up to play his new music.

Santana was ready to bolt Polydor but decided to

test the waters on yet another of Polygram's subsidiary labels—Island. Island had a reputation for being a haven for pure artists and so Carlos felt there would be more support for his work.

But Carlos was cautious in his dealings with Island. He began his relationship with his new label by using Island as the springboard for his Guts and Grace label. In 1993 he released *Live Forever*, an anthology recording that featured Jimi Hendrix, Marvin Gaye, Bob Marley, Stevie Ray Vaughan, and John Coltrane. The following year he released *Brothers*, an extended series of free-form guitar jams featuring Carlos, his brother Jorge, and a nephew, Carlos Hernandez. The records did acceptable business and *Brothers* would ultimately be nominated for a Grammy for Best Rock Instrumental.

But it was too little too late.

After nearly three decades of recording and nearly two decades without a major commercial success, Carlos Santana hit the wall. He did not see the point of rushing into the studio and doing yet another record that would only get halfhearted support. He did not have writer's block and was constantly working on material. But while he continued to tour throughout 1993 and 1994, and made a big splash at the second Woodstock festival, the thrill, to a large degree, was gone. It also did not do his damaged psyche a lot of good when, in 1995, Columbia, as was their right, began releasing the first of a series of Santana albums, a massive boxed set called *Dance of the Rainbow Serpent*.

Carlos was emotionally down and it began to show in a certain uneasiness around professional decisions. He was not as quick to jump at offers to help out others. But when he did, as on the albums of John Lee Hooker and Junior Wells, it tended to be a freeing experience that would block out the pressures of his own life.

However, his ego and insecurities did surface when he was approached to contribute to the song "Spanish Castle Magic" on a Jimi Hendrix tribute album entitled *In from the Storm*. Carlos felt insecure about "jumping in somebody else's footprints" and a bit intimidated when he discovered he would be doing the song with jazz greats Tony Williams and Stanley Clarke.

Twice Carlos declined the invitation. Williams called in an attempt to persuade him. He could think of no way to say no to Williams and so he agreed. But the day of the recording, he started to get cold feet. Carlos locked himself in a room, lit a candle, burned some incense, meditated, and asked for guidance. Finally a little voice came to Carlos and said, "Relax."

He went out into the studio and paid respect to the spirit of Hendrix.

Santana continued to grow increasingly moody and uncharacteristically quiet. The normally warm, smiling exterior was replaced by a seemingly constant look of abject frustration and dejection. Whereas Santana had always been an enthusiastic seeker of life and new experiences, he was now dour and noticeably withdrawn. Word among Carlos's closest circle of friends was that the musician was suffering a mild form of depression.

He remembered that his wife was seeing something else.

His wife was growing increasingly concerned that her husband's anger seemed to be growing. It had reached a point where she gave Carlos a strong ultimatum: See a therapist if he wanted to remain in the marriage.

Santana had known his wife long enough to know that she was not bluffing. Deborah, in looking back on that period of time, always sensed that her husband had secrets, and she had done her best to deal with his private thoughts. But she finally had had enough.

It reached a point where Carlos was given a final choice by his wife. He either had to deal with his issues or she was gone. Carlos saw the writing on the wall. He was upset. But he wanted to save his marriage.

Faced with this ultimatum, Carlos agreed to enter therapy early in 1995. This was not an easy step to take. His traditional Mexican upbringing had taught Carlos to keep things inside. To express one's feelings to a stranger was not the manly thing to do. But letting his marriage fall apart was too high a price to pay for his continued silence and secrets.

Santana's therapy was a long, often painful process of self-examination. With the therapist's help, Carlos was forced to deal with why he felt he awoke each morning with the idea that the world was out to fuck him over. He began to deal with the idea of being self-obsessed. There were the issues of his Catholic upbringing and, by association, the issues of guilt, shame, judgment, and fear. After weeks and months of therapy, there was a final breakthrough. After years of inner torment, Carlos Santana, now often in tears during his sessions, was facing the final demon.

Carlos admitted that he had been molested at a very young age. He had blocked out the fact that he had been seduced by toys and the idea of going to America.

But with the therapist's aid, Carlos was slowly able to untangle the evil that had overcome him. With this breakthrough, he was finally able to deal with the embarrassment and guilt. He was now ready to piece together and deal with the horror.

Between 1957 and 1959 (between the ages of ten and twelve) Carlos had made the acquaintance of an American, who Santana described as "this American guy from Burlington, Vermont, who dressed like a cowboy," who would come to Tijuana every couple of days, take Carlos across the border, buy him presents, and molest him. This perverted relationship went on for two years. A mere child, Carlos did not know what was happening to him was bad, at the time looking at the incident in his simplistic view of the world as an even exchange.

The molestation ended when Carlos fell in love with a girl. The American got jealous, one day, when he caught Carlos looking at the girl through a window. In a rage he slapped the youngster hard across the face. "At that point I woke up," he reflected. "I looked at him for the first time for what he was, a very sick person."

With the long-buried secret of childhood molestation finally out in the open, Carlos began the long process of healing his soul. He went through the phase where he beat himself up for not knowing better. He dealt with the guilt and shame of knowing that, through his naiveté, he had brought it on himself.

And finally he was able to come to grips with how being molested had impacted the rest of his life.

The guitarist painfully realized that when he had been angry with the original band members, his wife, and the first women in his life, his feelings had been blinded by the guilt of the childhood horror and his inability to express his feelings and to figure out how to begin the healing process.

Carlos Santana came out of the therapy at peace with his past and confident in his future. "It's just fuel now. Now I can use it to do something creative."

9

The Road Back

Carlos returned to his family a new man. The demons had been banished and, through a religious approach, a literal spiritual twelve-step program that combined Christianity, meditation, and dream interpretation, he was convinced they would stay away.

Not that the process was an easy one. Far from it. Once away from formal therapy, Carlos found himself in a highly vulnerable state. Logically he felt he was able to deal with the terrors of his childhood. But there were those moments when logic went out the window and the horrifying images would rush back into his life.

Deborah went through a range of emotions when Carlos revealed his dark secret. There was the anger at what had happened to her husband. There was also a sense of guilt and sadness that she had not been able to do more for him during the years of inner turmoil. But finally, like her husband, there were tears of happiness that the nightmare was finally over.

Carlos returned to his music. But while passionate, there was suddenly an unexpected sense of being tentative. He always had ideas and could regularly be found in his home studio, picking out melodic runs and experimenting with new sounds and ideas. But now he was not so anxious to waste them on a public that might not be interested anymore in the musings of a fifty-year-old rock star.

These were tough times for the guitarist. The passion to play and grow as a musician was stronger than ever. However, the disappointments of his recent releases and the nagging fear that the music scene had passed him by had created a mental block to his reentering the studio. Worse yet, in his darkest moments, Carlos speculated that, musically, maybe he had nothing more to say.

Through his spiritual explorations, Santana made the acquaintance of a group of people who were into channeling spirits and angels. It was a process that was new to him but, always having been the spiritual explorer, he was willing to test these waters. One day, a member of the group informed Carlos that he had heard the voice of an angel named Metatron who had advised them to tell Santana that he would soon be reconnected to the frequency of the radio.

Carlos took the information at face value . . . at first.

"I know it sounds like California New Age stuff," related Santana, "but then I started hearing Metatron in my meditations and dreams. Metatron said, 'We're gonna help get you back in the ring because we want you to utilize your sound, vibration, and resonance to hook up with a lot of new people.' "

This made sense to him. For a long time Carlos had been observing the way of the world through his charitable works and by keeping track, almost obsessively, with the social and moral conditions of the world. Unhappily, what he saw was a media that seemed hellbent on propagating sex, violence, and escape at any cost. In particular, he saw what these attitudes were doing to the young. In his mind, he felt that, through his music, there might be an answer to the world's ills.

Deborah was not surprised when Carlos told her about his latest spiritual breakthrough. Over the years Carlos would often excitedly bring her into his latest explorations. Once she got over her amazement at her husband's latest pronouncement and saw the look in his eye that meant he was serious, Deborah was supportive and encouraged Carlos to continue to form his spiritual plan to help the world and return to commercial prominence.

But one thing Carlos did know was that his next record would not be for Island. Despite what he perceived to be their best efforts, he felt strongly that Island was not up to the task of pushing his music. Through his management, he had made initial attempts at letting Island know he wanted out of his contract, but was met with all kinds of promises and excuses that did not ring true. There was an immediate stalemate. Carlos realized that he did owe Island product, based on the terms of his contract. He also knew that they could not force him to record another album. And, for his part, Santana was steadfastly refusing to go into the studio.

These were trying times for the musician. There were the inevitable hints of lawsuits and all the ugliness that goes along with a relationship gone sour. And for Carlos, there were also doubts. Even if he could get out of his contract, would anybody else want a fifty-something guitarist with a solid creative reputation but who had not had what would be considered a big commercial success in more than two decades? He did not know the answer and that kept him up nights.

"These were trying times for the guitarist. He felt in his soul that he had a positive musical masterpiece in his heart and soul. He felt he knew what the likes of Marvin Gaye and Bob Marley felt when they were about to record their classic songs."

While Santana was waiting out Island and hoping for other offers, he continued to find solace on the road. One particularly enjoyable round of shows was a series of 1995 concerts in which he opened for another world-class player, Jeff Beck.

Carlos was at ease with this supporting role. It also did not hurt that Beck and he had been good friends for a long time and that there was that mutual respect. He was happy to just bask in the glory of playing live and letting the emotions pour out of him. But he would be a liar if he did not claim, when the reviews of the tour began to appear, that he was being treated as a second-class citizen.

"After the concerts, you'll find Jeff getting praised and I'm chopped liver," said the obviously miffed Carlos. "It's just the media and how I'm perceived."

And at the time, many believed Carlos Santana was a rock-and-roll dinosaur. If you went by radio play in the mid-nineties, the perception would be that Carlos's career had peaked in 1970 with "Oye Como Va" and ended in 1974 with his *Greatest Hits* album. Nobody in the music industry was showing any inclination to acknowledge that anything Carlos Santana had done in the last twenty years was relevant.

While he was touring with Jeff Beck, his wife called one day and told him about a special event being planned to honor Clive Davis and asked if he would make some kind of statement about the event. Despite their creative differences over the years, the musician still considered the record executive a close friend and so he agreed.

"I said some things about how Clive Davis was one of the people who brought some balance into popular music and some other things. Clive liked what I said and got in touch with me. He asked what I was up to and what I wanted to do next. I told him I wanted to unify the molecules with the light through music."

Davis had been aware of Carlos's spiritual/cosmic side but he could not get around the sheer spaciness of what was coming out of his friend's mouth. Carlos laughingly recalled that his mentor's immediate response to his ramblings was, "What the hell does that mean?"

But he felt that Davis eventually got the message. He knew that he could once again make good, commercial Carlos Santana music. But he also knew that he would have to be very hands-on and that the friends would fight. But the upshot would be an album that people wanted to hear.

During his conversation with Davis, the guitarist, with more than a touch of irony in his voice, laid his cards on the table when he said, "I've got three kids at home and they want to know why they never hear me on the radio."

Carlos was encouraged by Davis's quiet confidence and enthusiasm. He felt that if anybody could bring him back from obscurity, it would be the man who had set him on the road to stardom so many years ago. Carlos was up front in telling Davis that he was still under contract to Island even though he had no intention of recording for that label again. Davis took it all in and then told Carlos that they would be in touch.

The meeting with Davis only served to push Santana to resolve his situation with Island as soon as possible. He realized that even if he could extricate himself from Island, there might be a price to be paid. His contract called for a certain number of albums and he might be forced to give them some new music. And given his lame-duck status, how hard would they try to market it? That he would have to give up yet another pound of flesh was something he did not relish. But, he determined, he would do whatever it took to be free.

He decided that the best way would be man-to-man and so, in October 1996, he flew to New York for a private meeting with Island Records president Chris

Blackwell. The meeting was cordial but there was an obvious tension as Carlos talked about his plans for a new record. Blackwell was well aware that Carlos was not happy and reluctant to record a new album for Island. Blackwell could have played hardball; wisely, he choose to listen instead.

"I looked him right in the eye and said, 'I feel that you know that your company is not equipped right now to deal with something like this.' "

Nothing was resolved at that meeting but, a short time later, Blackwell flew to Carlos's West Coast home in a last-ditch attempt to keep Santana on the label. But this meeting was quickly at a standstill. The musician wanted out in the worst way and Blackwell, with a whole lot of ego on the line, kept digging in with promises of better promotion and marketing if Carlos would stay with Island.

Finally Santana leaned forward, looked Blackwell right in the eyes and softly asked, "one artist to another," to free him from his contract. Now, Blackwell is not a stupid man. He could sense the sincerity and emotion in Santana's voice. He knew he had lost him. Blackwell gave in and said Carlos was free to go, without any kind of compensation.

Flushed with the idea of once again being a free agent, Santana set about letting the major labels know that he was available. There were a lot of calls that did not go very far. He received serious interest from three labels: Arista, EMI, and Tommy Boy. Carlos weighed the offers and, surprisingly, given his long-standing relationship with Clive Davis, he went with EMI.

Part of the reasoning was that Davit Sigerson, who was a big backer of Santana when he was at Polydor, had resurfaced as the president of EMI. The second reason was unabashed and uncharacteristic materialism.

Carlos, thinking with his wallet rather than his heart, went to EMI because they offered him four times the money that Arista was offering.

Santana's initial rush of enthusiasm for EMI led him back into the studio where he began working on ideas for a new album. Almost immediately his feelings began to change. The vibe was suddenly not right for Carlos. He felt he was forcing the music and that his ideas, when all was said and done, were not really focused or up to his standards. Frustrated at what he felt was his sudden inability to cross the line from thought to deed, he began having second thoughts about the deal with EMI and about how he had passed on his old friend, Clive Davis.

Davis, in their 1995 conversation, had warned Santana that working with him would not be easy. And Davis reasoned that not wanting to be in a combative situation in the studio may have initially put Carlos off Davis's offer. But Carlos knew that Davis did seem to have the Midas touch when it came to crafting radio-friendly hits, and that was Santana's ultimate goal. Unfortunately, he felt he had given his word to EMI and now he was stuck.

While Carlos was in creative limbo, a number of former band members were quite busy. The 1971 Santana band lineup, minus Carlos and Dave Brown, had decided to regroup, under the name Abraxas, to further explore the musical style pioneered by the band in their first three albums. Abraxas toured primarily on the West Coast and would produce an album, entitled *Abraxas Pool.*

Gregg Rolie would offer during interviews that the reason for re-forming as Abraxas was twofold. The first reason was to remind people that the band was never just Carlos and a bunch of faceless sidemen.

"The idea behind this was to go back and finish something we started," said Rolie. "Santana was never really the same after the demise of the first group. The fact is that the band Santana, when it was created, was six people. It was a total democracy and the sum of its parts was greater than any one individual. There was no individual genius there. We played on and off each other and developed it that way."

During those interviews, the inevitable question of

why Carlos was not involved in the group was broached. Rolie indicated that they had approached Carlos about playing on a couple of cuts when they did record an album, but he declined.

"I don't think he relishes the fact that we're doing this. He's made comments to the effect that the music was the only thing we had in common. Well, he doesn't know how right he is about that."

Carlos remained low-profile during the thinly veiled attacks by his former Santana bandmates and refused all comment on the band.

Santana's conflict with EMI was settled unexpectedly in May 1997 when, as part of a restructuring movement inside EMI Music Company, the EMI record label was folded. Santana was thrilled at the opportunity to work once again with Clive Davis at Arista. But he was concerned that, after his initial slight, Davis would not want him now. Happily, Carlos discovered that Clive Davis was a bigger man than that.

"To Mr. Davis's credit, he didn't rub it in my face. He said the company was still interested." With an emphasis on "interested."

Clive Davis's love of music had always been balanced out by his prowess as a bottom-line businessman. The reality was that he carried enough clout to get Santana signed to the label. But he was also privy to the rumor grapevine that, by even considering Santana for the label, he might be sending the music industry the message that he was losing his touch.

Yes, he loved Carlos like a son. But before he signed him to the label, he had to be convinced that Carlos Santana in the latter stages of the 1990s was still a viable attraction. He reasoned that there were many substantial artists. But Davis knew all too well that there were many veteran musicians who suddenly found themselves unable to connect with a '90's audience.

Santana was not offended that Davis was asking him to, in essence, audition. "That was okay. It's like, if I'm a horse, you still want to see me run the track."

Davis traveled to New York City in July 1997 to watch Carlos headline a show at Radio City Music Hall. A smile crossed his face as Santana's trademark "cry" soared out and washed over the crowd. By the end of the evening, Davis knew that Carlos had not lost a step. He approached Santana the next day with the offer of a contract. It was not as much money as EMI offered and, true to Davis's word, it did come with certain conditions.

In his own mind, Davis already had an idea of what the next Carlos Santana album should sound like. Part of the album would be a very nineties style of music, incorporating all the modern melodies and musical notions but, predictably, would be anchored by Santana's trademark guitar-playing. And the other half of the album would be vintage Santana in the spirit of 'Oye Como Va' which was the kind of thing he [Santana] wanted for himself.

Arista's point man, Pete Ganbarg, who was in on the early talk about the album, insisted that "while it was going to sound like a classic Santana album, it was not just going to be a tribute album or a museum piece."

Santana, whose entire history was marked by his dedication to total artistic freedom, did not blink at the prospect of compromise. His trust of Davis and his instincts overrode any fears of compromise. "He [Davis] is not a crass person. He would never ask me to do anything or play anything crass. I felt safe."

Safe enough to address the issue that, for the first time in his career, he was making an album that was totally directed toward getting radio airplay. That radio had accepted the first three Santana albums so readily was not lost on the guitarist.

"The first three Santana albums just happened because they happened," he said. "There was no premeditation there like, 'Okay, let's go after radio.' But with this record it's something different."

It was during this period that sadness descended upon Carlos when his father died of heart failure at the age of eighty-four. Carlos was devastated, but also philosophical about the death of his father.

"When he died, I didn't cry because I realized that

he's not really gone. It's like I'm on the first floor and he took an elevator to the second."

But at his core Carlos was extremely saddened. He did his best to be a rock of support for his mother and his family but deep inside he was hurting. So much so that he immediately went into a contemplative shell and would not play or listen to music of any kind. The isolation lasted four days. "I was numb," he recalled of those dark days.

But the isolation soon ended. "I was picking up my son from school and I thought, 'Okay, time to listen to some radio.' I turned on a classical station and the first thing I heard was this gentle, six-note melody. That melody just stayed with me. They didn't say who the composer was but I was sure it was Strauss. I wanted to find out what this was so I went to the classical-music section of a local record store and told the guy, 'All I have is this melody.' I sang it for him right there in the store and the guy goes, 'Oh yeah, Brahms Concerto no. 3.' He gets me the CD and that's the song!"

But that was not the end of the odyssey. Carlos would play the opus over and over in the ensuing days, falling in love with the complexity and simplicity all rolled into one and listening, with his heart as well as his head, as the simple six notes got into his heart and soul. Somehow, he reasoned, he would find a place for this wonderful piece of music.

Shortly after Santana signed with Arista, Carlos went into the studio and began putting together songs for his new album. There was a renewed sense of excitement in the guitarist and it resulted in a flurry of songwriting and playing. His hopes and dreams for positive, uplifting music were his guiding spirit. Carlos felt he was on the right track.

On Thanksgiving weekend 1997, a package arrived at Clive Davis's offices, containing the demos for more than thirty songs. One of the first to listen to the tapes was Senior Director of A&R Pete Ganbarg, who was excited but also disappointed at what he heard.

"Man, the guitar sound was amazing. But it was just bits and pieces. A cool lead here, a great melodic piece there, a cool chorus. But it needed some focus. There was a lot there but it wasn't jelling yet."

Ganbarg was looking for any bright spot in this sluggish start as he continued to pore over Santana's demos. And he found it in one song, "The Blind Leading the Blind." The song was not an original Santana composition, but rather a song written for Carlos by Dave Stewart of the Eurythmics and Mick Jagger of the Rolling Stones. The only thing missing was lyrics for the verse but Ganbarg felt that, with this song, there was something they could build upon.

Ganbarg suggested to Davis that, since Carlos was

not known for his verse-writing ability, someone be brought in from the outside to write the missing lyrics and, possibly, do a guest vocal on the song. The Arista brain trust scratched their heads and came up with John Popper of the Southern-styled rock group Blues Traveler. Popper, who had long ago gone on the record as being a big Santana fan, was thrilled at the opportunity to be involved and, after a positive first meeting, went away to write the verses to "The Blind Leading the Blind."

A few weeks later, Ganbarg received a fax from Popper, some lyrics literally scribbled on a piece of paper. The A&R director had his fingers crossed as he read the fax. The lyrics were confusing and abstract. It was hard to get a sense of how they would fit into the song. Upon reading them, Carlos expressed the same feeling. John Popper had given it his best shot but his contribution was not going to work. But amid the disappointment was a sign of encouragement and an idea of how to put Carlos Santana back on top.

Davis decided that he would approach other nineties singer-songwriters who had also expressed an affinity for Carlos in the past, and invite them to contribute a song and to sing the song. Ganbarg reflected that the idea was good in theory because Santana had never really been known for a trademark vocal sound. He also recalled that the criterion for this new approach to Santana's album was simple: "If you weren't delivering a hit song, you weren't on the record."

Davis and Ganbarg began rifling through their Rolodexes, placing telephone calls to some of the biggest names in the business who might be interested in lending Carlos a creative hand. Early attempts at securing an all-star lineup were hit-and-miss.

The Dust Brothers offered up a fantastic musical track. The first person approached for lyrics was Jamiroquai, who was too busy working on his own album to concentrate on any outside writing. Maxwell also had to decline, as he was busy working on the new R. Kelly album. But the people at Arista were persistent and finally landed Eagle-Eye Cherry to pen the lyrics for the track that ultimately became the song "Wishing It Was."

Carlos would later explain that the the idea to use others was fine with him and seemed to fit into some kind of cosmic plan. "A lot of people who are on this album said, 'I knew I was going to work with you because three days before you called you were in my dreams,' or 'I heard your music in a restaurant or I heard your name.' "

One of the early calls made in this Santana collaboration was to Wyclef Jean of the Fugees. Jean, a politically- and socially-conscious rapper, multi-instrumentalist, and an on-target songwriter, seemed the perfect complement to Carlos. Ganbarg approached Wyclef's manager with some trepidation; he had the reputation in the industry of driving a hard bargain and "yes" was not normally a part of his vocabulary. Consequently Ganbarg was shocked when he heard Wyclef's manager exclaim, "I don't even have to call Wyclef. Wyclef talks about Carlos all the time. He thinks he's the god of the guitar."

Wyclef was indeed thrilled when he received the offer to join Carlos in San Francisco to make some music. The singer-songwriter laughingly related, "I said yeah, I've already got a song." In fact he had nothing. "All of a sudden I was real kiddish about the whole thing. I wanted his autograph and everything." But when he arrived, empty-handed, in San Francisco a week later, he was not worried about delivering the goods.

"I knew I was such a fanatic of the guy that all I had to do was see him and I would know what to write," he said. "We got to the studio and it just came to me. I wrote the song ['Maria Maria'] in a couple of hours. Recording it was like smoking weed. I was just inhaling, exhaling, and vibing."

The recruiting process for the album would be marred by one major disappointment. Carlos had especially asked for his old friend Eric Clapton to be involved in the album but Clapton, who was involved in some charitable good works at the time and was also trying to find himself personally and creatively, had to respectfully decline. But not long after signing his contract, the guitarist received a bit of good news from Davis.

"He said, 'You know I was talking to Lauryn Hill on the phone and I found out that she really likes your music,' " recalled Santana. " 'I gave her your phone number. I hope you don't mind.' Eventually we got hooked up and she said, 'Oh man, I love your music. Since I was a child, I listened to "Samba Pa Ti." I even wanted to put words to it.' "

But there was more to Hill's phone call than mere fan praise. At the time, Hill was putting the finishing touches on her first solo album, *The Miseducation of Lauryn Hill*, and had written a very personal song to her son called "To Zion."

"The musical backing to that song included a part for some delicate flamenco guitar passages," recalled Lauryn's engineer, Che Guevara. "I had this guy who I actually wanted to lay down some flamenco guitar on it. But, at one point, Lauryn said she had a connection to Carlos Santana. I was excited when she mentioned it. That's the kind of opportunity that you don't want to miss."

Carlos was thrilled and humbled when Lauryn

asked him to participate. He immediately stopped work on his album and flew to New York for the express purpose of laying down a muted, haunting bit of flamenco to the song "To Zion." The spiritual side of the guitarist was immediately hooked by the the courage and conviction that Lauryn had invested in the song, and he literally had to fight back tears as he laid down his tracks.

"When I heard the song, it broke me up," he reflected. "The world is telling you to go one way, your record company is telling you to go another way, and you decide to go with your heart. It takes a lot of courage to do that."

Hill would return the favor when she brought her attention to spiritual matters to Santana's sessions with a set of lyrics all her own.

Carlos did have one lingering concern as the *Supernatural* sessions progressed. Over the years, he had heard the results of more than one so-called collaborative effort and the end result was never very appealing. Those sessions usually ended up disintegrating into a partylike atmosphere in which the music did not sound cohesive, and the impression was that the assembled talent did not seem to be listening to each other.

But as recording for what would become the album *Supernatural* progressed, Santana marveled at the ease with which a myriad of producers, engineers, and musicians meshed so effortlessly. He was finding much in the inherent good vibes that hearkened back to the Santana sessions circa 1969 to 1973.

"Now I could sense it happening again with this music," he rejoiced during a break in recording the album. "I'm in total awe of how fast and smooth things have been. Nobody has had a cow. Nobody has bugged out. And there are a lot of people involved with this record. They're putting their best foot forward and they're all being very gracious. I keep pinching myself. I feel very incidental. I just show up, we see each other's eyes, we hear the music, and we start recording."

K. C. Porter, one of several producers who worked on the album, could also see that the experiment was working. "There are so many styles on this record and they all seem to work."

Much of the credit for *Supernatural*'s cordial atmosphere had to go to Clive Davis, who was there just often enough and with just the right amount of encouragement to keep everybody on the same course. Matchbox 20's lead singer, Rob Thomas, in particular, credited Davis and his people skills with keeping the sessions in check "because there were enough egos to choke a horse."

Everlast, whose contribution to *Supernatural*, "Put

Your Lights On," would be perceived as one of the strongest tracks on the album, summed up the collective sentiment of the nineties superstars who had come together under the Santana banner. "It was a great experience," said the singer-songwriter. "I mean, I got to work with someone who has hung out with Bob Marley and Miles Davis. He probably even rapped with Jimi Hendrix. It was an honor to work with somebody like that."

Others had their own takes. Thomas felt particularly humbled by being in the presence of the master. "We all reverted back to that sixteen-year-old kid, playing air guitar in front of the mirror when we were around Carlos. I remember once, in the middle of a song, I looked over and thought, 'Holy fuck! That's Santana right there!' "

The singer-songwriter also recalled getting a new perspective on life and his music through the hours he spent hanging around with Santana.

"Carlos explained to me that the record we were making was put together so we could change people's molecular structure through sound and, as musicians, that is what we do. He told me, 'You can play one note and change the way people feel.' Carlos saying that gave me my new purpose on why I do what I do. It just put perspective on everything."

Typical of what Santana has described as the "synchronicity" that enveloped the *Supernatural* sessions was the process by which the song "Love of My Life," a collaboration between Santana and Dave Matthews, came into being.

One day, during a break in recording, Carlos mentally channeled those beloved Brahms melody lines and began running them, on a mental tape loop, over and over in his head. Finally, while looking at a picture of his wife on his nightstand, he picked up a pencil and paper and began playing around with lyrics. This was Carlos at his most vulnerable and heartfelt. Words of love and appreciation poured out of his heart and onto the page. The next time he was in the studio with Dave Matthews, he nonchalantly walked over and began reciting the lines to the by-now slightly disguised Brahms movement.

Matthews recalled, "He gave me some lyrics, just a couple of lines. He said something about hearing this with a 1999 bass behind it. I just kind of stood there. I didn't know what to do."

However, with Santana's encouragement ringing in his ears, Matthews sat down in a corner of the studio and wrote the lyrics to the song literally on the spot. It was recorded that same day. After the fact, Matthews offered, "I think he wrote it about his father. I wrote it about my lover. But in the end, it just worked out."

As had the entire Santana experiment to this point.

Ideas were flying thick and fast in the studio. There was the sense that every idea was important and, recalled Carlos, the spirit of cooperation and collaboration was not to be believed.

"I tell you, it's the most incidental I've ever felt on an album," he said. "You walk in like a chef. The water's boiling, the garlic's happening, the onions are in. And you just cook."

But not everybody involved in recording *Supernatural* was a big Santana fan. Sincere, a singer who was brought in to sing on the "Maria Maria" track did not have a clue. "Honestly, I never knew who Carlos was. After I did the song I'd tell people and they'd be, 'Carlos Santana! He's a legend!' I looked into it and found out that yeah, he is the bomb."

The recording sessions continued to be an exercise in creativity and spirituality. You could see it in the expressions on the musicians' faces when they nailed a particularly tasty lick or hammered out a lyric that moved people to tears and happiness. Visitors to the *Supernatural* sessions were likewise excited about what they were hearing. Santana's old-school stuff was sounding just as raw and relevant as it had thirty years earlier, and discerning ears were finding a whole slew of radio-oriented cuts in the mix. The song "Maria Maria," the aforementioned Wyclef Jean composition, was being touted as the first single off the album. But fate suddenly stepped in with a better offering.

Songwriter Itall Shur was always on the lookout to market his wares. Being in the right place at the right time had resulted in his cowriting the 1997 hit "Ascension" for soul singer Maxwell. When Shur heard that Santana was in the studio, he hustled right over to Arista Records with a song, entitled "Room 17," that he felt would be perfect for Santana.

Arista's Pete Ganbarg liked the musical backing but felt the lyrics were a little bit too sexy for Santana's current state of mind. In an effort to salvage the song, Ganbarg sent the backing track to Rob Thomas with the suggestion that he and Shur might work together to come up with some more appropriate lyrics and a different melody. The collaboration between Thomas and Shur worked and soon a demo of the song, retitled "Smooth," with Thomas singing vocals, was sent to Santana and Clive Davis. They both loved it.

Carlos, in looking back on his initial impressions of 'Smooth,' saw the song as a simple, good-time boogie. When he received the song, his instincts told him that there would be little he could do to improve upon it.

Now it was Thomas's turn to be surprised. "I had no intention of singing it at all. I thought Santana should use a vocalist like George Michael. But when Santana heard my vocals on the demo, he insisted that I do it myself."

The recording continued early into 1999. Santana was consumed with the album and the quality of music he was getting. His hopes for an album that would point the way to a positive vibe was becoming a reality. "Everything was just falling into place," exclaimed the happy guitarist. "It was like a chain reaction."

However Ganbarg echoed the sentiments of all involved when he offered, "Since things were coming along so well . . . we knew we wouldn't finish this record without Clapton on board." Unfortunately, Clapton had just split with his manager and so Ganbarg was faced with calling the label and his music publisher. The long and short of it was that nobody knew where Eric Clapton was or how to get ahold of him.

Carlos took a well-deserved break as the Grammys approached, when Lauryn Hill called and asked him to perform with her band onstage when she did "To Zion." Santana could not say no to the offer; especially since it would give him the opportunity to attend the Grammys for the very first time.

As the fates would have it, among those in the audience that night was Eric Clapton. His reaction to seeing his old friend onstage, playing his heart out as Hill sang, was an eye-opener. "All I could think was, 'What am I thinking?' " remembered Clapton. "I quickly sent him a message. 'I'm sorry. I've been a dick. Is there still room for me?' "

Santana received the message and his eyes lit up. He recalled that the message was followed by an equally apologetic telephone call from his friend. "He called and said, 'Look, man. I heard that people at Arista were trying to contact me to play on your new record. I've been going through some serious changes in my life and I was at a really critical point. But things are better now. Do you still hear me on your album? Is there room for me?' "

Santana held the phone away for a second and looked for guidance—from a rather unlikely source.

"Even though he had left the physical world, Bill Graham still comes to me in my dreams and gives me instructions. So when Eric asked if there was room for him on the record, I could hear Bill saying, 'No, you schmuck! You're too late!' So I'm on the phone, having a conversation with Bill and Eric at the same time. To Bill I said, 'Wait. Maybe you can talk to him like that. But I can't.' And to Eric I said, 'Yeah. But you know what? I wouldn't think of dipping you into something that has already been recorded. Why don't you come over and we'll write something from scratch.' "

The exchange between the two guitar legends was something to behold. Clapton, feeling a bit tentative at having initially blown Santana off and showing up at the studio with no songs, was feeling more than a bit uncomfortable. But Carlos made his friend believe that what had transpired between them was all right.

They went through a series of extended jams. Then they started playing around with an old Santana song that had been gathering dust. The result was a very John Lee Hooker–Staple Singers hybrid of bluesy swamp rock, entitled "The Calling," that fit easily into the song list that was rounding into shape on *Supernatural*.

Supernatural was completed just before Memorial Day 1999. The initial good feeling about the recording process carried over into the first informal listening parties at the Arista offices. Those hearing the album for the first time drew an immediate comparison to albums like *Abraxas* and songs like "Soul Sacrifice." "We knew we had a really great record," reflected Ganbarg. "It was a record that we would all take home to listen to because we loved it."

Supernatural was poised for a midsummer 1999 release. After much deliberation, "Smooth" was chosen as the all-important first single on Carlos Santana's road back to the Top 40. The song had that distinctive guitar sound that would be an instant hook for Santana's longtime fans. It also had that hipness of lyric and production that would most certainly plug him in to the younger group of nineties music lovers. "Smooth" had "hit" written all over it.

Now all Arista had to do was convince radio stations that they should play it.

Easier said than done—1999 was the year of prefab boy groups, teeny-bop girl singers, alternative rock, and rap. Most groups who had had any measure of stardom in the late sixties and early seventies were either dead, had long since broken up, or were hanging on by their fingertips with oldies shows or a seemingly endless string of small-club dates. That Santana had managed to continue to be viable as a musician and to continue to release albums of new material for nearly thirty years meant one thing: He was respected.

But respect would not necessarily get his record played. Not that a good many radio stations were not behind Santana. For years they had been frustrated at every turn in their attempts to get Carlos's music back on the air. But they were inevitably handcuffed by a too-stringent playlist and, to be honest, the musician's often noncommercial attitude. But the buzz had already begun on *Supernatural,* and programmers were holding out for any excuse to put Santana back on the radio.

Richard Palmese, Arista's Senior Vice President of Promotion, recalled sending advance copies of

"Smooth" to the program directors of five of the top radio stations in the country. He was shocked to discover that none of them would add the song to their playlists on the grounds that Santana was too old for their target audience. Palmese rolled up his sleeves and went to war.

"I always liken convincing radio stations to play a record to having to go into a courtroom," he revealed of his approach to getting "Smooth" played. "You've got to prove your case, in this case with statistics, that the music will appeal to the station's audience. And that's what we did with 'Smooth.' "

Palmese accomplished this by working backward from Santana's perceived base, which was older adults. When the more youth-oriented stations discovered that, in fact, other stations had already added the record to their playlist, they found themselves in a position of having to play catch-up. They immediately added "Smooth" to their lists.

Santana was not sitting on the sidelines while all the behind-the-scenes maneuvering was going on. Nearly thirty years in the business had taught him how to play the game and he willingly stepped into the promotion of *Supernatural* with both feet. "It was a bloody war to get that CD on the radio," he remembered with equal parts amusement and exasperation. "I went personally to talk to the radio-station managers and to try to get them to change their minds."

Everybody held their breath as to whether "Smooth" would find that all-important younger demographic. Six weeks later, they had their answer. Teenagers had rediscovered Carlos Santana in a monster way.

Supernatural debuted at number one on the album charts and would remain there for an astounding six weeks. It finally fell to number two but, propelled by the Top 40 smash that "Smooth" had become, remained in that coveted spot for over six months. At the height of its popularity, *Supernatural* was selling a quarter of a million copies a week. By December 31, *Supernatural* had already sold in excess of four million copies.

Reviewers fell all over themselves in praise of the album. *Rolling Stone*, in a rave review, gave the album three and a half stars out of five, stating, "The album is eclectic, lively and only occasionally goofy. *Supernatural* offers a glossy but winning context of musical fusion that highlights Santana's unique ability to make that guitar of his cry expressively."

The influential music publication *CMJ* included the album in its Top 5 for 1999, offering, "This record proves in 1999 that veteran rockers don't have to burn out or fade away." *Entertainment Weekly* capped a literal flood of positive reviews when they said, "Whether he's spraying lyrical notes over a soulful Lauryn Hill composition, trading molten licks with Eric Clapton or playing spacey blues with Everlast, Santana still has that old 'Black Magic Woman' thing going on."

Supernatural began to take on a life of its own. People were sampling the album and telling their friends. Record-store clerks were going out of their way to buttonhole customers and sing the praises of Santana's latest efforts. A video had been recorded for "Smooth." But in terms of the street response to the album, the video as a promotional tool was almost unnecessary.

Hollywood could not write a better comeback story if it tried. Music-industry pundits were scratching their heads, attempting to figure out how and why Carlos Santana had come back from the dead. For Carlos, the answer was simple.

"It has a lot to do with grace and synchronicity."

Nobody had a better explanation.

10

The Ride into 2000

The smile was rarely off Carlos Santana's face.

It was there when he was doing the sudden rush of press interviews. It was there when he was holding his wife and playing with his children. It was there when he was alone in meditation.

And the smile was there in words when he would speak.

"In my heart, it feels like it still hasn't hit the ceiling yet," said a truly humble Santana not long after *Supernatural* cracked the four million sales barrier. "It feels like it's still going up."

Santana was referring, to a large extent, to the material side of his success. He could not help but note that he was all over the radio, and making a lot of money. But the spiritual driving force what had compelled him to make *Supernatural* was never very far from his thoughts.

The most gratifying thing to the guitarist was that everyone was responding to the message as well as the music. Carlos reveled in the fact that he was getting letters and e-mails from seven-year-olds, teenagers, parents, and grandparents, as well as other artists. They were all sending their best wishes. But he was equally heartened by the fact that there was a sense of understanding that he had set out to make more than a pop record that people would hear in their car radio and could dance to. For Carlos it was like a dream come true—a dream he was not in any hurry to wake up from.

Sharing in the joy of *Supernatural*'s success was Clive Davis who, typically, deflected the praise directed toward him back to Santana.

"Never in my wildest imagination did I think the album would be the commercial phenomenon that it has turned out to be," he enthused. "But when you work with someone whose music is as timeless as Carlos's, there is always the chance of coming up with that magic that touches everyone."

Davis chuckled as he recalled how, the day *Supernatural* passed the seven million sales mark, he was on the phone to Carlos with the good news.

"Carlos had been telling me that he kept pinching himself to make sure it was not a dream. When I called him and told him that the album just went seven times platinum, he said, 'Oh my God, I'm glad I'm lying down or else I'd fall.'"

How enthusiastically people were responding to Santana's new music became evident when the musician took to the road for a series of U.S. dates that showcased a good number of *Supernatural*'s songs in a live setting for the first time. Despite the overwhelming response to the record and the massive amount of radio play he was receiving, Carlos was still a shade tentative about how the songs would be received in concert. Carlos was amazed to see both the old, familiar faces, and a new generation of 1990s teenagers screaming their lungs out for the new songs.

It was a whole new experience for this elder statesman to see an influx of this entirely new, young audience that was screaming louder for the new songs than for the older songs. And while he cherished the people who had been with him through the years, he was excited that now there was a whole new audience to embrace. Excitement mixed with a knowing smile when he would paint the scenario of these children of the nineties coming to see him, expecting to hear the music of *Supernatural*, and discovering that there was a thirty-year backlog of great music they were experiencing for the first time.

Encouraged by the response to *Supernatural*, Carlos was already making grand plans for a follow-up album which, like his current music, would be a collaborative effort. But this time Carlos would recruit people like Ry Cooder, Alice Coltrane, Ali Akbar Khan, and Cuba's Buena Vista Social Club. These artists, much like Carlos, have been shunned by commercial radio. However the guitarist, insisting that his album was an example of how quality and quantity can be combined, feels he can make radio-friendly music with these esoteric talents.

Carlos was spending as much time as possible around home during the early days of 2000. With an extensive world tour due to begin shortly, he was enjoying as much time as he could with his family and in quiet meditation. During daily periods of quiet introspection, Santana would fill up a legal pad with messages and picture images that he says were coming from Metatron and, he offered, by the presence of other angels in the room.

Yes, it was Carlos Santana talking of angels and spirituality in that cosmic, sixties way guaranteed to drive many observers to distraction. But it had been his way for a number of years, and who could deny that it had not provided him the way?

The music industry could not deny that the success of *Supernatural* was the comeback story of the year. And so it was to be expected that, when the Grammy nominations were announced, Carlos would be well represented in a number of categories. What nobody, including Carlos, expected was that, in a year dominated by the likes of Britney Spears, the Backstreet Boys, and 'N Sync that Santana would end up leading the pack with eleven nominations.

"I had just gotten out of the shower," he remembered of the moment he heard the news, "and my wife had this beatific smile. She said, 'Hey, Mr. Eleven Nominations.' There I was all butt-naked and wet and all I could say was, 'You're kidding me.'"

Speculation ran rampant in the days and weeks leading up to the Grammys. There was the camp that insisted that Santana deserved every one of the nominations and more. There was the somewhat cynical group that said while *Supernatural* was a solid album, it was not a spectacular one, and that the nominations were more a reward for a long and distinguished career than for anything he had done in the past year. Finally, there were those who worried about the embarrassment if Santana, after getting all the nods, ended up losing the big honors to the likes of the Backstreet Boys.

Carlos's attitude was that the success of *Supernatural* with the public was all the reward he needed. Which is why on the night of the Grammy Awards, it was a Carlos Santana totally at peace with the world who walked down the red carpet of Los Angeles's Staples Center arena, hand in hand with Deborah, to the applause of fans and fellow musicians alike.

His excitement was much in evidence during an early, nontelevised segment of the awards ceremony when he effusedly said, "To live is to dream. To die is to awaken. Please don't wake me up."

It was not long after the ceremonies began that the world knew this was going to be Carlos Santana's night.

Santana was elated that awards for Best Pop Collaboration, Best Performance Duo or Group, Best Pop Performance Duo or Group, and Best Rock Instrumental highlighted the efforts of his collaborators Rob Thomas, Eric Clapton, Everlast, and Wyclef Jean. And he clapped long and loud when "El Farol" captured honors for Best Pop Instrumental.

"This is for my daddy," said Carlos as he accepted the Best Pop Instrumental award. "He taught me the value of music when I was growing up in Tijuana. This is for all the people who don't have running water or electricity. If I can do it, you can do it."

But he began to get a little antsy as the evening wore on, anticipating the announcement of the big honors and the validation of the year and the career he had had. A smile creased his face when *Supernatural* was announced the winner of Best Rock Album of the Year. He was positively ecstatic when "Smooth" was named Song of the Year and *Supernatural* was named Album of the Year.

Winning album of the year on the heels of all the other awards left Carlos humbled as he once again stepped to the stage. "Music is a vehicle for the magic of healing," said Carlos, his eyes wide in happiness.

He had agreed, as part of the evening's live performances, to play "Smooth" and as he played the now familiar guitar lines to an enthusiastic audience, he felt at one with his world and his universe. Carlos Santana was a happy man.

"And the winner for Record of the Year . . . 'Smooth'!"

Carlos, Rob Thomas, and a multitude of producers and musicians raced to the stage amid deafening applause. At the moment when audiences expected Carlos to be effusive and over-the-top in his acceptance, he was humble, offering thanks to all his earthly partners and to the angels up above.

During his long life and career, Carlos Santana has given new meaning to the word "survivor." He has been up and down more times than a roller coaster. He has endured much. But as we go into the millennium, Carlos Santana has discovered his spiritual way and, although, his utterings don't always make sense to others, he is comforted in the fact that there are angels up above looking out for him.

"I know it sounds really crazy to a lot of people but it's okay because I'm not afraid of what people think. My reality is my reality. I'm not going to deny it at all. I stand in front of people. I look for the perfect melody.

"Behold my reality."

Discography

SANTANA BAND ALBUMS

SANTANA
Release Date: October 1969
Songs: Waiting; Evil Ways; Shades of Time; Savor; Jingo; Persuasion; Treat; You Just Don't Care; Soul Sacrifice.

ABRAXAS
Release Date: October 1970
Songs: Singing Winds–Crying Beasts; Black Magic Woman–Gypsy Queen; Oye Como Va; Incident at Neshabur; Se a Cabo; Mother's Daughter; Samba Pa Ti; Hope You're Feeling Better; El Nicoya.

SANTANA III
Release Date: October 1971

SONGS: Batuka; No One to Depend On; Taboo; Toussaint L'Overture; Everybody's Everything; Guajira; Jungle Strut; Everything's Coming Our Way; Para los Rumberos.

CARAVANSERAI
Release Date: November 1972

SONGS: Eternal Caravan of Reincarnation; Waves Within; Look Up (To See What's Coming Down); Just in Time to See the Sun; Song of the Wind; All the Love of the Universe; Future Primitive; Stone Flower; La Puente del Ritmo; Every Step of the Way.

WELCOME
Release Date: November 1973

SONGS: Going Home; Love Devotion and Surrender; Samba de Sausalito; When I Look into Your Eyes; Yours Is the Light; Mother Africa; Light of Life; Flame Sky; Welcome.

GREATEST HITS
Release Date: August 1974

SONGS: Evil Ways; Jingo; Hope You're Feeling Better; Samba Pa Ti; Persuasion; Black Magic Woman; Oye Como Va; Everything's Coming Our Way; Se a Cabo; Everybody's Everything.

BORBOLETTA
Release Date: October 1974
SONGS: Spring Manifestations; Canto de los Flores; Life Is Anew; Give and Take; One with the Sun; Aspirations; Practice What You Preach; Mirage; Here and Now; Flor de Canela; Promise of a Fisherman; Borboletta.

LOTUS
Release Date: December 1975
SONGS: Going Home; A-1 Funk; Every Step of the Way; Black Magic Woman; Gypsy Queen; Oye Como Va; Yours Is the Light; Batuka; Xibaba; Stone Flower (Introduction); Waiting; Castillos de Arena Part 1 (Sand Castle); Free Angela; Samba de Sausalito; Mantra; Kyoto; Castillos de Arena Part 2 (Sand Castle).

AMIGOS
Release Date: March 1976
SONGS: Dance Sister Dance (Baila Mi Hermana); Take Me with You; Let Me; Gitano; Tell Me Are You Tired; Europa (Earth's Cry Heaven's Smile); Let It Shine.

FESTIVAL
Release Date: December 1976
SONGS: Carnaval; Let the Children Play; Jugando; Give Me Love; Verão Vermelho; Let the Music Set You Free; Revelations; Reach Up; The River; Try a Little Harder; María Caracóles.

MOONFLOWER
Release Date: September 1977

SONGS: Dawn / Go Within; Carnaval; Let the Children Play; Jugando; I'll Be Waiting; Zulu; Bahia; Black Magic Woman / Gypsy Queen; Dance Sister Dance (Baila Mi Hermana); Europa (Earth's Cry Heaven's Smile); She's Not There; Flor D'Luna (Moonflower); Soul Sacrifice / Head Hands and Feet (drum solo); El Morocco; Transcendence; Savor Toussaint L'Overture.

INNER SECRETS
Release Date: October 1978

SONGS: Dealer / Spanish Rose; Move On; One Chain (Don't Make No Prison); Stormy; Well All Right; Open Invitation; Life Is a Lady / Holiday; The Facts of Love; Wham!

MARATHON
Release Date: September 1979

SONGS: Marathon; Lightning in the Sky; Aqua Marine; You Know That I Love You; All I Ever Wanted; Stand Up; Runnin'; Summer Lady; Love; Stay (Beside Me); Hard Times.

ZEBOP!
Release Date: March 1981

SONGS: Changes; E Papa Re; Primera Invasion; Searchin'; Over and Over; Winning; Tales of Kilimanjaro; The Sensitive Kind; American Gypsy; I Love You Much Too Much; Brightest Star; Hannibal.

SHANGO
Release Date: August 1982
SONGS: The Nile; Hold On; Night Hunting Time; Nowhere to Run; Nueva York; Oxun (Oshùn); Body Surfing; What Does It Take (To Win Your Love); Let Me Inside; Warrior; Shango.

BEYOND APPEARANCES
Release Date: February 1985
SONGS: Breaking Out; Written in Sand; Brotherhood; Spirit; Right Now; Who Loves You; I'm the One Who Loves You; Say It Again; Two Points of View; How Long; Touchdown Raiders.

FREEDOM
Release Date: February 1987
SONGS: Vera Cruz; She Can't Let Go; Once It's Gotcha; Love Is You; Songs of Freedom; Deeper Dig Deeper; Praise; Mandela; Before We Go; Victim of Circumstance; Brotherhood; Open Invitation; Aqua Marine; Dance Sister Dance (Baila Mi Hermana); Europa (Earth's Cry Heaven's Smile); Peraza I; She's Not There; Bambele; Evil Ways; Daughter of the Night; Peraza II; Black Magic Woman / Gypsy Queen; Oye Como Va; Persuasion; Soul Sacrifice.

VIVA SANTANA!
Release Date: October 1988
SONGS: Everybody's Everything; Black Magic Woman / Gypsy Queen; Guajira; Jungle Strut; Jingo; Ballin'; Bam-

bara; Angel Negro; Incident at Neshabur; Just Let the Music Speak; Super Boogie / Hong Kong Blues; Song of the Wind; Abi Cama; Vilato; Paris Finale; We Don't Have to Wait; A Dios.

MILAGRO
Release Date: April 1992
SONGS: Milagro; Somewhere in Heaven; Saja / Right On; Your Touch; Life Is for Living; Red Prophet; Agua Que Va Caer; Make Somebody Happy; Free All the People (South Africa); Gypsy / Grajonca; Samba Pa Ti; Guajira; Make Somebody Happy; Toussaint L'Overture; Soul Sacrifice / Don't Try This at Home; Europa; Ji-Go-Lo-Ba.

SACRED FIRE
Release Date: November 1993
SONGS: Angels All Around Us; Vive La Vida (Life Is for Living); Esperando; No One to Depend On; Black Magic Woman / Gypsy Queen; Oye Como Va.

DANCE OF THE RAINBOW SERPENT
Release Date: January 1995
SONGS: Evil Ways; Soul Sacrifice; Black Magic Woman / Gypsy Queen; Oye Como Va; Samba Pa Ti; Everybody's Everything; Song of the Wind; Toussaint L'Overture; In a Silent Way; Waves Within; Flame Sky; Naima; I Love You Much Too Much; Blues for Salvador; Aqua Marine; Bella; The River; I'll Be Waiting; Love Is You; Europa; Move On; Somewhere in Heaven; Open Invitation; Test;

All I Ever Wanted; Hannibal; Brightest Star; Wings of Grace; Se Eni a Fe l'Amo–Kere Kere; Mudbone; The Healer; Chill Out (Things Gonna Change); Sweet Black Cherry Pie; Every Now and Then; This Is This.

LIVE AT THE FILLMORE '68
Release Date: May 1997

SONGS: Jingo; Persuasion; Treat; Chunk a Funk; Fried Neckbones; Conquistador Rides Again; Soul Sacrifice; As the Years Go Passing By; Freeway.

SANTANA (REISSUE)
Release Date: March 1998

SONGS: Waiting; Evil Ways; Shades of Time; Savor; Jingo; Persuasion; Treat; You Just Don't Care; Soul Sacrifice; Savor; Soul Sacrifice; Fried Neckbones.

ABRAXAS (REISSUE)
Release Date: March 1998

SONGS: Singing Winds / Crying Beasts; Black Magic Woman / Gypsy Queen; Oye Como Va; Incident at Neshabur; Se a Cabo; Mother's Daughter; Samba Pa Ti; Hope You're Feeling Better; El Nicoya; Se a Cabo; Toussaint L'Overture; Black Magic Woman / Gypsy Woman.

SANTANA III (REISSUE)
Release Date: March 1998

SONGS: Batuka; No One to Depend On; Taboo; Toussaint L'Overture; Everybody's Everything; Guajira; Jungle

Strut; Everything's Coming Our Way; Para los Rumberos; Batuka; Jungle Strut; Gumbo.

SUPERNATURAL
Release Date: June 1999
SONGS: (Da le) Yaleo; Love of My Life; Put Your Lights On; Africa Bamba; Smooth; Do You Like the Way; Maria Maria; Migra; Corazón Espinado; Wishing It Was; El Farol; Primavera; The Calling; Day of Celebration.

CARLOS SANTANA SOLO PROJECTS

LIVE CARLOS SANTANA
Release Date: August 1972
SONGS: Marbles; Lava; Evil Ways; Faith Interlude; Them Changes; Free Form Funkafide Filth.

LOVE DEVOTION SURRENDER
Release Date: July 1973
SONGS: A Love Supreme; Naima; The Life Divine; Let's Go into the House of the Lord; Meditation.

ILLUMINATIONS
Release Date: July 1974
SONGS: Guru Sri Chinmoy Aphorism; Angel of Air; Angel of Water; Bliss: The Eternal Now; Angel of Sunlight; Illuminations.

ONENESS SILVER DREAMS GOLDEN REALITY
Release Date: February 1979

Songs: The Chosen Hour; Arise Awake; Light Verses Darkness; Jinr Geannie; Transformation Day; Victory; Silver Dreams Golden Smiles; Cry of the Wilderness; Guru's Song; Oneness; Life Is Just a Passing Parade; Golden Dawn; Free as the Morning Sun; I Am Free; Song for Devadip.

THE SWING OF DELIGHT
Release Date: February 1980

Songs: Swapan Tari; Love Theme from *Spartacus*; Phuler Matan; Song for My Brother; Jharma Kala; Gardenia; La Llave; Golden Hours; Sher Khan, The Tiger.

HAVANA MOON
Release Date: April 1983

Songs: Watch Your Step; Lightnin'; Who Do You Love; Mudbone; One with You; Equador; Tales of Kilimanjaro; Havana Moon; Daughter of the Night; They All Went to Mexico; Vereda Tropical.

BLUES FOR SALVADOR
Release Date: October 1987

Songs: Bailando / Aquatic Park; Bella; I'm Gone; 'Trane; Deeper, Dig Deeper; Mingus; Now That You Know; Hannibal; Blues for Salvador.

SPIRITS DANCING IN THE FLESH
Release Date: June 1990

SONGS: Let There Be Light / Spirits Dancing in the Flesh; Gypsy Woman; It's a Jungle Out There; Soweto (Africa Libre); Choose; Peace on Earth...Mother Earth...Third Stone from the Sun; Full Moon; Who's That Lady; Jin-Go-Lo-Ba; Goodness and Mercy.

CARLOS SANTANA GUEST APPEARANCES

MIKE BLOOMFIELD AND AL KOOPER
THE LIVE ADVENTURES OF
Release Date: 1968

SONG: Sonny Boy Williamson.

JEFFERSON AIRPLANE
BARK
Release Date: 1971

SONG: Pretty As You Feel.

PAPA JOHN CREACH
PAPA JOHN CREACH
Release Date: 1971

SONG: Papa John's Down Home Blues.

LUIS GASCA
LUIS GASCA
Release Date: 1971

SONGS: Street Dude; Spanish Gypsy; Little Mama.

GIANTS
GIANTS
Release Date: 1978

Song: Fried Neckbones and Home Fries.

FLORA PURIM
STORIES TO TELL
Release Date: 1974

Song: Silver Sword.

ERIC CLAPTON
CROSSROADS 2
Release Date: 1996

Songs: Eyesight to the Blind; Why Does Love Have to Be So Sad.

ALICE COLTRANE
ETERNITY
Release Date: 1973

Songs: Los Caballos; Morning Worship.

NARADA MICHAEL WALDEN
GARDEN OF LOVE LIGHT
Release Date: 1976

Song: First Love.

JOHN McLAUGHLIN
ELECTRIC GUITARIST
Release Date: 1978

Song: Friendship.

GATO BARBIERI
TROPICO
Release Date: 1978

Song: Latin Lady.

NARADA MICHAEL WALDEN
AWAKENING
Release Date: 1979

Song: The Awakening.

HERBIE HANCOCK
MONSTER
Release Date: 1980

Song: Saturday Night.

BOZ SCAGGS
MIDDLE MAN
Release Date: 1980

Song: You Can Have Me Any Time.

JOSÉ FELICIANO
ESCENAS DE AMOR
Release Date: 1982

Song: Samba Pa Ti.

LEON PATILLO
I'LL NEVER STOP LOVIN' YOU
Release Date: 1982

SONGS: I'll Never Stop Lovin' You, Saved.

STANLEY CLARKE
LET ME KNOW YOU
Release Date: 1982

SONGS: Straight to the Top; I Just Want to Be Your Brother.

McCOY TYNER
LOOKING OUT
Release Date: 1982

SONGS: Hannibal; Señor Carlos.

JIM CAPALDI
ONE MAN MISSION
Release Date: 1984

SONGS: Lost Inside Your Love; Nobody Loves You.

BOB DYLAN
REAL LIVE
Release Date: 1988

SONG: Tombstone Blues.

ARETHA FRANKLIN
WHO'S ZOOMIN' WHO
Release Date: 1985

SONG: Push.

GREGG ROLIE
GREGG ROLIE
Release Date: 1985

SONG: Marianne.

WEATHER REPORT
THIS IS THIS
Release Date: 1986

SONGS: This Is This; Man with the Copper Fingers.

BABATUNDE OLATUNJI
DANCE TO THE BEAT OF MY DRUM
Release Date: 1986

SONGS: The Beat of My Drum; Loyin Loyin; Ife L'oju L'aiye; Akiwowo Ensamble; Se Eni a Fe L'Amo–Kere Kere; Ilere Ilere Ilere.

GREGG ROLIE
GRINGO
Release Date: 1987

SONGS: Fire at Night; Too Late.

NEVILLE BROTHERS
UPTOWN
Release Date: 1987
SONG: Forever . . . For Tonight.

CLYDE CRINER
BEHIND THE SUN
Release Date: 1988
SONGS: Black Manhattan; Kinesis; Behind the Sun.

BABATUNDE OLATUNJI
DRUMS OF PASSION: THE BEAT
Release Date: 1989
SONGS: The Beat of My Drum; Loyin Loyin; Ife L'oju
L'aiye; Akiwowo; Se Eni A Fe L'Amo–Kere Kere.

TERRI LYNE CARRINGTON
REAL LIFE STORY
Release Date: 1989
SONG: Human Revolution.

NDUGU LEON CHANCLER
OLD FRIENDS NEW FRIENDS
Release Date:1989
SONGS: Oh Yah Yeh; Trying Again.

Discography

JOHN LEE HOOKER
THE HEALER
Release Date: 1994
Song: The Healer.

BOBBY WOMACK
SAVE THE CHILDREN
Release Date : 1989
Song: Too Close for Comfort; Tough Job.

MORY KANTE
TOUMA
Release Date: 1991
Song: Soumba.

TREMAINE HAWKINS
LIVE
Release Date: 1990
Songs: Who Is He; Lift Me Up.

ALEX ACUNA AND THE UNKNOWNS
THINKING OF YOU
Release Date: 1990
Song: Psalms.

SALIF KEITA
AMEN
Release Date: 1991
Songs: Yele n Na; Nyananfin; N B I Fe.

JOHN LEE HOOKER
MR. LUCKY
Release Date: 1991

Song: Stripped Me Naked.

OTTMAR LIEBERT
SOLO PARA TI
Release Date: 1992

Songs: Reaching Out 2 U; Todos Bajo la Misma Luna; Samba Pa Ti (Thru Every Step in Life U Find Freedom from Within).

PAOLO RUSTICHELLI
MYSTIC JAZZ
Release Date: 1995

Song: Full Moon.

BLUES TRAVELER
ON TOUR FOREVER
Release Date: 1992

Song: Mountain Cry.

CARIBBEAN ALL STARS
PATHS TO GREATNESS
Release Date: 1992

Songs: Sette Massgana; Caught in the Middle; Ras Clatt Ridd'm.

JOHN LEE HOOKER
CHILL OUT
Release Date: 1995

Song: Chill Out.

JUNIOR WELLS
EVERYBODY'S GETTIN' SOME
Release Date: 1995

Song: Get Down

JIMI HENDRIX TRIBUTE
IN FROM THE STORM
Release Date: 1995

Song: Spanish Castle Magic.

ANGELIQUE KIDJO
FIFA
Release Date: 1996

Song: Naima.

PAOLO RUSTICHELLI
MYSTIC MAN
Release Date: 1996

Songs: Get On; Rastafario; Vers le Soleil.

EL TRI
CUANDO TU NO ESTAS
Release Date:1997

Song: Virgen Morena.

LAURYN HILL
THE MISEDUCATION OF LAURYN HILL
Release Date: 1998

Song: To Zion.

Carlos Santana Album Awards

RIAA Double Platinum Album for *Santana*—1969

RIAA Quadruple Platinum Album for *Abraxas*—1970

RIAA Double Platinum Album for *Santana III*—1971

RIAA Platinum Album for *Caravanserai*—1972

RIAA Platinum Album for *Live Carlos Santana*—1972

RIAA Gold Album for *Love Devotion Surrender*—1973

RIAA Gold Album for *Welcome*—1973

RIAA Double Platinum Album for *Santana's Greatest Hits*—1974

RIAA Gold Album for *Borboletta*—1974

RIAA Gold Album for *Amigos*—1976

RIAA Gold Album for *Festival*—1976

RIAA Platinum Album for *Moonflower*—1977

RIAA Gold Album for *Inner Secrets*—1978

RIAA Gold Album for *Marathon*—1979

RIAA Gold Album for *Zebop!*—1981

RIAA Triple Platinum Album for *Supernatural*—1999

Sources

Like all good biographies, *Carlos Santana: Back on Top* has benefited from myriad sources and an emphasis on solid journalism.

The following books have helped the cause: *Bill Graham Presents* by Bill Graham and Robert Greenfield; *Beneath the Diamond Sky: Haight-Ashbury 1965–1970* by Barney Hoskins; *Summer of Love* by Joel Selvin; *Not Fade Away* by Ben Fong-Torres; *Rock Movers and Shakers* by Dafydd Rees and Luke Crampton; and *My Rules: The Lauryn Hill Story* by Marc Shapiro.

The following magazines and newspapers opened

my eyes to infinite ideas: the *Los Angeles Times*; the *Chicago Tribune*; *The Beat*; *Guitar World*; *Billboard*; *Guitar Player*; *Down Beat*; *Classic Rock*; *Time*; *Musician*; *Latin Style*; *NY Rock*; *Entertainment Weekly*; *People*; *CMJ*; *Q* magazine; *Rolling Stone*; *Nuestro*; *Newsweek*; *Music Connection*; the *New York Times*; *Goldmine*; the *San Jose Mercury-News*; the *San Diego Union-Tribune*; *BAM* magazine; the *Philadelphia Inquirer*; the *San Francisco Chronicle*; and *Pulse*.

The following recommended Santana Web sites helped set the record straight: The Santana Official Website; Santana World; Sonic Net.

The following television programs helped turn the dark to light: CNN's *Show Biz Today*, *60 Minutes*.

Liner notes from the rerelease of the albums *Santana* and *Abraxas* and *Santana III*.